PERFORMING SALOME, REVEALING STORIES

ASHGATE INTERDISCIPLINARY STUDIES IN OPERA

The *Ashgate Interdisciplinary Studies in Opera* series provides a centralized and prominent forum for the presentation of cutting-edge scholarship that draws on numerous disciplinary approaches to a wide range of subjects associated with the creation, performance, and reception of opera (and related genres) in various historical and social contexts. There is great need for a broader approach to scholarship about opera. In recent years, the course of study has developed significantly, going beyond traditional musicological approaches to reflect new perspectives from literary criticism and comparative literature, cultural history, philosophy, art history, theatre history, gender studies, film studies, political science, philology, psycho-analysis, and medicine. The new brands of scholarship have allowed a more comprehensive interrogation of the complex nexus of means of artistic expression operative in opera, one that has meaningfully challenged prevalent historicist and formalist musical approaches. The *Ashgate Interdisciplinary Studies in Opera* series continues to move this important trend forward by including essay collections and monographs that reflect the ever-increasing interest in opera in non-musical contexts. Books in the series will be linked by their emphasis on the study of a single genre—opera—yet will be distinguished by their individualized and novel approaches by scholars from various disciplines/fields of inquiry. The remit of the series welcomes studies of seventeenth century to contemporary opera from all geographical locations, including non-Western topics.

Performing Salome, Revealing Stories

Edited by

CLAIR ROWDEN
Cardiff University, UK

ASHGATE

Published by
Ashgate Publishing Limited
Wey Court East
Union Road
Farnham
Surrey, GU9 7PT
England

Ashgate Publishing Company
110 Cherry Street
Suite 3-1
Burlington, VT 05401-3818
USA

www.ashgate.com

British Library Cataloguing in Publication Data
A catalogue record for this book is available from the British Library

The Library of Congress has cataloged the printed edition as follows:
Performing Salome, revealing stories / edited by Clair Rowden.
   pages cm. -- (Ashgate interdisciplinary studies in opera)
   Includes bibliographical references and index.
   ISBN 978-1-4094-4567-8 (hardcover) -- ISBN 978-1-4094-4568-5 (ebook) --
ISBN 978-1-4094-7422-7 (epub) 1. Strauss, Richard, 1864-1949. Salome. 2. Wilde, Oscar, 1854-1900. Salome. 3. Salome (Biblical figure)--Drama--History and criticism. I. Rowden, Clair.
   ML410.S93P34 2013
   809.2'9351--dc23
                                                                                    2012049939
   ISBN 9781409445678 (hbk)
   ISBN 9781409445685 (ebk – PDF)
   ISBN 9781409474227 (ebk – ePUB)

MIX
Paper from
responsible sources
FSC® C013985

Printed in the United Kingdom by Henry Ling Limited, at the Dorset Press, Dorchester, DT1 1HD

Contents

List of Figures   vii
List of Plates   ix
Notes on Contributors   xi
Series Editor's Preface   xv
Acknowledgements   xvii

    Introduction: Performing Salome, Revealing Stories   1
    Clair Rowden

1   Decadent Senses: The Dissemination of Oscar Wilde's
    Salomé across the Arts   15
    Polina Dimova

2   Visions of Salome, Visions of Wilde: Critical Readings of
    Oscar Wilde's Salome in Early Twentieth-Century Vienna   49
    Sandra Mayer

3   Whose/Who's Salome? Natalia Trouhanowa, a Dancing Diva   71
    Clair Rowden

4   Salome's Slow Dance with the Lord Chamberlain,
    London 1909–10   99
    Anne Sivuoja-Kauppala

5   Seven Veils, Seven Rooms, Four Walls and Countless Contexts 133
    Hedda Høgåsen-Hallesby

6   The Dirt on Salome   155
    Caryl Clark

7   Outrageous Salome: Grace and Fury in Carmelo Bene's Salomè
    and Ken Russell's Salome's Last Dance   171
    Tristan Grünberg

Bibliography   191
Index   211

List of Figures

Figures

1.1   Alice Guszalewicz as Salome   16
1.2   Alice Guszalewicz as Salome   18
1.3   Aubrey Beardsley, *Black Cape*, 1894   35
1.4   Aubrey Beardsley, *The Toilette of Salome – I*, 1894   37
1.5   Aubrey Beardsley, *The Climax*, 1894   38

2.1   Lili Marberg as Salome, Munich 1905   62

3.1   Natalia Trouhanowa in Strauss's *Salome*   74
3.2   Natalia Trouhanowa in Schmitt's *La Tragédie de Salomé*   80
3.3   *La Tragédie de Salomé*   81
3.4   Lucienne Bréval in Mariotte's *Salomé*   85
3.5   Production drawing of *La Tragédie de Salomé*   86

4.1   Short musical excerpt indicating a change in Kalisch's
      bowdlerized *Salome* libretto which Ackté had requested in
      rehearsal, drawn from Alfred Kalisch's letter to Aino Ackté,
      4 December 1910   119
4.2   Engraving by F. Matania of the Covent Garden production with
      Aino Ackté as Salome, holding the charger aloft, *The Sphere*,
      17 December 1910   123
4.3   Engraving by Gilbert Holiday of the Covent Garden production
      with Aino Ackté as Salome and Clarence Whitehall as the Prophet,
      The Graphic, 17 December 1910   127

5.1   Franz Lechleichner as Herod and Constance Shacklock as
      Herodias in the Covent Garden production of *Salome* (1949)
      produced by Peter Brook, designs by Salvador Dali   147

6.1   A scene from the Canadian Opera Company's production
      of *Salome*, 2002   168

List of Plates

1   Gustave Moreau, *Salome Dancing before Herod*, 1874–76. Oil on canvas, 56 1/2 × 41 1/16 in (143.5 × 104.3 cm). [The Armand Hammer Collection. Gift of the Armand Hammer Foundation. Hammer Museum, Los Angeles, California. Photo by Robert Wedemeyer.]

2   Scenery design by Maxime Dethomas for *La Tragédie de Salomé*. [Reproduced in Concerts de danse. N. Trouhanowa (Paris, 1912). Private Collection.]

3   The Dover Street Studios had exclusive rights for Ackté's Salome photographs. This only remaining colour photograph allows observation not only of the colours but also the textures of the cloth. Ackté's costume was tailored by the Parisian Worth, according to her own model. Supplement to *The Sketch*, December 1910. [Aino Ackté–Jalander Archive Coll. 4.49, National Library of Finland.]

4   Peter Konwitschny's production of *Salome* at De Nederlandse Opera, Amsterdam, 2009. [Photo by Monika Rittershaus.]

5   Robert Tear as Herod surrounded by the Five Jews, from the Canadian Opera Company's production of *Salome*, 2002. [Photo by Michael Cooper.]

6   Veruschka as Myrrhina in Carmelo Bene's *Salomè* (Italy, 1972). [© General Video.]

7   Franco Leo as Jesus Christ in Carmelo Bene's *Salomè* (Italy, 1972). [© General Video.]

8   Donyale Luna as Salomè in Carmelo Bene's *Salomè* (Italy, 1972). [© General Video.]

9   Carmelo Bene as Herod in *Salomè* (Italy, 1972). [© General Video.]

Notes on Contributors

Caryl Clark is Professor of Musicology at the Faculty of Music, University of Toronto, and a senior fellow at Trinity College. Her research interests include Haydn studies, gender and performance, opera and ethnicity, and the politics of musical reception. She edited the *Cambridge Companion to Haydn* (2005), and is the author of *Haydn's Jews: Representation and Reception on the Operatic Stage* (Cambridge 2009; ebook 2012). She has co-edited several special journal issues devoted to opera, including one on Wagner's *Ring Cycle* for *The Opera Quarterly* (2007), Dryden's and Purcell's *King Arthur* for *Restoration – Studies in English Literary Culture 1660–1700* (2010), and five special issues of *The University of Toronto Quarterly* (1998; 2003; 2005; 2006; 2012) on opera and interdisciplinarity. Together with art historian Thomas Tolley, she is currently engaged in a new book project on Haydn, Orpheus, and the French Revolution funded by the Social Science and Humanities Research Council of Canada.

Polina Dimova is Mellon Assistant Professor in Comparative Literature and Russian at Oberlin College. Previously, she taught at the University of California, Berkeley, where she completed her PhD in Comparative Literature in 2010, specializing in English, German, and Russian Modernist literature in its relation to music, visual art, and the historical and scientific discourses of synaesthesia. She has published on Oscar Wilde's *Salomé*, on Alexander Skriabin's synaesthetic symphony *Prometheus* and the Russian Symbolist poetics of light; and on Skriabin, Viacheslav Ivanov, and Russian religious philosophy. Dimova is currently reworking her thesis into a book, *The Synaesthetic Metaphor Across the Arts in European Modernism*. Her project surveys the intellectual history of synaesthesia in art, aesthetics, technology and science, and examines specific modernist sites of artistic intersection, such as R.M. Rilke's Orphic poetry and Rodin's sculptural fragments, to develop a theory of interartistic adaptation based on synaesthesia.

Tristan Grünberg holds a doctorate in cinematographic and audiovisual studies from the University of Paris III – Sorbonne Nouvelle where he teaches aesthetics and semiology of cinema. His thesis, *Hantises: visages du fantastique dans le cinéma de Rainer Werner Fassbinder*, explores the genealogy of the fantasy and ghostly world which informs the works of the German director. Between aesthetics and psychoanalysis, his research examines the formal and mythical traces that survive in the 'film noir', such as fantasy cinema, Renaissance art and nineteenth-century literature. He has published several articles on the representation of body, space and time in the films of Victor Sjöström, Josef von Sternberg, Fritz Lang,

Paul Verhoeven and Atom Egoyan. In 2009, he co-organized study days for the association GRADIVA (http://gradiva.org.free.fr) dedicated to the representation of blondness in the arts, and the volume, co-edited with Marie-Camille Bouchindomme, *Blondes mythiques: représentation de la blondeur dans les art* (Dijon: Editions du Murmure) was published in 2012.

Hedda Høgåsen-Hallesby is a musicologist working as a research fellow at the Centre for Gender Research at the University of Oslo, where she has recently completed a PhD thesis on productions of Richard Strauss's *Salome*. Her work forms part of a larger interdisciplinary project entitled 'Canonicity, Gender and Critique: The Hermeneutics of Feminism and Canon-Transformations', sponsored by the Research Council of Norway. Høgåsen-Hallesby has previously published on opera, Orientalism and gender critique in *Tidsskrift for kjønnsforskning* (The Norwegian Journal for Gender Research), *Studia Musicologica Norvegica*, and in the anthology *Music and Identity in Norway and Beyond: Essays Commemorating Edvard Grieg the Humanist* (Oslo: Fagbokforlaget, 2011).

Sandra Mayer is a lecturer and research assistant in the Department of English at the University of Vienna, in the areas of English Literature, Irish Studies and Cultural Studies. She studied English and History at the universities of Sussex, Graz and Vienna and submitted her PhD thesis on the reception of Oscar Wilde's plays on twentieth-century Viennese stages in 2011. Her research forms part of the project *World Stage Vienna*, which investigates the reception of Anglophone drama in Vienna during the twentieth century. She has lectured and published extensively on the British and European reception of Oscar Wilde and has contributed to the volume *The Reception of Oscar Wilde in Europe* (Continuum, 2010). She is also a member of the editorial board of *The Oscholars*, an e-journal devoted to current research on Oscar Wilde and *Fin-de-Siècle* Studies.

Clair Rowden is Senior Lecturer in the School of Music, Cardiff University. Her research deals with opera, dance and nineteenth-century France; her book *Republican Morality and Catholic Tradition at the Opera: Massenet's* Hérodiade *and* Thaïs was published in 2004. She is a member of the 'Francophone Music Criticism 1789–1914' network and is responsible for the preparation of on-line editions of various corpora of nineteenth-century French music criticism. Current research comprises a book on opera, parody and caricature in the French *fin-de-siècle* press, and an edited volume (with Alexandra Wilson) *Transforming Opera*. Clair Rowden has published articles in *Cambridge Opera Journal, La Revue de musicologie, Music in Art, Franco–British Studies, Avant-Scène Opéra* and regularly contributes chapters concerning opera and dance to the *Cahiers de l'Esplanade* (Saint-Etienne, France), and programme notes for the Royal Opera House, Covent Garden.

Anne Sivuoja-Kauppala is Professor of Music Performance Research at the Sibelius Academy of the University of the Arts Helsinki, Finland. Her research fields include opera, musical semiotics, cultural studies of art music (including performance), as well as gender studies and opera. Besides *Narrating with Twelve Tones. Einojuhani Rautavaara's First Serial Period (ca. 1957–1965)* (Helsinki, 1997), her publications include articles in international and Finnish periodicals as well as editorial work, including an anthology of Kaija Saariaho's music *Elektronisia unelmia* [*Electronic Dreams*]. From 2010 to 2013, she ran a research project entitled 'The Finnish Opera Company (1873–1879) from a Microhistorical Perspective', funded by the Academy of Finland. She is also working on the project 'The Cantarices Achté' which concentrates on the operatic careers of Aino Ackté, her sister Irma Tervani and their mother Emmy Achté at the turn of the nineteenth and twentieth centuries. In addition, she has recently launched an inter-Nordic research project on opera funded by NOS-HS, whose most recent outcome is a co-edited anthology *Opera on the Move in the Nordic Countries during the Long 19th Century* (Helsinki, 2012), also published in open-access electronic format.

Series Editor's Preface

Roberta Montemorra Marvin

Ashgate Interdisciplinary Studies in Opera provides a centralized and prominent forum for the presentation of cutting-edge scholarship that draws on numerous disciplinary approaches on a wide range of subjects associated with the creation, performance, dissemination, and reception of opera and related genres in various historical and social contexts. The series includes topics from the seventeenth century to the present and from all geographical locations, including non-Western traditions.

In recent years, the field of opera studies has not only come into its own but has developed significantly, going beyond traditional musicological approaches to reflect new perspectives from literary criticism and comparative literature, cultural history, philosophy, art history, theatre history, gender studies, film studies, political science, philology, psychoanalysis, and even medicine. The new brands of scholarship have allowed a more comprehensive and intensive interrogation of the complex nexus of means of artistic expression operative in opera, one that has meaningfully challenged prevalent historicist and formalist musical approaches. Today, interdisciplinary, or as some prefer cross-disciplinary, opera studies are receiving increasingly widespread attention, and the ways in which scholars, practitioners, and the public think about the artform known as opera continue to change and expand. *Ashgate Interdisciplinary Studies in Opera* seeks to move this important trend forward by including essay collections and monographs that reflect the ever-increasing interest in opera in non-musical contexts.

Performing Salome, Revealing Stories takes as a starting point Richard Strauss's *Salome*, an iconic work that resonated throughout the twentieth century. It treats the subject of Salome in new ways, through focussing on the perspective of performers and the performative aspects of Strauss's opera and related works from which it is derived, as well as manifestations of the figure of Salome in dance and film. The collection of essays thereby illuminates the opera by placing it in a broad cultural framework that permits discussion of reception, appropriation, translation, embodiment, and performance. An international array of scholars from a variety of disciplines including musicology, film studies and comparative literature, address topics within diverse geographical contexts throughout Western Europe and the United States. The contributors also aim at breadth in intellectual scope, drawing on a broad range of methodologies from genetic analysis to reception studies, and from micro-history to spatial theory. The volume as a whole builds and substantially expands on the critical mass of published scholarship to offer new and valuable insights into Salome's appropriation across the arts of the late-nineteenth and early twentieth centuries.

Acknowledgements

The idea for this volume first arose out of the conference 'Opera, Exoticism and Visual Culture: The *Fin de Siècle* and Its Legacy', hosted jointly by the Institute of Germanic & Romance Studies and the Institute of Musical Research in London in September 2008. Four of the contributors to this volume – Caryl Clark, Hedda Høgåsen-Hallesby, Anne Sivuoja-Kauppala and myself – presented papers on the theme of Salome, and Marcia Citron suggested that we 'take this show on the road'. Which is precisely what we did. New papers from each of these contributors were presented in a Salome session at the 16th Biennial Conference on Nineteenth-Century Music at the University of Southampton in July 2010 and form the basis for this volume. My thanks go to all the contributors, but particularly to these three for accompanying me from the very conception to fruition, to Caryl Clark for procuring and purchasing the cover image, and to Hedda Høgåsen-Hallesby especially for her help with introductory material and for providing the title to this volume. The project also benefitted from discussion with and the friendship of Emily Eells, to whom I am most grateful.

Thanks are also due to Sandra Mayer for proofreading German text, and to John Nelson for proofreading Finnish text. I am grateful also to Daniel Bickerton for the preparation of score extracts, and to the School of Music, Cardiff University for a semester's study leave during the preparation of this volume which allowed for extended periods of research in Paris. Technical, material and moral support were willingly and lovingly provided by Pierre-Maurice Barlier, to whom, along with our children Joseph and Rose, I dedicate this book.

Clair Rowden
Cardiff, April 2013

Introduction:
Performing Salome, Revealing Stories

Clair Rowden

More of a *succès de scandale* than a real critical triumph, Wilde's *Salomé* was first performed on stage in Paris on 11 February 1896 by Lina Munte and the Théâtre de l'Œuvre, a theatre company run by Aurélien Lugné-Poë at the Comédie-Parisienne.[1] I begin this book, not with the Gospel versions of Salome's story, nor her various incarnations over the centuries, nor with the publication of Wilde's play, the catalyst that lit the 'Salomania' fuse in Europe just before the turn of the twentieth century.[2] I begin with the play's first performance, as the embodiment of Salome is the focus of this volume, with onstage (or on film) performance of Salome central to most of the chapters presented. Much has been written, particularly in literary and gender studies, about Wilde's Jewish princess, her perverse appetites and tragic end. This volume, whose contributors are drawn from musicology, comparative literature and film studies, builds on the critical mass already published to offer insights into Salome's appropriation across the arts of the late-nineteenth and twentieth centuries, and specifically investigates performances of Salome, indeed, not just Wilde's or Strauss's *Salome*, but Salome as a cultural icon in *fin-de-siècle* society, whose appeal for ever new interpretations of the biblical story still endures.

Richard Strauss was a member of the hand-picked audience which attended the private German premiere of Wilde's drama in Berlin, in a staging by

---

[1] Aurélien Lugné-Poë played Herod. Emily Eells demonstrates how the reception of this one performance of Wilde's *Salomé* coincided with press reports of Wilde's imprisonment in Reading Gaol. A revival opened at the Nouveau Théâtre with Lina Munte in the title role on 28 October 1896. Emily Eells, 'Naturalizing Oscar Wilde as an *homme de lettres*: The French Reception of *Dorian Gray* and *Salomé* (1895–1922)', in Stefano Evangelista (ed.), *The Reception of Oscar Wilde in Europe*, The Athlone Critical Traditions Series: The Reception of British and Irish Authors in Europe (London, 2010), pp. 80–94.

[2] In English prose, 'Salome' will be used. However, *Salomé* and *Salome* will be used to distinguish between performances of different works in French and German, and original spelling has been retained in all quotations. Similarly, the character from Richard Strauss's opera is referred to as Jochanaan, while for the character in Wilde's play, Jokanaan is used.

Max Reinhardt on 15 November 1902.[3] As Strauss recounted, on leaving the theatre, his companion Heinrich Grünfeld suggested *Salome* was ripe operatic material, to which Strauss responded that he had already begun composing it.[4] Strauss used Hedwig Lachmann's powerful German translation of the play to create his libretto, and the opera was premiered at the Hofoper in Dresden on 9 December 1905. But of course, by this time, Oscar Wilde was no longer the dandy and *raconteur extraordinaire* of the 1880s and early 1890s, but a convicted homosexual, spurned by many, whose ill-health, worsened by hard manual labour in prison, brought about his early death in 1900 at the age of 46. By the time of the premiere of Strauss's opera, the decadent morality of Wilde's play *Salomé* was inextricably linked in public perception to that of his private life.[5] Despite wide-ranging acceptance of the play and recognition of the 'pathology' of its heroine in the Freudian era, the notion that Strauss's music had transformed, or transfigured the subject was much debated throughout the opera's European reception. Anne Seshadri's close reading of the Dresden press in 1905 reveals a critical body obsessed with a Wagnerian conception of redemption, whereby Strauss's musical power and the greatness of the last scene 'transforms the pure animalistic longing and transfigures a love that has been driven to madness'.[6] The power of this music then, allied to traditional operatic narrative and musical closure, could only lead to such an interpretation; any alternative was too monstrous to behold, and in Seshadri's reading of *Salome*'s reception, Strauss is more a prophet than the pervert identified by Sander Gilman. Moreover, Joy H. Calico has recently linked this interpretation to the first Salome in Strauss's opera, Marie Wittich, a well-known Isolde who, at the same time as rehearsing *Salome*, was preparing for a performance of *Tristan und Isolde* at Bayreuth, the press thus being unable to escape reading Salome's death in the terms of Isolde's transfiguration.[7] But as Morten Kristiansen points out, very few critics were willing to recognize not only an inversion of Wagnerian ideology – Strauss positing Salome as an extreme physicalization of Isolde's

---

[3]   Rainer Kohlmayer and Lucia Krämer, '*Bunbury* in Germany: Alive and Kicking', in Evangelista (ed.), *The Reception of Oscar Wilde*, pp. 189–202.

[4]   Richard Strauss, *Recollections and Reflections*, ed. Willi Schuh, trans. L.J. Lawrence (London, 1953), p. 150.

[5]   Sander L. Gilman, 'Strauss and the Pervert', in Arthur Groos and Roger Parker (eds), *Reading Opera* (Princeton, NJ, 1988), pp. 306–27, p. 311.

[6]   H. St., 'Konigl. Hofoper', *Dresdener Nachrichten*, 11 December 1905, quoted in Anne L. Seshadri, 'The Taste of Love: Salome's Transfiguration', *Women & Music*, 10 (2006), pp. 24–44, p. 39.

[7]   Joy H. Calico, 'Staging Scandal with *Salome* and *Elektra*', in Rachel Cowgill and Hilary Poriss (eds), *The Arts of the Prima Donna in the Long Nineteenth Century* (London and New York, 2012), pp. 61–82, p. 67.

metaphysical love – but also Strauss's calculated affront on 'music drama' as the title character seduces the redeemer, who is not redeemed but beheaded.[8]

The original French reception of Strauss's opera offered a similar perspective to that in Dresden, believing Strauss's music more pure than the libretto based on Wilde's text, and having succeeded in ennobling the play from base sentiments to a higher spiritual plane.[9] And yet if Salome's necrophilic desires could be interpreted as her 'Wagnerian' redemption through love,[10] the French were left with an uneasy feeling, and a challenge to their definition of the word 'love'.[11] Terms such as desire or lust in relation to Salome's behaviour were rarely substituted, and many critics had to settle for a warped *fin-de-siècle* definition of 'love' in order to skate round the discussion of Salome's pathology. Despite these qualms, Wilde's drama held an important place in French contemporary culture, and at the same time as Strauss conceived his opera, the little-known French composer, Antoine Mariotte also wrote an opera based directly on Wilde's French play. A long and drawn-out public controversy ensued in France as Strauss's editor Adolph Fürstner had acquired the rights to Wilde's play, something Mariotte only sought to do once his score was finished.[12] Nevertheless, Strauss's opera was first performed (in German) in Paris at the Théâtre du Châtelet on 8 May 1907, then at the Paris Opéra in May 1910 in French translation, Mariotte's opera eventually making it to the capital just two weeks before the latter performances of Strauss's work, in April 1910. But the day before the 1907 Parisian premiere of Strauss's work, Maud Allan had rocked the town with her raunchy dance version of the drama,[13] and in November of that year, another famous North American dancer, Loïe Fuller, danced *La Tragédie de Salomé*, whose music was written by Florent Schmitt in the

---

[8]   Morten Kristiansen, 'Strauss's road to operatic success: *Guntram, Feuersnot,* and *Salome*', in Charles Youmans (ed.), *The Cambridge Companion to Richard Strauss* (Cambridge and New York, 2010), pp. 105–18, pp. 116–17; Bryan Gilliam, 'Strauss and the sexual body: the erotics of humour, philosophy, and ego-assertion', in Youmans (ed.), *The Cambridge Companion*, pp. 269–79, pp. 274–5.

[9]   See, for example, M.K. [Maurice Kufferath], 'Salomé', *Le Guide musical*, 24 March 1907, pp. 227–9; Pierre Lalo, 'La Musique', Feuilleton du *Temps*, *Le Temps*, 28 December 1905, pp. 2–3; Pierre Lalo, 'La Musique', Feuilleton du *Temps*, *Le Temps*, 15 May 1907, p. 3.

[10]   And often, by extension, through Christianity.

[11]   This tension is also revealed in the Berlin reception of Wilde's play *Salome* (in Max Reinhardt's production) by W. Eugene Davis, 'Oscar Wilde, *Salome*, and the German Press, 1902–1905', *English Literature in Transition 1880–1920*, 44/2 (2001): pp. 149–80.

[12]   See my chapter, '*Salome* and modern opera: a Parisian perspective', in Günter Brosche and Jürgen May (eds), *Richard Strauss–Jahrbuch 2011*, herausgegeben von der Internationalen Richard Strauss–Gesellschaft in Wien und dem Richard Strauss–Institut in Garmisch-Partenkirchen (Tutzing, 2011), pp. 163–76.

[13]   *La Vision de Salomé*, Théâtre des Variétés, 7 May 1907. The first performance of Allan's dance, given in Vienna in December 1906, is briefly discussed in Sandra Mayer's chapter.

wake of hearing Strauss's opera. The Russian actors/dancers then made a play for the Jewish princess; first Ida Rubinstein starred in Wilde's drama and danced to music by Alexander Glazunov, while Natalia Trouhanowa and Tamara Karsavina, followed by Rubinstein, had all tackled *La Tragédie de Salomé* by 1919.[14] On the other side of the English channel, Sarah Bernhardt's early attempts to stage Wilde's drama were thwarted by the Lord Chamberlain, who only gave permission for Strauss's opera to be performed with a bastardized libretto at Covent Garden in December 1910.[15] This list is meant in no way to be exhaustive, but merely demonstrates the engouement of 'high-art' Salomes at the start of the twentieth century – let alone the proliferation of Salomes on the vaudeville and cabaret stages – and introduces some of the early productions which will be considered in this volume.[16]

Wilde and Strauss: *une entente cordiale*

Scholars in the past 30 years have increasingly identified Wilde's *Salomé* as a forward-looking Modernist text.[17] Wilde thus emerges as a transitional figure whose interests in symbolist drama and synthetic spectacle as shaped in *Salomé* anticipate developments in poetic drama such as those made by William Butler Yeats.[18] Yeats, in Dublin, was pursuing a similar, Maeterlinck-influenced dramatic vision to Wilde, and both men used the imagery of acting as a way of expressing a profound psychological and metaphysical concept of human nature.[19] This notwithstanding, Yeats expressed his dislike of *Salomé* in 1906,[20] yet acknowledged his debt to, fascination with, and exorcism of *Salomé* in his late plays *The King of the Great Clock Tower* (1934) and *A Full Moon in March* (1935, the latter being a versified version of the former), describing *Salomé* as a 'fragment of the past I had

---

[14]   This work and its subsequent performances are further discussed in my chapter 'Whose/Who's Salome? Natalia Trouhanowa, a Dancing Diva'.

[15]   Anne Sivuoja-Kauppala's chapter deals with Finnish soprano Aino Ackté's performance in the London premiere of Strauss's *Salome* in 1910.

[16]   The appendix 'Chronological Table of Selected Productions', in William Tydeman and Steven Price, *Wilde: Salome*, Plays in Production (Cambridge and New York, 1996), pp. 184–7, is a useful resource.

[17]   From Katharine Worth, *Oscar Wilde* (London and Basingstoke, 1983) to Petra Dierkes-Thrun, *Salome's Modernity: Oscar Wilde and the Aesthetics of Transgression* (Ann Arbor, MI, 2011).

[18]   Richard Allen Cave, 'Wilde's plays: Some lines of influence', in Peter Raby (ed.), *The Cambridge Companion to Oscar Wilde* (Cambridge, 1997), pp. 219–48.

[19]   Worth, *Oscar Wilde*, pp. 4, 53.

[20]   In a letter to art critic, engraver, poet and dramatist T. Sturge Moore, dated 6 May 1906. See Ursula Bridge (ed.), *W.B. Yeats and T. Sturge Moore: Their Correspondence, 1901–1937* (London, 1953), pp. 8–9.

to get rid of'.[21] The decadent style of Wilde's *Salomé* is thus now understood to point forwards, decadence and the avant-garde being two aspects of Modernism's discontent with bourgeois institutions, mores and morality, values and hopes of cultural progress.[22] Decadent literature is thus a self-conscious critique of the same through the denigration of wholeness and wholesomeness and the celebration of the toxic and taboo.[23] Decadent literature usually toyed with themes of deviance and degeneration; it is described as excessive and artificial; it is understood as based upon processes of deformation and ornamentation. In this way, decadent literature is already a performative genre; in a post-Derridean, post-Butlerian sense, it 'strikes a pose'.[24] Wilde's *Salomé* is thus a self-conscious performance, or process of representation, which was in turn appropriated by hundreds (if not thousands) of others as a vehicle for the manipulation of the concepts of performance and representation. Wilde's text has also been equated with mannerism and camp – love of artifice and exaggeration, victory of style over content, aesthetics over morality, irony over tragedy – both of which share many defining characteristics with decadence.[25] But as Susan Sontag affirmed in her ground-breaking essay nearly 50 years ago, camp treads a fine line between parody and self-parody; if the latter lacks ebullience and reveals the slightest hint of contempt for one's themes and materials, self-parody reeks of self-love. Thus camp rests on innocence and naivety, but can also corrupt it.[26]

Sontag categorizes Strauss's operas as camp, and an element of parody was important both to Strauss and to the reception of his works, as Wayne Heisler

---

[21]   Worth, *Oscar Wilde*, p. 72. For a detailed study of Yeats's late plays, see F.A.C. Wilson, *W.B. Yeats and Tradition* (London, 1958). This chain of influence continued also to Ezra Pound. Yeats discovered Japanese Noh theatre, which inspired his late plays, through his friendship and association with Pound (who acted as Yeats's secretary from 1913), and who also wrote his own, Jules Laforgue-inspired ironic version of the Salome tale as *Our Tetrarchal précieuse*. Ezra Pound, *Instigations of Ezra Pound together with an essay on the Chinese Written Character by Ernest Fenollosa* (New York, 1920). On the relationship between Yeats and Pound, see Richard Ellmann, *Yeats: The Man and the Masks* (New York and London, 1948, reissued 1999), pp. 215–17.

[22]   Stephen Downes, *Music and Decadence in European Modernism: The Case of Central and Eastern Europe* (Cambridge, 2010), pp. 31, 246.

[23]   Ibid., p. 1.

[24]   See James Loxley, *Performativity* (London and New York, 2007) for an excellent and concise history of the term performativity and its associated branch of study. I refer to the works of Jacques Derrida and Judith Butler (particularly *Gender Trouble*, 1990).

[25]   Susan Sontag, 'Notes on Camp', in *Against Interpretation and Other Essays* (London, 2009), pp. 275–92. Originally published in *Partisan Review*, 31/4 (Fall 1964): pp. 515–30. Sontag's essay is problematized, and its reception – and the polemic responses it provoked (particularly from gay writers) – is clearly examined in Fabio Cleto's introduction to Fabio Cleto (ed.), *Camp: Queer Aesthetics and the Performing Subject. A Reader* (Edinburgh, 1999), pp. 1–42.

[26]   Sontag, 'Notes on Camp', pp. 282–3.

Jnr.'s recent study of Strauss's ballets has shown.[27] Strauss was at the forefront of musical Modernism in the period before the First World War, but his retreat from a radical tonal language after *Elektra* – a 'retreat' now informed by perceptive modern scholarship which demonstrates the continuities in Strauss's approach to tonality, form and aesthetics[28] – discredited him among the younger generation of Modernist composers who saw his works as decadent, superficial, even banal. Yet our understanding of Modernism has also been expanded to include a more complex, pluralistic approach to the question of style,[29] Heisler identifying parody as an alternative to Modernism in Strauss's works after *Elektra*. Yet Heisler qualifies Strauss's use of parody, suggesting it occasionally slips into self-parody due to Strauss's compositional virtuosity and performance conditions out of the composer's control. While this occasional 'excess of technique over expression' was a compositional flaw in nineteenth-century aesthetic terms,[30] it is also a marker of Strauss's twentieth-century modernity.[31] But this issue of self-parody haunts Strauss's music and academic writings thereof,[32] commentators readily defining both *Salome*, and particularly the 'Dance of the Seven Veils', as camp and kitsch.[33] Charles Youmans recently affirmed not only that the music of the dance is kitsch and vulgar as a mirror of Herod's taste, but also that it functions as a necessary pendant to the nauseating dissonance and radical tone-painting of the score, as well as the overblown seriousness of the music of Jochanaan.[34] The

---

[27] Wayne Heisler Jnr., *The Ballet Collaborations of Richard Strauss* (Rochester, NY, 2009). While Sontag's inclusion of Strauss's operas on her 'camp list' could be seen as referring to only those works post *Elektra*, the camp of Wilde's text has led to readings of Strauss's opera which deal with these aspects also.

[28] Alex Ross, 'Strauss's place in the twentieth century', in Youmans (ed.), *The Cambridge Companion*, pp. 195–212, p. 196.

[29] Ibid., p. 197.

[30] For a discussion of this issue in the original French reception of *Salome*, see my chapter, '*Salome* and modern opera: A Parisian perspective', in Brosche and May (eds), *Richard Strauss Jahrbuch 2011*.

[31] Lawrence Kramer, *Opera and Modern Culture: Wagner and Strauss* (Berkeley, CA, 2004), p. 189.

[32] Hugo von Hofmannsthal admonished Strauss as early as September 1912 for contempt of his subject, and thus his narcissistic parody and caricatural manner, in relation to their collaboration for Diaghilev's Ballet Russes *Josephslegende*, premiered in Paris as *La Légende de Joseph* in May 1914. See *A Working Relationship: The Correspondence between Richard Strauss and Hugo von Hofmannsthal*, trans. Hanns Hammelmann and Ewald Osers (New York, 1961), pp. 142–4.

[33] This is a relatively common trope in modern Strauss scholarship. See, for example, Robin Holloway's chapter '*Salome*: art or kitsch?', in Derrick Puffett (ed.), *Richard Strauss: Salome*, Cambridge Opera Handbooks (Cambridge, 1989), pp. 145–64.

[34] Charles Youmans, 'Strauss and the nature of music', in Charles Youmans (ed.), *The Cambridge Companion to Richard Strauss*, pp. 280–293, p. 285.

dance's 'ostentatious tastelessness' and 'weakness', according to Youmans, create an appealing, alternative reality which draws the listener in but which abandons the realm of the composer's own musical experience.

And yet, while later readings of the 'Dance of the Seven Veils' and title role may inhabit this interpretative paradigm, for many early performers, Salome was (deadly) serious business. Thus *Salome* remains a musical and theatrical stylization of a stylized text, seized upon by many for its highly fashionable *fin-de-siècle* themes of desire, transgression, hysteria and erotic dance, taken up by others to create camp, Orientalist, extravagant theatrical spectacles, and by many more for an exploration of subjectivity, sexuality and representation. For, in *Salomé/Salome*, the site of subjectivity (and objectivity) is dislodged: who is performing and for whom? Craig Owens has identified the enactment of objectification in transgressive sexualities, such as those represented in Wilde's play, whereby the subject poses as an object in order to be a subject,[35] Emily Apter demonstrating how Orientalist stereotypes were self-consciously mobilized by French *fin-de-siècle* feminists (and lesbians) to fashion 'new' sexual identities which functioned as props on which to hang a pose.[36] Thus, understanding of the performative nature of *Salome* – the way in which meaning is inscribed and reinscribed with each successive iteration or performance – is key: Strauss's opera, both its performance and discussion of it, is a ripe site for the negotiation of multiple meanings, tensions and agency between its different interpretative layers.

Strauss's Opera, Musicology and the 'Dance of the Seven Veils'

Despite the centrality of the themes of representation and performance in both Wilde's play and Strauss's 'performative' opera, much musicological writing on *Salome* has not taken the actual performers into account.[37] Inevitably, attention has been given to the artwork, particularly two key scenes and pivotal events in Strauss's opera, the dance – exaggerated to extraordinary proportions in comparison with literary versions due to the media within which Strauss was working – and Salome's monologue with the dismembered head. They are nevertheless both associated with physical bodies, and form two visual components which help

---

[35]   Craig Owens, 'The Medusa Effect, or, The Spectacular Ruse', in Scott Bryson et al. (eds), *Beyond Recognition: Representation, Power and Culture* (Berkeley, CA, 1992), cited in Emily Apter, 'Acting Out Orientalism: Sapphic Theatricality in Turn-of-the-Century Paris', in Elin Diamond (ed.), *Performance and Cultural Politics* (New York and London, 1996), pp. 15–34, p. 18.

[36]   Apter, 'Acting Out Orientalism', p. 19.

[37]   For instance, in Linda Hutcheon and Michael Hutcheon's *Bodily Charm: Living Opera* (Lincoln and London, 2000), despite claims that the body on stage is the centre of their attention (rather than music or disembodied voice), they do not actually deal with performers of *Salome*, but rather with the performer that is Salome.

establish the phenomenon of spectacle and the act of seeing as a textual leitmotif – an *idée fixe* – in Wilde's symbolist drama. Although every character is caught within this observational chain,[38] it is Herod's gaze on Salome's body that has become the locus of much scholarly writing.[39] In musicology, this obsession with the male gaze is contested in more feminist readings of the opera which investigate how both the body and voice might challenge such structures, encouraging different and often conflicting interpretations. Lawrence Kramer describes Salome as disrupting and usurping the male gaze during her dance; Linda and Michael Hutcheon go further to declare the dance as a triumph: to be the object of the gaze is to be empowered.[40] Carolyn Abbate finds a similar kind of power in the opera's envoicing of Salome.[41] Like Kramer and Susan McClary,[42] Abbate interprets Salome (notably both the character and the singer that embodies her) as the object of the gaze, but she does not understand the score as supporting the visual (and confining) structures of the libretto. Instead, at times she identifies Strauss's refusal to use traditional operatic compositional power and music (such as leitmotifs, etc.) to reveal the objectified, relinquishing an 'authorial voice' in favour of other voices and alternative perspectives, thus deconstructing one established viewpoint. In this way the female body on stage and her strong and seducing female voice may be heard across the narrative. In Kramer's and McClary's analyses, Salome's position as 'Other' is explained through the way she functions as a threat to operatic unity; her moral transgressions are equated with the musical transgressions that surround her,[43] McClary explaining Salome's death in terms of the restoration of both

---

[38]   As Charles Bernheimer points out, the tragic psychological truth conveyed by the play's naturalistic mimesis is that desire never coincides with its object: the Page wants Narraboth, Narraboth and Herod want Salome, Salome wants Jokanaan. Charles Bernheimer, *Decadent Subjects: The Idea of Decadence in Art, Literature, Philosophy, and Culture of the* Fin de Siècle *in Europe*, eds T. Jefferson Kline and Naomi Schor (Baltimore, MD and London, 2002), p. 125.

[39]   On the act of looking and the gaze as structuring principle in Wilde's drama, see Helen Tookey, '"The fiend that smites with a look": The Monstrous/Menstruous Woman and the Danger of the Gaze in Oscar Wilde's *Salomé*', *Literature and Theology*, 18/1 (2004): pp. 23–37; Brad Bucknell, 'On "Seeing" Salome', *English Literary History*, 60/2 (1993): pp. 503–26; Joseph Donohue, 'Distance, Death and Desire in *Salome*', in Peter Raby (ed.), *The Cambridge Companion to Oscar Wilde* (Cambridge, 1997), pp. 118–42.

[40]   Hutcheon and Hutcheon, *Bodily Charm*, p. 109. It should be noted that Kramer finds that Salome eventually loses the power of the gaze she usurped in the dance. Lawrence Kramer, 'Culture and musical hermeneutics: the Salome complex', *Cambridge Opera Journal*, 2/3 (1990): pp. 269–94.

[41]   Carolyn Abbate, 'Opera; or, the Envoicing of Women', in Ruth A. Solie (ed.), *Musicology and Difference* (Berkeley, CA, 1992), pp. 225–58.

[42]   Susan McClary, *Feminine Endings: Music, Gender, and Sexuality* (Minneapolis, MN, 1991).

[43]   Kramer, 'Culture and musical hermeneutics', p. 291.

social and tonal order.[44] For Abbate, when Salome manages to break out of what McClary defines as the patriarchal established frame of the narrative, or when a strong performance manages to subvert that frame, a new unity, or rather an alternative multiplicity can be seen to be established.

Wilde's stage directions for the dance are infamously laconic, specifying simply 'Salomé dances the dance of the seven veils'.[45] Biblical sources from the Gospels of Saints Matthew and Mark give no detail of the dance which over the centuries has been left to the imagination of artists, writers and dancers. The most influential Salome precedent for Wilde's drama was no doubt Gustave Flaubert's 'Hérodias', one of his *Trois Contes*, published in 1877.[46] Joris-Karl Huysmans's *A Rebours* (1884) contained a graphically decadent and sensual description of Salome dancing, but his version is not a straightforward 'creation', more an influential literary elaboration of what he saw in Gustave Moreau's famous Salome paintings (*L'Apparition* and *Salomé dansant devant Hérode*), both exhibited in Paris in the late 1870s before being sold to private owners and becoming unavailable for public viewing.[47] The detail Flaubert gives specifically about Salome's dance – rather than the effect it has on its audience – is also remarkably concise.[48] The most vivid details evoke a highly supple young woman who bends from the hips, sweeping her chin to the floor, as well as an acrobatic ability to walk swiftly on her hands, the nape of her neck and her vertebrae at right angles to one another. At the premiere in Paris in 1896, René Darlay, a young 'chansonnier', provided

---

[44]   McClary, *Feminine Endings*, p. 100.

[45]   Oscar Wilde, 'Salomé', in *Complete Works of Oscar Wilde* (London and Glasgow, 1948, rpt. 1977), pp. 552–75, p. 570. Bernheimer suggests that Wilde did not describe the dance precisely in order to maintain ambiguity about how the author 'looks on' his heroine. Bernheimer, *Decadent Subjects*, p. 128.

[46]   Eells, 'Naturalizing Oscar Wilde', p. 84.

[47]   Bernheimer, *Decadent Subjects*, p. 111. Thus Huysmans's text became a proxy for Moreau's artworks. For an excellent, succinct examination of Huysmans's Salome, see Dierkes-Thrun, *Salome's Modernity*, pp. 34–42.

[48]   Flaubert, 'Hérodias', in *Trois Contes*, Le Livre de Poche (Paris, 1983), pp. 141–2: 'Elle se renversait de tous les côtés, pareille à une fleur que la tempête agite. Les brillants de ses oreilles sautaient, l'étoffe de son dos chatoyait; de ses bras, de ses pieds, de ses vêtements jaillissaient d'invisibles étincelles qui enflammaient les hommes. ... Sans fléchir ses genoux en écartant les jambes, elle se courba si bien que son menton frôlait le plancher; ... Ensuite elle tourna autour de la table d'Antipas, frénétiquement, comme le rhombe des sorcières; ... Elle se jeta sur les mains, les talons en l'air, parcourut ainsi l'estrade comme un grand scarabée; et s'arrêta, brusquement. Sa nuque et ses vertèbres faisaient un angle droit. Les fourreaux de couleur qui enveloppaient ses jambes, lui passant par-dessus l'épaule, comme des arcs-en-ciel, accompagnaient sa figure, à une coudée du sol. Ses lèvres étaient peintes, ses sourcils très noirs, ses yeux presque terribles, et des gouttelettes à son front semblaient une vapeur sur du marbre blanc. Elle ne parlait pas. Ils se regardaient.'

the music for Lina Munte's dance,[49] a rather ironic 'soiriste' describing a music 'of curious rhythm, with an original melody, played on an out-of-tune piano and a flute which ignored the pulse'.[50] No more is known of the music to which the first 'embodied' Wildean Salome danced. The dance expected by today's audiences of Strauss's opera is far from that described by Flaubert, and Hedda Høgåsen-Hallesby's chapter in this volume discusses 'the impossibility of staging the dance',[51] or rather the possible ways of staging the dance in modern productions to bring new meaning to Salome's story. From early in the opera's performance history, singers have danced (with varying degrees of success) themselves (Franchette Verhunk, Aino Ackté, Mary Garden, Gemma Bellincioni), but many more have been replaced by professional dancers. Theatrical illusion has taken precedence so that the dance may become a truly embodied experience, yet it takes a fine dancer and choreography to break free from the merely voyeuristic nature of the on- and offstage experience.[52] Strauss himself was unsatisfied with the general salacious trend of interpretations of the dance, and nearly 20 years after its first performance, wrote concise stage directions, but which referred constantly to different poses from Orientalist paintings, including those by Gustave Moreau, which should be struck by the dancer at various moments.[53] Thus the 'real', embodied, unrestrainable Salome – whose presence calls into question social and political relationships, ideological and emotional positions – was not what Strauss had in mind, as here he seems to want to reimpose the 'frame', and Salome as the object of the gaze. In this case, arguments for the dance as empowerment, or Abbate's reading of Strauss's relinquishing of authorial control seem to crumble beneath the weight and corporeality of a dancing body that risks 'stealing the show'.

---

[49] Louis Schneider, 'Salomé', *Le Théâtre* (202) May 1907, pp. 3–8, p. 3. Darlay is given here, as elsewhere, as Darlé. My thanks to Emily Eells for her sharing of this information.

[50] 'musique au rythme curieux, à la mélodie originale, jouée par un piano faux, et une flûte qui ignorait la mesure'. Le Pompier de Service, 'La Soirée parisienne', 'Recueil factice du Théâtre de l'Œuvre', Département des Arts du Spectacle, Bibliothèque nationale de France, RE 10889 (Microfilm 102070).

[51] Abbate, 'Opera; or, the Envoicing of Women', p. 240.

[52] As Susan Leigh Foster reminds us, 'choreographic choices constitute a theorization of embodiment – how bodies express and interact in a given cultural moment.' Susan Leigh Foster, 'Pygmalion's No-Body and the Body of Dance', in Diamond (ed.), *Performance and Cultural Politics*, pp. 131–54, p. 137.

[53] Reprinted as an appendix in Puffet (ed.), *Richard Strauss: Salome*, pp. 165–7. Strauss later wrote: 'Anyone who has been in the east and has observed the decorum with which women there behave, will appreciate that Salome, being a chaste virgin and an oriental princess, must be played with the simplest and most restrained of gestures, unless her defeat by the miracle of a great world is to excite only disgust and horror instead of sympathy' (pp. 166–7).

Since Roland Barthes's 'The Death of the Author' (1967) and since the post-structuralist era,[54] no 'text' can be read as having a stable meaning, the signified being dependent on varying cultural contexts. Barthes also proposed the rebirth of the author inside the artwork, one that is revealed through voices that speak what we read/see/hear.[55] Feminist writing has claimed those voices as female, and in a study of artworks featuring one of the all-time great female protagonists, this volume invariably deals with feminist critical perspectives in its interdisciplinary mix. Moreover, while issues of gender and sexuality necessarily underpin all discussions in this book, gender studies and queer theory are not the main theoretical focus of its investigations.

The volume begins with Polina Dimova's eclectic and 'synaesthetic' chapter which situates Wilde's *Salomé* within the long tradition of Salome artistic interpretations, and locates decadent literature in the transitional period which resolves into the avant-garde and the beginnings of Modernism in order to discuss transformations of *Salomé* across the arts and into the twentieth century. Indeed, Dimova sets out to prove not only that Wilde's text was ripe for intermedial adaptations, but indeed, that these reinterpretations were demanded by the play's very construction and language. Thus by minimizing the importance of the word and giving preference to other sensory perceptions and manifestations, Wilde facilitated, indeed negotiated *Salomé*'s transformation in music and the fine arts. Thus, under the weight of decadent concerns, Wilde consciously permitted his play to transcend itself, allowing it to relive, or live again in other media.

This chapter sets the tone for the rest of the volume which develops many of the ideas already set out in relation to specific case studies. The three following chapters deal with reception, reputation, appropriation, embodiment and performance. Sandra Mayer examines the critical Viennese reception of Wilde's play, attempting to assess its impact on the formation of Wilde's authorial image and literary status, demonstrating the way in which censorship operated with regard to different theatres and publics, as well as highlighting pseudo-scientific theories which were used to explain deviance and transgression. The reception of Wilde's play in German-speaking countries is central also to the creation and reception of Richard Strauss's operatic version, and Mayer addresses how in less than 10 years, the fame and popularity of the operatic version had completely

---

[54]   Roland Barthes, 'La Mort de l'auteur', in Eric Marty (ed.), *Roland Barthes Œuvres complètes, Tome III, 1966–1973* (Paris, 1994), pp. 491–5. Originally published in English in *Aspen Magazine*, 5–6 (Autumn/Winter 1967).

[55]   Drawn from Carolyn Abbate's discussion of Kaja Silverman's interpretation of Barthes's 'author politics' in 'Opera; or, the Envoicing of Women', pp. 231–2. Kaja Silverman, *The Acoustic Mirror: The Female Voice in Psychoanalysis and Cinema* (Bloomington, IN, 1988). See also the collection of essays by Barthes from the 1970s, regrouped as 'Le Corps de la Musique', in *L'Obvie et l'obtus: Essais critiques III* (Paris, 1982). The discussion in Abbate's book, *Unsung Voices: Opera and Musical Narrative in the Nineteenth Century* (Princeton, NJ, 1991), develops from similar premises.

eclipsed Wilde's tragedy. As Petra Dierkes-Thrun writes, Wilde's play, despite what some commentators have read as the crushing narrative of the death of a *femme fatale* at the end, stops short of making sense of its own ending,[56] unlike Strauss's opera which, by allying Wilde's story to narrative musical techniques, necessarily achieves closure of a more affirmative nature. Indeed, it is perhaps in part this 'popular avant-garde' stance which reconciles the expectations of many different audiences that has allowed the bourgeois Strauss and his opera to succeed where the highly controversial Wilde and his play failed.

The focus of chapters 3 and 4 is specific performers of Salome from the period before World War One. Performance as cultural practice – its concern for historical and cultural specificity of individual performances – gives rise also to performance as cultural process. Performance studies and writings on performativity tend to focalize on one performance, but discussions in this volume take a step back to attempt a genetic analysis of performance.[57] While the reception of a show may shed light on a performance's meaning and aesthetic (as well as social and political) status, genetic analysis deals with a performance in the process of being made, examining the preliminary materials and choices made that characterize the final staged event, in an attempt to uncover how an aesthetic was constituted.[58] Chapters by Anne Sivuoja-Kauppala and me look at how two historic performers – the singer Aino Ackté in London and the dancer Natalia Trouhanowa in Paris – went about authoring the role of Salome, their preparatory procedures and collaborative strategies. While all was permitted in Paris, London performances of Strauss's opera were plagued by issues of censorship, and Sivuoja-Kauppala's chapter reifies Mayer's discussion of Austrian debates by problematizing the workings of the censors in Edwardian Britain. The study of performance as process also counterbalances those readings of opera which revel in the sound and image of the female performer, such as those proposed by Paul Robinson and Wayne Koestenbaum in their debunking of Catherine Clément's all-crushing narrative frame.[59] Both these chapters provide access to hitherto unexplored primary sources, press and iconographical materials in order to build up a picture of both the artists' working methods and the spectacles they created. Both use techniques from reception studies and microhistory, whereby examination of a performance catalyses the study of a constellation of broadly held values to which it relates, and

[56]   Dierkes-Thrun, *Salome's Modernity*, pp. 45–6.

[57]   Josette Féral, 'Introduction: Towards a Genetic Study of Performance – Take 2', *Theatre Research International* 35 (2008): pp. 223–33.

[58]   Ibid., p. 229.

[59]   Catherine Clément, *Opera or the Undoing of Women*, trans. Betsy Wing (London, 1989). (First published in French in 1979). Paul Robinson, 'A Deconstructive Postscript: Reading Libretti and Misreading Opera', in Arthur Groos and Roger Parker (eds), *Reading Opera* (Princeton, NJ, 1988), pp. 328–46. Wayne Koestenbaum, *The Queen's Throat: Opera, Homosexuality, and the Mystery of Desire* (New York and London, 1993).

reveals how that global context inflects forces which in turn affect performance.[60] Thus these chapters offer insights into the role and agency of early performers in the production and complex negotiation of meaning inherent in the role of Salome.

The final three chapters explore performance as cultural practice which reinscribes and continuously reinvents the ideas, icons, symbols and gestures that shape both the performance itself, and its reception.[61] Thus the death of Barthes's author can give life to other 'authors' – performers, directors, designers, choreographers, conductors – to present (yet) another version of the signified, if they dare to control it. Choreographic choices can play with the relations between one body and another, between body and subject, between subject and its setting.[62] Directors of both opera and film have specific ideas and messages to convey, but in this post-everything era, they are perhaps just as comfortable with the multiple meanings that their readings offer. In this section, Hedda Høgåsen-Hallesby uses critical space theory, adapted from the work of French sociologist and philosopher Henri Lefebvre,[63] to re-examine the rooms and spaces created by different interpretations of the 'Dance of the Seven Veils' in operatic productions since 1945, and what those empty yet resonant rooms may mean. Caryl Clark focusses on just one recent production of *Salome* by the award-winning Armenian–Canadian film director Atom Egoyan, which nevertheless privileges the eye of the *auteur* and that of the voyeuristic audience over embodied performance, problematizing the narrative to operate a powerful reorientation onto the young woman's psychologically and sexually dysfunctional family.

Tristan Grünberg's chapter opens the door to cinematographic portrayals of Salome who continues to fascinate the film world as actor/director Al Pacino showed in his *Wilde Salomé* in 2011. Grünberg, however, chooses to focus on two Salome films from the last quarter of the twentieth century which embrace and celebrate camp and decadent aesthetics with their focus on ornamentation, excess, parody and performativity, discussed at the start of this introduction. Thus the volume comes full circle, from the opening chapters dealing not only with the reception of Wilde's heroine and how her transgressive sexuality and that of Wilde were indissolubly linked in public perception, but also with Modernist representation, to melodramatic and ambivalent filmic renderings of Salome where the frontiers between life and art, stage and backstage are continuously blurred. In

---

[60] Microhistory as found in the work of Robert Darnton (*The Great Cat Massacre and Other Episodes in French Cultural History* (London, 1984)) or Edward Berenson (*The Trial of Madame Caillaux* (Berkeley, CA, 1992)) informs these chapters. See also the edited collection, Jacques Revel (ed.), *Jeux d'échelles: La micro-analyse à l'expérience* (Paris, 1996).

[61] Here I paraphrase Elin Diamond's introduction to her edited volume, *Performance and Cultural Politics*, pp. 1–14.

[62] Foster, 'Pygmalion's No-Body', p. 136.

[63] Henri Lefebvre, *The Production of Space*, trans. Donald Nicholson-Smith (Oxford, 1991). First published in French as *La production de l'espace* in 1974.

its wide-ranging presentation of subject materials, theoretical tools, and authors, this interdisciplinary volume aims at breadth in terms of intellectual scope and audience. Using Salome as a common starting point, each chapter suggests new ways in which corporeal performing bodies reveal alternative stories, narratives, perspectives. By crossing and challenging disciplinary boundaries, this volume may shed new light on Salome, Wilde, Strauss and the many other artists examined here, and hence how they and, more importantly, how we appreciate Salome as a cultural icon of our era.

Chapter 1

Decadent Senses: The Dissemination of Oscar Wilde's *Salomé* across the Arts

Polina Dimova

The Vicissitudes of Photography

In a 1987 article on Oscar Wilde, the French newspaper *Le Monde* published a photograph of the playwright, dressed up and posing as his *femme fatale* heroine Salome.[1] The picture appeared in Richard Ellmann's 1987 biography, captioned: 'Wilde in costume as Salomé'[2] (see Figure 1.1). In the following decade, the photograph titillated the imagination of gender critics, opening up a myriad of interpretative possibilities by alerting scholars to Wilde's supposed transvestite tendencies. Marjorie Garber proposed that Salome's dance should be construed as a transvestite dance: 'the dancer is neither male nor female, but rather, transvestitic – that is the essence of the dance itself.'[3] Though exposing the fetishistic tendencies of Garber's reading, Megan Becker-Leckrone herself lovingly describes the photo in an apposition she could not resist interpolating: 'a self-consciously staged photograph of Wilde in drag, on bended knee, reaching toward a dummy head on a platter.'[4] After situating Wilde's *Salomé* 'within the Paterian tradition … [as] a male transvestite', even Richard Dellamora, who is quick to put forward his argument about *Salomé* as 'a significant document in the history of a specifically female sexuality', continues to deal with the picture by describing it in detail: 'a semi-nude photograph of Wilde dressed as Salomé and reaching for the decapitated head of John'.[5] The picture seems to possess enormous argumentative value. As an image, an indexical sign, and an existential trace of historical truth, the photograph proves its insurmountable power.

---

[1] Information on the 'photograph affair' is drawn from Steven Morris, 'Importance of not being Salome', *The Guardian*, Monday 17 July 2000.

[2] Richard Ellmann, *Oscar Wilde* (New York, 1988), facing p. 428.

[3] Marjorie Garber, *Vested Interests: Cross-Dressing and Cultural Anxiety* (New York, 1992), p. 342.

[4] Megan Becker-Leckrone, 'Salome ©: The Fetishization of a Textual Corpus', *New Literary History*, 26/2 (1995): pp. 239–60, p. 253.

[5] Richard Dellamora, 'Traversing the Feminine in Oscar Wilde's *Salomé*', in Thaïs E. Morgan (ed.), *Victorian Sages and Cultural Discourses: Renegotiating Gender and Power* (New Brunswick, NJ and London, 1990), pp. 246–64, pp. 247–8.

Figure 1.1   Alice Guszalewicz as Salome
Source: Guillot de Saix Collection. © Roger-Viollet.

Not convinced of Wilde's alleged transvestitism, Merlin Holland joined forces with the German scholar Horst Schroeder to demystify the photograph.[6] Merlin Holland, Wilde's grandson and co-editor of his complete letters, was lucky to be presented with a photograph of Alice Guszalewicz, the Hungarian soprano who sang Salome in Cologne in 1906/07, six years after Wilde's death in Paris (see Figure 1.2). Her jewellery and garment appear identical to those in the 'Wilde-in-drag' picture. This new attribution of the photograph suggests that its identification, and our recognition of Wilde in the picture, was over-determined. Due to Salome's professed virility, androgyny or even male homosexuality and Paterism, her identification with Wilde himself had sedimented in the critical consciousness over the years. Practices of cross-dressing in various productions, most notably Lindsay Kemp's all-male 1977 production and Ken Russell's film *Salome's Last Dance* (1987), discussed in detail in the final chapter to this volume, made it possible for us to envision a Wilde in drag.[7] Indeed, Becker-Leckrone is completely justified in pointing out the series of 'mystifications' informing the Salome myth, although the critic herself was caught up in them. Elaine Showalter, also fascinated with the picture of Wilde as Salome 'in a wig and jeweled costume, slave bracelets around his arms', realizes that the photograph is veiled in mystery. Nevertheless, while raising questions, she never doubts its authenticity; rather, she keeps weaving out its story by further asking rhetorically, 'At what private theatricals did Wilde decide "Salomé, ç'est [*sic*] moi"?'[8] Critics wistfully desired this image of Wilde, and their fantasy finally produced it.

The new interpretation of the photograph gives us a curious insight into what critics have come to emphasize in recent years, namely, Wilde's homosexuality, and what they have neglected, namely, his play's involvement with the other arts. An all-too-vulnerable photograph opens up new interpretative possibilities for the study of Wilde's *Salomé* across the arts and urges us to shift our critical focus away from Wilde's gay flamboyance toward his *Salomé*'s transformations on the stage, in the theatre and in the opera houses, as well as in drawings.

The resurgence of the Salome myth in *fin-de-siècle* literature, visual arts and music has produced a tremendous body of critical writing, which traces influences and intertextual connections in various representations of the irresistible *femme fatale*. While much scholarly work strives to cross disciplinary boundaries by discussing the decadent incarnations of Salome in more than one medium,

---

[6]   Horst Schroeder drew attention to the misreading of the Wilde picture by presenting four other pictures of Alice Guszalewicz as Salome in his *Alice in Wildeland* (Braunschweig, 1994). See also Ian Small, *Oscar Wilde: Recent Research* (Greensboro, NC, 2000), pp. 27–8.

[7]   For a discussion of all-male or gender-ambiguous performances of *Salomé*, see Elaine Showalter, *Sexual Anarchy: Gender and Culture at the Fin-de-Siècle* (New York, 1990), pp. 167–8. About Kemp's production in particular, see William Tydeman and Steven Price, *Wilde: Salome* (Cambridge and New York, 1996), pp. 98–105.

[8]   Showalter, *Sexual Anarchy*, p. 156.

Figure 1.2   Alice Guszalewicz as Salome
Note: Published in Horst Schroeder, *Alice in Wildeland* (Braunschweig, 1994), p. 33.
Originally published in *Bühne und Welt*, 9 (1907), p. 444.

intermediality,[9] as an issue in itself, has been eclipsed by psychoanalysis, feminism, sexuality and gender and queer studies as a focus of investigation.[10] This critical preoccupation, of course, reflects well the content of the myth of the *femme fatale* or 'dragon lady' Salome, as decadents and symbolists construed her at the turn of the twentieth century. Rather than reading Salome's various embodiments across the arts as a mere symptom of a *fin-de-siècle* obsession revealing male anxieties about female sexuality or enacting a masculine wish-fulfilment, as many critics have done, this essay disentangles the discourse of gender from the discourse of intermediality.[11] It shifts the focus of Salome criticism toward issues of intermedial translation, mirroring the dynamics of the 'Wilde-in-drag' picture.

By examining the intermedial drive that has propelled the Salome tradition over the centuries, this chapter construes Wilde's play as self-consciously looking back on its multifarious interartistic sources on the one hand, and, on the other, as looking forward to its future artistic interpretations. Over the course of this examination, I will trace the internal logic of the play's synaesthetic principles – its interweaving of vision, voice and dance – as motivating and, in fact, necessitating *Salomé*'s dissemination across the arts. In order to disentangle the

---

[9]   I use the term 'intermediality' as shorthand for the relations between interartistic endeavours and the processes that inform these relations. I opt for 'intermediality' and 'intermedial' rather than 'intertextuality' and 'intertextual' so as not to give preponderance to text over the visual arts, music and dance. Peter Wagner defines 'intermediality' as the intertextual use of one medium (for instance, painting or music) in the realm of another medium (for instance, poetry or drama). Peter Wagner (ed.), *Icons, Texts, Iconotexts: Essays on Ekphrasis and Intermediality* (Berlin and New York, 1996). The term 'intermedium', and hence 'intermediality', goes back to the theoretical essays of the fluxus artist Dick Higgins in the 1960s. More recently in the 1990s, the term intermediality has established itself in German criticism as *Intermedialität*.

[10]   Lawrence Kramer approaches the 'Salome complex' by using feminist criticism, while his other goal is to find common methodological space for literary criticism and musicology. Lawrence Kramer, 'Culture and musical hermeneutics: the Salome complex', *Cambridge Opera Journal*, 2/3 (1990): pp. 269–94. Brad Bucknell suggests that various representations of Salome rely on the interaction of visual and verbal signs which make Salome available to the male gaze of the reader, the viewer and the writer. In this vein, Bucknell carefully traces the interplay of words and images in the biblical Salome sources, Huysmans's *A Rebours*, Moreau's paintings and Wilde's play but always interprets them as simply misogynistic. Brad Bucknell, 'On "Seeing" Salome', *English Literary History*, 60/2 (1993): pp. 503–26. An exception to the rule of scholarly neglect of one medium in favour of another is Tydeman and Price's stage history of Salome, *Wilde: Salome*, which, however, does not analyze the intermedial processes informing the Salome tradition.

[11]   See Mario Praz about Salome as the embodiment of the eternal feminine evil, Bram Dijkstra on the misogynistic subtext of this *fin-de-siècle* myth, and Kramer on the vindication of the male artist against Salome as an artist figure. Mario Praz, *The Romantic Agony*, trans. Angus Davidson (Oxford and New York, 1970), pp. 304–19; Bram Dijkstra, *Idols of Perversity: Fantasies of Feminine Evil in Fin-de-Siècle Culture* (Oxford and New York, 1986), pp. 376–401; Kramer, 'Culture and musical hermeneutics', pp. 279–81.

late-Victorian and decadent conflation of homosexuality, Wagnerism, the total artwork (*Gesamtkunstwerk*) and synaesthesia, this chapter draws attention to the interartistic transformations of Wilde's play in Aubrey Beardsley's drawings and in Richard Strauss's opera. It enquires into how Wilde's play can anticipate its future aesthetic elaborations.

The Legend of Salome across Media

Through the ages, the Salome legend has captured the imagination of Medieval, Renaissance, and *fin-de-siècle* visual artists, poets and composers, and has thus produced a rich, intricately layered, and resonant history of interartistic endeavours. The two compressed Biblical accounts of John the Baptist's death in the Gospels of Saint Matthew (Chapter 14, verses 1 to 13) and Saint Mark (Chapter 6, verses 14 to 29) lay the foundations of the myth.[12] But the narrative is sparse and austere, lacking in sensory detail. If anything, the story creates an aural frame, as in both biblical accounts, Herod hears about Jesus and the miracles he performs and mistakes John the Baptist for the Messiah. The interpolation emerges as a memory in Herod's mind upon his hearing of Jesus, and Jesus's hearing of Herod's beheading of John the Baptist, in turn, closes the framed narrative.[13] In this aural frame, sound and hearing are also associated with the Word. Still, the story appears to retain enough emblematic vividness for the artistic imagination to be kindled: Salome's supple figure, a severed head on a silver charger, a dance which literally triggers music, rhythms and gestures in an artist's mind, all cry out for artistic treatment. Thus, the artistic production evolving from the Biblical accounts arose out of a lack that would be perpetually elaborated upon to the point of repletion and, in fact, surfeit.

The biblical account depicts the nameless princess as a docile girl, observing the instructions of her mother Herodias. Only after the fourth century AD did Salome's vilification commence with the growing veneration of Saint John. His spirituality was thus contrasted with the carnality Salome came to embody. The opposition between the spirit and the flesh informed also the first artistic depictions of Salome that appeared on the tympanums of cathedrals, on stained glass windows and on the pages of illuminated manuscripts during the Middle Ages.

Gradually, the accent on Salome's notoriety faded away, as the Renaissance painters began to emphasize Salome's idealized beauty. Italian, Flemish and German artists created a rich iconographic tradition of Salome paintings. Humanist

---

[12]   In my account of the history of the Salome myth, I follow Helen Grace Zagona, *The Legend of Salome and the Principle of Art for Art's Sake* (Geneve, 1960), pp. 13–22.

[13]   Françoise Meltzer offers an excellent discussion of the framing techniques at work in the Biblical stories, as well as those in Huysmans's *A Rebours*. Françoise Meltzer, *Salome and the Dance of Writing: Portraits of Mimesis in Literature* (Chicago, IL, 1987), pp. 13–46.

paintings of Salome portray a graceful, dignified princess dancing before Herod at his opulent feast, or, alternatively, a pensive girl gazing at Saint John's head. Following earlier Medieval renditions of Saint John's martyrdom, many Renaissance Salome representations preserve the narrative entirety of the story by combining into one painting, fresco or panel a number of plot elements such as the feast, the dance, the beheading and the presentation of the Baptist's head to Herodias.

In the nineteenth century, the interchange among the arts and the senses fascinated poets, artists, composers and philosophers alike, and informed the transmutations of the Salome legend across the arts. Figures of sensory and artistic synthesis emerged prominently in the Symbolist and Decadent most-treasured trope of synaesthesia, the mixing of sense–impressions, for instance, in the perception of sound as colour. Richard Wagner's music dramas and theoretical writings on the *Gesamtkunstwerk* exalted the emotional, sensory and aesthetic potential of the multi-media artwork. The French Symbolist poets interpreted Wagner's synthesis of the arts as a synthesis of the senses. In Charles Baudelaire's experience, Wagner's prelude to *Lohengrin* musically evoked a synaesthetic blend of visual, spatial and tactile percepts: 'brightness' and 'intensity of light', levitation and 'increase of incandescence and heat'.[14] Baudelaire called Wagner's ability to paint space with music his 'art of translating', and this for him was a synaesthetic translation among the arts. Moreover, in *The Renaissance*, Walter Pater adopted and reformulated the German Romantic idea of *Anders-streben*, the artistic impulse to transmute into another art.[15] In all their endeavours, the early Modernist artists inexorably followed the logic of synaesthesia by transforming works of art across medial and linguistic boundaries.

Heinrich Heine revived the Salome legend in the nineteenth century in his long, unfinished poem *Atta Troll* (1841), and his own French translation of 1847 marked the beginning of the renewed interest in Salome in France. In his incomplete dramatic poem *Hérodiade*, begun in 1864, Stéphane Mallarmé portrayed Salome as a solipsistic virgin visually obsessed with her mirror image, which reflects the 'melodious light' ['clarté melodieuse'] of jewels. Gustave Moreau staged Salome's dance against an opulent, exotic backdrop in his painting *Salomé dansant devant Hérode* (see Plate 1), and his watercolour *L'Apparition*, both presented at the 1876 Paris Salon. Gustave Flaubert's archaeological, historico–artistic recreation of the myth appeared as 'Hérodias' in his *Trois Contes* within months of the 1876 Salon exhibition of Moreau's paintings. 'Hérodias' was possibly directly inspired by them, as well as by an image of Salome dancing on her hands that Flaubert saw in his youth on the tympanum of Rouen Cathedral, and which made its way into Flaubert's description of the 'Dance of the Seven Veils', as demonstrated in the introduction to this volume. Flaubert's story was quickly followed by Jules Massenet's opera

---

14   Charles Baudelaire, 'Richard Wagner and the Tannhäuser in Paris', *The Painter of Modern Life and Other Essays*, trans. Jonathan Mayne (London, 1995), pp. 113–17. Originally published in 1861.

15   Walter Pater, *The Renaissance* (Charleston, SC, 2007), p. 95.

Hérodiade, premiered in Brussels in 1881, whose libretto paints the unusual picture of a sentimental Salome in love with John the Baptist – for whose beheading she is not directly responsible – and who, in turn, professes his love for her.[16]

Huysmans's *A Rebours* (1884) captures the bejewelled Salome of Gustave Moreau's paintings in luxurious, erotically charged ekphrases which fuse the visual and the verbal. In his flagrant misogyny, Huysmans delineates Salome as 'the symbolic incarnation of undying Lust, the Goddess of immortal Hysteria', an 'accursed Beauty' and a 'monstrous Beast'; as an Othered aesthetic object, she epitomizes woman.[17] Huysmans's *A Rebours* further consists of endless lists and catalogues of sense–perceptions, synaesthetically conflating colours, sounds, tastes and perfumes. We need only think of the anti-hero Des Esseintes and his mouth organ, where alcohols with particular flavours recreate the sounds of particular symphonic instruments on his palate. In turn, Jules Laforgue parodied Salome and the French obsession with her in his *Moralités légendaires* (1886–87).[18] In Laforgue's treatment, Salome's passion leads to her inadvertent death. After fervently kissing the lifeless head to no effect, she tries to dispose of the gory thing by casting it into the sea. Unwittingly, she slips, topples down a cliff and dies, mutilated by the rocks, as well as by her jewels, of which Laforgue does not fail to remind us. Indeed, one scholar painstakingly counted 2,789 French poetic treatments of the Salome motif during its Post-Romantic flourish.[19]

The Importance of Oscar Wilde's *Salomé* for the Salome Tradition

This vibrant interartistic tradition inspired Oscar Wilde's notorious and immensely popular *Salomé* (1891) that would in turn serve as the basis for Aubrey Beardsley's illustrations and Richard Strauss's eponymous opera. Strikingly, despite its aesthetic appeal to artists, Oscar Wilde's *Salomé* has almost invariably provoked negative judgements, denounced as inferior by critics.[20] As an interesting foil to

---

[16]   For detailed treatment of Massenet's *Hérodiade*, see Clair Rowden, *Republican Morality and Catholic Tradition at the Opera: Massenet's* Hérodiade *and* Thaïs (Weinsberg, 2004).

[17]   Joris-Karl Huysmans, *Against Nature (A Rebours)*, trans. Robert Baldick (Harmondsworth, 1959), p. 65.

[18]   Jules Laforgue, 'Salomé', *Moralités légendaires* (Paris, 1887), pp. 119–53.

[19]   Cited in Rita Severi, 'Oscar Wilde, La Femme Fatale and the Salomé Myth', in Anna Balakian and James J. Wilhelm (eds), *Proceedings of the Xth Congress of the International Comparative Literature Association* (New York, 1985), p. 458.

[20]   Mario Praz (*The Romantic Agony*, p. 316), in his uncompromising survey of and search for originality in the *fin-de-siècle* Salome tradition, completely dismisses Wilde's play: 'Yet, as generally happens with specious second-hand works, it was precisely Wilde's Salome which became popular.' Philippe Jullian calls Wilde's *Salomé* 'one of the most famous and one of the worst of his works'. Philippe Jullian, *Oscar Wilde*, trans. Violet Wyndham (New York, 1969), p. 247.

this disparaging attitude toward the play come the commendations of various art projects inspired by Wilde's *Salomé*. While Wilde's play is deemed trite, derivative and banal, Beardsley's drawings are considered innovative and daring. In his correspondence with Richard Strauss, Romain Rolland also lamented the composer's poor choice of source for his opera: 'Oscar Wilde's *Salomé* was not worthy of you …: you transcend your subject, but you can't make one forget it.'[21] Yet, can there be a law of artistic exchange governing the artistic ferment stirred by Wilde's play in particular? Given the presumed mediocrity of the play, what can explain the artistic excitement and creativity it provoked, other than its implicit scandalous sensationalism?

I propose that the repeated representations of Salome function within the iconographic or intermedial memory of the Salome tradition. This is why the repetitive structure of Wilde's *Salomé* reflects most saliently this tradition of infinite copies, imitations and repetitions. The sense of foreboding and déjà vu evoked by the compulsive repetitions in Wilde's play – 'Something terrible may happen!' – is amplified by repetition on the level of tradition.[22] The tradition remembers the story of Saint John's decollation; although we know about its tragic end, we will experience it again. This perhaps motivates also Wilde's decision to make Herod give his unconditional promise to Salome before she dances.[23] This decision, much lamented by critics of the play, reveals Wilde's awareness of a tradition in which Herod has experienced the dance an infinite number of times. The promise is given because of Herod's remembrance of Salome's previous dances and not because Herod was subdued by *Salomé*'s irresistible, erotically titillating performance in the play itself.

Furthermore, the verbal repetitions in the play curiously encapsulate Salome's inherent intermediality looking backward to the Salome tradition, as well as anticipating its new manifestations. The persistent verbal snippets 'look', 'voice', 'see', 'hear' and 'dance' recur more than 20 times each within the taut, compact structure of the text to conjoin the synaesthetic and interartistic impulses behind the play. Thus, the repetitions in the text reveal its heightened self-consciousness, as Wilde's *Salomé* knows of its previous intermedial beings. It also knows of itself as an iconographic exemplum, as a precious item in a list.

Wilde described his play as 'a piece of music'; his lyrical text bifurcates, straddling both the visual, in its obsession with reflections, and the musical, in its

---

[21]   Letter to Strauss, dated 'Tuesday evening, 14th May, 1907. (After the 3rd performance of *Salomé*)', in Rollo Myers (ed.), *Richard Strauss & Romain Rolland: Correspondence* (London, 1968), pp. 82–3. Rolland's date refers to the Parisian premiere of *Salome* (in German) in May 1907.

[22]   Oscar Wilde, 'Salomé', in *Complete Works of Oscar Wilde* (London and Glasgow, 1948, reprinted 1977), pp. 552–75, p. 553.

[23]   Of course, Herod's promise to give Salome anything she desires reinforces the sense of Salome's psychological motivation to dance. By reversing the Biblical order of promise and dance, Salome dances with the clear purpose to obtain the head of John the Baptist and to kiss it.

'recurring *motifs*'.[24] Moreover, these qualities necessitate the traverse of the play across media. In its persistent self-reflections and reiterations, the play asserts the possibility of transcending its own medium,[25] as the play's future transformations in pictures, music, dance and film more than testify. In respect to the vast iconographic Salome tradition, Wilde's play is the paradigmatic Salome text.

Production History of Wilde's *Salomé*

Wilde's self-created legend reads as follows: the story and image of Salome had preoccupied the playwright for a long time before he actually wrote the play in a night, in a blank notebook. After Wilde had been writing uninterruptedly for some considerable time, he took a break to go to the Grand Café where he asked the leader of a gypsy band to play music in harmony with his current thoughts about a woman dancing barefoot in the blood of a man she had desired, but could not have and, therefore, had slain. The orchestra played some 'wild and terrible music' that frightened and silenced the guests of the café.[26] It will be inaccurate to say that this musical, spur-of-the-moment creative stimulus simply influenced Wilde in his creative process; in fact, Wilde consciously sought the music as a further creative incentive. Again according to Richard Ellmann, Wilde was a connoisseur of the iconography of Salome in Western Art, but Rubens, Leonardo, Dürer, Ghirlandaio, van Thulden, and Henri Regnault's attempts at rendering her seemed unsatisfactory to him. Only the Salome of Gustave Moreau satisfied him, and he often quoted Huysmans's passages on Salome from *A Rebours*. Wilde was also eager to visit the Prado to view Stanzioni's and Titian's paintings of Salome, while Bernardo (Bernardino) Luini's rendition likewise became important for Wilde's conception of Salome.[27] Wilde was further inspired after a visit to the Moulin Rouge where he saw a Romanian acrobat dance on her hands just as Flaubert's Salome,[28] and, according to his friends, Wilde also seemed to want the actress playing Salome to be an accomplished dancer.[29]

The production history of Wilde's play is punctuated by synaesthetic and intermedial elements. Suffice it to mention Wilde's conception of the banned first

---

[24]   Wilde, 'De Profundis', in *Complete Works*, pp. 873–957, p. 922.

[25]   David Wayne Thomas affirms that Wilde's *Salomé* is not only about reflections but also a reflection on reflections; it is 'a text about that very distinction, about the slippage between a logic and a metalogic'. Thomas, 'The "Strange Music" of Salome: Oscar Wilde's Rhetoric of Verbal Musicality', *Mosaic: A Journal for the Interdisciplinary Study of Literature*, 30/1 (2000): pp. 15–38, p. 21. However, Thomas is locked in the Lessingean strictures of the limits between the arts and suggests that verbal music in *Salomé* fails in the precarious slippage of the figuring of figuration.

[26]   Ellmann, *Oscar Wilde*, p. 344.

[27]   Ibid., p. 342.

[28]   Wilde declared, 'I want her [Salome] to dance on her hands, as in Flaubert's story.' Ibid., p. 343.

[29]   Tydeman and Price, *Wilde: Salome*, p. 13.

performance of *Salomé* in 1892, in which Sarah Bernhardt was supposed to play the title role. Wilde suggested that the orchestra be replaced with perfumes to correspond to each new emotion in the play.[30] Charles Ricketts designed the sets for another thwarted staging nine months later in Paris.[31] The discussions of the sets and costumes revolved around the different colours the characters would be assigned: the sky was to be rich turquoise green or violet, the Jews were to be in yellow, while Herod and Herodias were envisaged in blood-red or purple. Salome was wavering between the silver, the green and the golden. The thwarted Sarah Bernhard and Ricketts productions, as well as the French edition and subsequent English translation of the book emphasized the synaesthetic, the pictorial, the textural and the aesthetic qualities of the play.[32] Thus, though the Biblical account is sparse on sensuous detail, Wilde's play, together with the vast iconographic and literary Salome tradition, elaborates on the sensory gaps.

In Wilde's play, gazing (implicit in the painterly tradition), dance, and voice (suggested by the Biblical account where voice and hearing predominate) take over. This is a troubled space to occupy for a drama often described by critics as unperformable, while Wilde himself thought of it as opening up new artistic horizons for the stage.[33] How do we reconcile the musical and the pictorial dimensions of the play, its provocative stagings in the twentieth and twenty-first centuries, its February 1893 French edition bound in 'Tyrian purple' wrappers with lettering of 'tired silver',[34] and the Beardsley-illustrated English translation of February 1894? The ordinary edition was bound in coarse-grained blue canvas while the luxury edition was rendered in green silk.[35] Ada Leverson's reminiscences of the literary practices of the 1890s provide us with a telling anecdote about Wilde's aesthetic motivations concerning his play's artistic status:

> There was more margin; margin in every sense of the word was in demand, and I remember looking at the poems of John Gray (then considered the incomparable poet of the age), when I saw the tiniest rivulets of text meandering through the very largest meadow of margin, I suggested to Oscar Wilde that he should

---

[30]   Ellmann, *Oscar Wilde*, p. 372.

[31]   Ibid. Also Horst Schroeder, *Additions and Corrections to Richard Ellmann's Oscar Wilde*, second edition, revised and enlarged (Braunschweig, 2002), p. 128.

[32]   For an excellent study of Wilde's *Salomé* in its decorated book form, see Nicholas Frankel, *Oscar Wilde's Decorated Books* (Ann Arbor, MI, 2000).

[33]   Wilde, *The Complete Letters of Oscar Wilde*, Merlin Holland and Rupert Hart-Davis (eds) (New York, 2000), p. 874. Western thinkers, among them Hegel, Wagner and Emil Staiger, have long described drama as the medium of the future, and Wilde's use of the dramatic medium, as well as the sensory impulses underlying the play, indeed facilitate its forward artistic movement and aesthetic anticipation of future Salome projects.

[34]   Ibid., p. 555.

[35]   Ibid., p. 578.

go a step further than these minor poets; he should publish a book all margin; full of beautiful unwritten thoughts, and have this blank volume bound in some Nile-green skin powdered with gilt nenuphars and smoothed with hard ivory, decorated with gold by Ricketts and printed on Japanese paper, each volume must be a collector's piece, a numbered one of a limited "first" (and last) edition: "very rare."

He approved.

"It shall be dedicated to you, and the unwritten text illustrated by Aubrey Beardsley. There must be five hundred signed copies for particular friends, six for the general public, and one for America."[36]

Oscar Wilde's *Salomé* is indeed the book, and the play, 'all margin'. The text vanishes, beckoning the alluring and pleasing surface of a rare collector's piece, inviting pictures, and defiantly subverting its textual origins. The images, the music, the texture, and the scents informing Wilde's concept of his play suggest that his *Salomé* is not interested in its textuality; it deliberately undermines it and thus transcends it. The sensory richness of the Salome tradition, Wilde's preliminary aesthetic explorations and interartistic conception of the play, and his *Salomé*'s synaesthetic organization determine the transition from the play's intermedial reflection back on the Salome tradition to its aesthetic anticipation of future intermedial translations of Salome.

Translation and Intermediality

Both culturally and textually, the Salome legend seems to be tangled up in translation. Heine's translation of *Atta Troll* into French commenced the obsessive recapturing of Salomé/Hérodiade in the second half of the nineteenth century in France. According to Oscar Wilde's own account, *Salomé* (with *accent aigu*) was written initially in French, and Derrick Puffett appropriately summarizes the linguistic complications stemming from Wilde's play in his discussion of Richard Strauss's opera: 'Any attempt to impose linguistic consistency on a work involving a character called Jochanaan – the German version of an English transliteration of the Hebrew form of the name of a character in a German opera based on a play written in French by an Irishman – is probably doomed from the outset.'[37] *Salomé* was translated into English by Sir Alfred Douglas, but his translation was published only after Oscar

---

[36] Quoted in Frankel, *Oscar Wilde's Decorated Books*, p. 1.

[37] Derrick Puffett (ed.), *Richard Strauss: Salome*, Cambridge Opera Handbooks (Cambridge, 1989), p. 9. To complicate the matter, Ellmann actually maintains that Wilde borrows Flaubert's use in French of the Greek for Saint John's name, Iokanaan. Ellmann, *Oscar Wilde*, p. 84.

Wilde revised it heavily. Furthermore, Aubrey Beardsley, who illustrated the first English edition of *Salomé*, desired to translate the play more than to picture it.[38] Richard Strauss used Hedwig Lachmann's translation, the German version used in Max Reinhardt's production of the play. Anton Lindner had also sent his translation of the play to Strauss, but eventually the composer opted for Lachmann's translation as the basis for his libretto.

Still, can we trace a relation between this linguistic inconsistency of translation and the interartistic dispersal of the play? How do we proceed from the play's actual translation from French into English to intermedial translation?[39] Why did Wilde's creative mind, conditioned by his literary mastery of his native English language, venture into the foreign French and only then journey back into English? In an interview for the *Pall Mall Budget*, Wilde plays with a number of intermedial metaphors to recognize the interartistic resonance that his translinguistic play achieves:

> I have one instrument that I know that I can command, and that is the English Language. There was another instrument to which I had listened all my life, and I wanted once to touch this new instrument to see whether I could make any beautiful thing out of it. The play was written in Paris some six months ago, where I read it to some young poets, who admired it immensely. Of course there are modes of expression that a Frenchman of letters would not have used, but they give a certain relief or colour to the play. A great deal of the curious effect that Maeterlinck produces comes from the fact that he, a Flamand by race, writes in an alien language. The same thing is true of Rossetti who, though he wrote in English, was essentially Latin in temperament.[40]

The defamiliarization of the verbal creative process seems to parallel the medial defamiliarization of the play. By writing *Salomé* in French, Wilde appears to be touching a 'new instrument', and we can further infer, a musical instrument. His writing in French lends the play 'a certain relief or colour', visual aspects that, Wilde suggests, would be impossible for a Frenchman to capture. The

---

[38]   Beardsley expressed his wish to 'translate' *Salomé* in November or October 1893 when he read and found inadequate Douglas's translation of the play. Ellmann, *Oscar Wilde*, p. 403.

[39]   For a theoretical discussion of intermedial translation as a creative act securing the artwork's 'afterlife' in Walter Benjamin's terms, see Polina Dimcheva Dimova, *'Beautiful, Colored Musical Things': Metaphors and Strategies for Interartistic Exchange in Early European Modernism* (University of California, Berkeley, ProQuest, UMI Dissertations Publishing, 2010, 3526569), pp. 53–4 and 59–60. See also Walter Benjamin, 'The Task of the Translator', *Illuminations*, trans. Harry Zohn (New York, 1969), pp. 69–82.

[40]   Oscar Wilde, *Pall Mall Budget*, XL (30 June 1892): p. 947. Quoted in E.H. Mikhail (ed.), *Oscar Wilde, Interviews and Recollections*, Vol. 1 (London, 1979), p. 188. In the penultimate sentence of the above quotation, I give Ellmann's replacement or interpretation of 'grace' (as it appears in Mikhail's reprint) as 'race'. Ellmann, *Oscar Wilde*, pp. 372–3.

typical *fin-de-siècle* intermedial metaphoricity is here transposed onto language, implying the kinship between the crossing of medial and linguistic boundaries. Wilde traces this figurative intermedial translation of the creative self into a new language to a line of predecessors, who had also become intimately connected with the other arts: Maeterlinck, whose lyric drama *La Princesse Maleine* (1889) influenced Wilde's *Salomé* in its 'repetitious, incantatory ... cadences', and the Pre-Raphaelite poet-painter, Dante Gabriel Rossetti.[41]

Unsurprisingly, French artists heatedly debated whether Wilde's French was good enough for the playwright to have written *Salomé* in French; moreover, they all detected the self-conscious aesthetic posture that Wilde took up in the act of translation. While Ransome deems Wilde's French child-like, André Gide claims Wilde spoke French 'admirably'.[42] Gide continues to reflect on, psychologize, and reinvent Wilde's thought processes by suggesting that Wilde 'pretended' to look for words with the intention of making his listeners wait. He interprets Wilde's almost imperceptible accent in French synaesthetically, as a deliberately retained sound inflection, which gave Wilde's words 'a new and strange aspect'. Felix Paul Grewe also recounts his impressions that Wilde took up the foreigner's disguise when he wanted to make his audience wait for his words. Significantly, the dramatic effect of Wilde's performance of his foreignness results again in an intermedial metaphor. The word he searches for and finds is in fact a difficult French word that would challenge even native speakers of French. According to Grewe, this newly found French word struggling and fumbling its way out of the Englishman's mouth and mind resembles 'a statue emerging from the relief of his speech'.[43]

The complicated materialization of Wilde's French word, deliberate or not, gives grounds for romanticized synaesthetic interpretations of its coming into being. Thus, in their intermediality, Wilde's translated words metaphorically endorse the possibility for transfer between language and the arts while, at the same time, embodying in their own right the aesthetics of artistic synthesis. In Wilde's case, linguistic translation parallels closely interartistic experimentation.

---

[41]   See Tydeman and Price, *Wilde: Salome*, pp. 4–6, where Maeterlinck's *Princesse Maleine* is described in musical and visual terms.

[42]   Arthur Ransome, *Oscar Wilde: A Critical Study* (London, 1912), p. 146. For Gide's and Ransome's opinions, see Christa Satzinger, *French Influences on Oscar Wilde's 'The Picture of Dorian Gray' and 'Salome'* (Lewiston, NY, 1994), p. 207.

[43]   'ein Wort, das er wie eine Statue hinausstellte aus dem Relief seiner Rede'. Karl Lück, *Das französische Fremdwort bei Oscar Wilde als Stilistisches Kunstmittel* (Greifswald, 1927). For Grewe's opinion cited in Lück, see Satzinger, *French Influences*, pp. 207–8. Translation by Polina Dimova.

Vision and Voice in *Salomé*

At first sight, Wilde's *Salomé* is structured neatly around two pairs of oppositions: that of the idolatrous eye and the iconoclastic and iconophobic voice, and that of the material and spiritual worlds.[44] The eye seems to be bound exclusively to the material realm of sense–perceptions and the body, while the prophetic voice seems to transcend the material and access the spiritual realm:

Eye	versus	**Ear (Voice)**
Material	versus	**Spiritual**
Body/Senses	versus	**Soul**

The characters who belong to the corrupted Oriental court are obsessed with gazing, a gaze that generates and perpetuates desire. Hypnotized by his compulsive gazing, Narraboth opens the play with a statement prompted by his sighting of the princess: 'How beautiful is the princess Salomé to-night!'[45] The young Syrian's infatuated exclamation is followed by an urgent imperative: 'Look at the moon!' Herodias's Page, in his homoerotic desire for the young Syrian, attempts to divert Narraboth's fixed gaze, but unsuccessfully. Although Narraboth looks at the moon, he is able to see only Salome in the moon, which to him looks 'like a little princess'. Narraboth's similes internalize his visual desire, and now his language, rather than his gaze, pursues and fixes on Salome. The vicious circle of visual desires keeps haunting the play until the end. Salome's stepfather Herod, too, desires the princess, and, in his ocularcentric infatuation, he looks at her 'with his mole's *eyes* under his shaking *eye*lids'.[46] Herod later attempts to deflect Salome's determination to possess the head of Jokanaan by offering her topazes 'yellow as are the *eyes* of tigers, … pink as the *eyes* of a wood-pigeon, and green … as the *eyes* of cats', as well as 'onyxes like the *eye*balls of a dead woman.'[47] Thus, the *eye* itself as the organ of sight becomes an obsession, recurring compulsively in the

---

[44]   The opposition of sight and sound, as aligned with that of matter and mind, informs Bram Dijkstra's reading of Wilde's *Salomé*. Yet, to serve his discussion of misogyny in *fin-de-siècle* representations of Salome, he concentrates solely on the figures of Salome (the flesh), Jokanaan (the spirit), and Herod, as torn between body and soul. Thus, Dijkstra's account misses the intricacies of the exchange between voice and vision in *Salomé*, despite his sensitivity to the pictorial and verbal dimensions of the Salome iconographic tradition. Dijkstra, *Idols of Perversity*, pp. 396–8.

[45]   Wilde, 'Salomé', p. 552.

[46]   Ibid., p. 555. The emphases here and below are mine unless otherwise indicated.

[47]   Ibid., p. 572.

text. Finally, Salome's own obsession with Jokanaan emerges visually in the play: 'I would but *look* at this strange prophet.'[48]

At the other end of the *eye–ear* opposition stands Jokanaan. The Hebraic prohibition against graven images resounds through all his speeches. In one of his most iconoclastic prophetic outbursts, he verbally abuses the woman who succumbs to her visual lust:

> Where is she who, having seen the images of men painted on the walls, the images of the Chaldeans limned in colours, gave herself up unto the lust of her eyes …[49]

Jokanaan condemns eyesight, the visual art of painting, and the sacrilegious image-making as idol-making in their naturalized relation to sensual lust. Lust is defined as essentially visual, the lust of the eyes. The apparently obscure referent, the abstract 'she' whom Jokanaan invokes, remains incomprehensible to the soldiers of the court. Salome and Herodias, however, cannot be deceived; they see through the abstractness of the feminine third-person singular pronoun, tracing back the imaginary genealogy of visual lust: woman–Herodias–Salome.

Yet if we look at another of the proclamations of Jokanaan's voice, the opposition between vision and voice becomes entangled: 'The *eyes* of the blind shall *see* the day, and the *ears* of the *deaf* shall be opened.'[50] Here vision and hearing both exist in a spiritual dimension. A new opposition develops: that of seeing and mere looking. This is a Platonic opposition implying a double vision: that of the inner eye of the intellect, perceiving the truth, and that of the deceptive senses apprehending only the shadow-world of illusions.[51] In this sense, the initial alignment of the eye and the ear with the material and the spiritual is now unsettled, and we have to ask whether the concept of voice in the play undergoes a similar splitting.

Overcome by desire for Jokanaan, Salome first figures her fascination with him in aural terms. In fact, we first encounter the prophet in the auditory realm, as a disembodied voice, to which Salome responds: 'What a strange voice! I would speak with him.'[52] Salome reads or misreads the exuberantly allegorical prophecies of John the Baptist as the elocutions of 'a strange voice'; she reduces the figurative import of his words to a timbre, a strange tone of voice. This desire for the voice turns, on the spur of the moment, into a desire for verbal communication, for 'speaking'. The mysterious quality of the voice blends with what may seem an obscure or hackneyed prophecy and necessitates Salome's further exploration.

---

[48]   Ibid., p. 556.

[49]   Ibid., p. 557.

[50]   Ibid., p. 554.

[51]   On double vision in Plato's dialogues, see Martin Jay, *Downcast Eyes: The Denigration of Vision in Twentieth-Century French Thought* (Berkeley, CA, 1993), pp. 26–7.

[52]   Wilde, 'Salomé', p. 556.

Certainly, Jokanaan's prophecies perplex the rest of the court members in a similar manner: 'What is he talking of? // We can never tell. Sometimes he says terrible things; but it is impossible to understand what he says.'[53] The prophetic words of Jokanaan prove unintelligible and disintegrate into gibberish in the perception of the other characters. His voice is figured as sheer aural presence, lacking in meaning: 'He is always saying ridiculous things.'[54]

Thus, we witness how voice splits into physical timbre and spiritual message. Salome further equates this corrupted, material function of the prophetic voice not with comprehensible words but with music: 'Speak again, Jokanaan. Thy *voice* is as *music* to mine *ear*.'[55] In this sense, the voice that Salome perceives is sheer timbre, and in the perception of the characters, words are confused with music and act only in what is commonly understood as musical sensuous terms. Thus, the perception of voice as music without any intellectual or spiritual meaning is the material side of the voice, which is coupled with looking and gazing in the text.

Strikingly, the musical and auditory simile Salome uses to describe her perception of John the Baptist's voice has undergone a curious transformation from the original French, in which she intones: 'Ta voix m'enivre.'[56] The princess is 'drunk' on Jokanaan's voice. Thus in *Salomé*'s first translation into English in 1894, a radical, yet poetically motivated act of translation has performed simultaneously a linguistic and a synaesthetic leap. The ecstasy of intoxication transmutes into the ravishing sounds of music, and we know from the German Romantics and Nietzsche that the conflation of drunkenness and music is appropriate. The murky fate of the actual translation into English attributed in various degrees to Sir Alfred Douglas and Wilde does not allow us to identify precisely who of the two took the liberty of translating intoxicating taste into exhilarating sound. Nevertheless, the creative departure from the original gives us a reason to believe the change was made by the author in accordance with his own aesthetic philosophy of translation as synaesthesia. In this sense, in addition to performing Wilde's synaesthetic translation, the English version also bears the seal of authorial self-consciousness, and thus deliberately chooses music and ear as the appropriately intoxicating art and sense for Salome's ravishing experience of voice as sensuous sound, bereft of traditional and easily comprehensible meaning.

---

[53] Ibid., p. 554.

[54] Ibid.

[55] Wilde, *Salomé* (Boston, MA, 1996), p. 10. This edition reproduces the first English translation of Wilde's play, by Lord Alfred Douglas with illustrations by Aubrey Beardsley (London: Elkin Matthews and John Lane, 1894). Electronic transcript, Oberlin College. Accessed on 15 April 2012. In later critical editions of Wilde's collected works, such as the *Complete Works of Oscar Wilde* (London and Glasgow, 1948, rpt. 1977) used for reference throughout this volume, the editors revert to a more literal English translation of the French 'Ta voix m'enivre', as 'Thy voice is wine to me'.

[56] Wilde, *Salomé*, in *Oscar Wilde: Œuvres*, Jean Gattégno (ed.), Bibliothèque de la Pléiade (Paris, 1996), pp. 1229–59, p. 1237.

The initial oppositions of eye and ear can now be seen in a new light, and the modes of perception in Wilde's *Salomé* realigned:

Material		Spiritual
Music	**Voice**	Words
Looking/Gazing	**Vision**	Seeing

The phenomenology of voice in Wilde's novel *The Picture of Dorian Gray* similarly foregrounds the musical quality of speech, giving it a sensuous dimension. In *Dorian Gray*, Lord Henry's musical voice seduces Dorian and exercises the decisive influence in his corruption. Arousing Dorian's senses, Harry's mellifluous words are able to touch 'some secret chord that had never been touched before, but that he [Dorian] felt was now vibrating and throbbing to curious pulses.'[57]

> *Music* had stirred him [Dorian] like that. *Music* had troubled him many times. But *music* was not articulate. It was not a new world, but rather another chaos, that it created in us. Words! Mere words! How terrible they were! ... They seemed to be able to give a plastic form to formless things, and to have a *music* of their own as sweet as that of viol or of lute.[58]

> And how charming he [Dorian] had been at dinner the night before, as, with startled eyes and lips parted in frightened pleasure, he had sat opposite to him at the club, the red candleshades staining to a richer rose the wakening wonder of his face. Talking to him was like playing upon an exquisite *violin*. He answered to every touch and thrill of the *bow*. ... There was something terribly enthralling in the exercise of influence. No other activity was like it. To project one's soul into some gracious form, and let it tarry there for a moment; to hear one's own intellectual views echoed back to one with all the added *music* of passion and youth ...[59]

These passages not only figure seductive words and rhetoric as music, but also capture the invasive act of the voice entering the body of another subject as influence. Influence empties out the body of a subject, making it an object to be possessed. This act is not innocuous, as the subject who exerts its influence is also 'enthralled'. The fetters of influence enslave in both directions. In *Salomé*, voice and vision function in a similar fashion. The male gaze (Herod's or Narraboth's)

---

[57]   Oscar Wilde, 'The Picture of Dorian Grey', *Complete Works*, pp. 17–167, pp. 29–30. All emphases are mine.

[58]   Ibid., p. 30.

[59]   Ibid., p. 41.

is active and powerful, but the power dynamic is completely reversed when the gazer is also enthralled and hypnotized in his gazing. The voice of Jokanaan has impact upon the world around him, but it also becomes the agent of his own demise. His powerful melodious voice is figured as the physical act of penetration, for Salome claims that Jokanaan 'didst take my [her] virginity' from her.[60] The bondage between subject and object of the gaze and the voice denies access to transcendence in the play. Both voice and gaze become bound to the sensual, the physical and the material.

Still, what is the function of language and words here? Language is entirely corrupted in the play, turned into music. As Wilde himself said, he wanted the play to be a ballad in its repetitive structure, like a piece of music with 'recurring *motifs*'.[61] Charles Bernheimer suggests that the word in the play is foregrounded.[62] This might be so, but it is foregrounded only to experience its own demise. It is emptied out of meaning to be occupied by the eye and the ear, by music and painting. The disembodied voice of Jokanaan, first resounding off-stage from the cistern and then literally severed from the body, cannot overpower any more.

Ultimately, in Wilde's play we witness the decay of the word, that is, what Oscar Wilde had called earlier the 'decay of lying'.[63] Herod gives a binding promise to fulfil Salome's wish if she obliges him by dancing for him. After the 'Dance of the Seven Veils', when Herod hears Salome's inexorable wish to be presented with Jokanaan's head on a silver platter, he does not dare violate his promise despite his compunctions and misgivings. What contemporary speech act theorists would call in this case 'the power of language' is dramatized in the play and figured in Wilde's typically paradoxical terms as the opposite of powerful language and imaginative fiction, that is, as the decay of lying, the decay of the aesthetic (aestheticized) word. The word (or Word) is reified. Its inflexibility and rigidity render it weak. Furthermore, in *Salomé*, the word is waning in the incommunicability of its language, which persists throughout the play in the infinite chain of similes, which fail to reach, represent or construct a referent.[64] Thus, the senses followed by the arts kill and resurrect the word. Although critics have often condemned the play as bad, I suggest that we see in it the word performing its own death.

Ultimately, instead of construing Herod's outraged exhortation 'Kill that woman!' as a virulent misogynistic pronouncement in Dijkstra's vein, I interpret it as an appeal for transformation. As Wilde postulates in *The Ballad of Reading*

---

[60] Wilde, 'Salomé', p. 574.

[61] Wilde, 'De Profundis', p. 922.

[62] Charles Bernheimer, *Decadent Subjects: The Idea of Decadence in Art, Literature, Philosophy, and Culture of the* Fin de Siècle *in Europe*, T. Jefferson Kline and Naomi Schor (eds) (Baltimore, MD and London, 2002), p. 123.

[63] Oscar Wilde, 'The Decay of Lying', in Richard Ellmann (ed.), *The Artist as Critic: The Critical Writings of Oscar Wilde* (New York, 1969), pp. 290–320.

[64] See Linda Saladin's chapter on Wilde's *Salomé* in her *Fetishism and the Femme Fatale: Gender, Power, and Reflexive Discourse* (New York, 1993), pp. 125–47.

Gaol, 'each man kills the thing he loves'.[65] Here I do not mean just Herod, but also Wilde as the artist of Salome, who associates tightly art and criminality, or 'pen, pencil and poison'.[66] This murderous yet transformative impulse of Wilde's aesthetic views is recorded in André Gide's recollection that, according to Wilde, 'in order to know an essence, one must eliminate it. ... Each thing is made up only of its emptiness ...'.[67] Thus, to reveal itself, art needs to kill its essence and become a surface, a mask, or a veil. The arts imitate each other so as to create the illusion of another art, which is their way of murdering their essence so as to become themselves.

The violent plot of murders in Wilde's *Salomé* lays bare the self-reflexivity of the text, which is conscious of its decadent renunciation of the word for the other sensory and artistic realms, for the other arts. Thus, *Salomé* is a text that does not want to be one. It transcends itself by wishing to be music. The text keeps emphasizing that which is beyond its words: the non-existent referent, Jokanaan's voice, which is not contained by the play, as well as the dance, which takes over the play. Ultimately, music and the sensualized word as music, look, gaze and vision become so overpowering that the word loses its meaning, killed by the senses. Music and painting, therefore, take on the next transformations of Oscar Wilde's *Salomé* in Aubrey Beardsley's illustrations to the play and in Richard Strauss's opera. The play is transformed into the other media in what I will call the decadent procedure of reviving and animating a dead thing or a dead language, and thus engendering new extra-verbal life.[68]

Salomé's Visual and Musical Afterlife

The decadent process of interartistic translation keeps unfolding in Aubrey Beardsley's Japanese-influenced black-and-white illustrations.[69] His *Black Cape* emerges as such a new organism, a 'beautiful and quite irrelevant' substitution for

---

[65] Wilde, 'The Ballad of Reading Gaol', in *Complete Works*, pp. 843–60, p. 844.

[66] Wilde, 'Pen Pencil and Poison', in Ellmann (ed.), *The Artist as Critic*, pp. 320–41.

[67] Jullian, *Oscar Wilde*, p. 239.

[68] On the necessary process of artistic transformation in modernity, and of the aesthetic death of old things and their Modernist resurrection in Pater and Wilde, see Jonah Siegel, *Desire and Excess: The Nineteenth-Century Culture of Art* (Princeton, NJ, 2000), pp. 227–62. Of Beardsley he remarks (p. 262), '[he] certainly has captured ... the fascination of mortality in a world of excess, and the manner in which death marks not a complete end, but a transformation into a new beginning.'

[69] On Japonisme in Aubrey Beardsley's *Salomé* drawings, see Klaus Berger, *Japonisme in Western Painting from Whistler to Matisse*, trans. David Britt (Cambridge, 1992), pp. 250–57.

Figure 1.3　　Aubrey Beardsley, *Black Cape*, 1894
Source: Reprinted from *Best Works of Aubrey Beardsley* (New York, 1990), p. 28.

a censored drawing[70] (see Figure 1.3). Silhouetted against a white background, the flamboyantly tiered black cape is imposing, with the flow of the curvaceously voluminous black skirt beckoning the viewer. The virile *femme fatale* of the other drawings such as *The Climax* vanishes in the sensuously rounded black fabric, which is only subtly accentuated in white by a miniature feminine baby face, two barely perceptible hands, and the vulnerably white flesh revealed by a v-shaped neckline, plunging down to the delicately dotted black navel. The drawing completely erases the Salome story by transforming it into a Japanese-inspired fashion fantasy. Beardsley's unorthodox drawings further refuse to illustrate the text and prefer to translate its synaesthetic figurations and net of desires into unexpectedly varying sexual desires, ambiguous gender and character representations, and physical aberrations.[71] Beardsley's figures range from a fœtus with a poorly concealed monstrous erection to an effeminate page not aroused by a gorgeous Herodias in his provocative *Enter Herodias*, or from autoerotically occupied figures, hands blissfully in lap, to a hermaphroditic servant and an artistic Pierrot, whose human identity is defined by a mask in *The Toilette of Salome – I* (see Figure 1.4). Like the gaze in Wilde's play, the sinuous lines and the quivering white flesh of the paper generate desire in this pleasing drawing about self-pleasure. Beardsley thus maps out the play's multiplicity of senses onto a multiplicity of genders and human forms. In her discussion of Huysmans's *A Rebours*, Barbara Spackman insightfully shows that in decadent practice both synaesthetic and sexual diversity are meant to compound systems based on simple binaries that describe woman as the negation of man, or, in my terms, vision as the negation of voice.[72] By translating sensory diversity into sexual diversity, Beardsley does not simply kill off Wilde's synaesthetically informed drama, but also enriches it in this subversive decadent intermedial translation of synaesthetic desires into sexually experimental pictures.

Finally, Beardsley's *The Climax* presents an allegorical instance of death transformed into life where the dripping blood of Jokanaan's severed head generates a flower in the foreground; a living thing burgeons out of the dead body (see Figure 1.5). In a similar aesthetically murderous vein, Strauss's 'Dance of the Seven Veils' is a kitsch, exoticizing pastiche of previous themes in the opera, a festering corpse, which does not fit within the musical logic of the opera. The dance was composed in a rush only a number of months after the completion of the opera itself, and it does away with the intricately woven fabric of Strauss's

---

[70]   Beardsley commented on new *Salomé* illustrations destined to replace suppressed ones in his letter to Robert Ross in November 1893. Quoted in Ellmann, *Oscar Wilde*, p. 404.

[71]   Both early and contemporary critics of Wilde's and Beardsley's *Salomé* seem to agree that Beardsley's drawings do not illustrate the text; rather, they challenge it or parody it. On the collaboration between Beardsley and Wilde, see Ian Fletcher, *Aubrey Beardsley* (Boston, MA, 1987), pp. 57–63.

[72]   Barbara Spackman, 'Interversions', in Liz Constable, Dennis Denisoff and Matthew Potolsky (eds), *Perennial Decay* (Philadelphia, PA, 1999), pp. 35–49.

Figure 1.4   Aubrey Beardsley, *The Toilette of Salome – I*, 1894
Source: Reprinted from *Best Works of Aubrey Beardsley* (New York, 1990), p. 34.

Figure 1.5   Aubrey Beardsley, *The Climax*, 1894
Source: Reprinted from *Best Works of Aubrey Beardsley* (New York, 1990), p. 36.

Salome.[73] By transmuting into dance, the opera seeks its future realization rhythmical, expressive movement. That is how Wilde's laconic parenthetical stage direction came to hold a sway on the *fin-de-siècle* imagination, as it decides the fate of the characters in the play. If we see the play as staging a battle between the verbal and the non-verbal – dance, gesture, rhythm and music – the mellifluous voice and the dance clearly prevail in *Salomé*'s artistic adaptations.

The Voice

At the end of Wilde's play, Salome gradually vanishes from sight after being initiated with a lethal kiss into the mystery of love and the mystery of death. Herod orders that the stars and the moon be hidden, and the stage directions state: 'The great black cloud crosses the moon and conceals it completely. The stage becomes very dark.'[74] Salome as a visual presence transforms into a sheer vocal presence, into 'The Voice of Salomé'. In her last lines, Salome relinquishes her sensuous appearance and adopts Jokanaan's essence as a disembodied voice. The shields of the soldiers cover and crush the princess of Judaea. The word is dead, and the image is dead at the end of this tragedy, but the voice perseveres and continues to resound, as if music emanated from Salome herself, as Hofmannsthal's and Strauss's Elektra would have it.

In Richard Strauss's opera *Salome*, the most (in)famous adaptation of Wilde's *Salomé* in the early twentieth century, the composer adopts and complicates the opposition of spiritual voice or Word and sensuous voice and music. Taking up Wilde's synaesthetic ideas, Richard Strauss envoices the characters in his *Salome* and translates spiritual Word and sensuous voice into a musical idiom. On the one hand, Strauss's Jochanaan inhabits the spiritual edifice of Western tonal music with its overarching scheme of tonal development and resolution, and the diatonic, pure, 'white-note', heroic tonal area of C. On the other hand, Salome's musical character is centred around the 'black-note' key of C♯ minor (and C♯ major at the climax of the opera), replete with seductive chromaticisms and tonal colours, proliferating ambiguous and luxuriant harmonic progressions. Thus, Strauss perpetuates Wilde's conception of Jokanaan as a disembodied voice, now a bass-baritone initially singing off-stage, and of Salome as the sensual, alluring, embodied voice of a soprano.

Nevertheless, Strauss's lack of empathy with Jochanaan is well documented, and the composer later referred to his musical motif for the prophet as 'pedantic'

---

[73]   Robin Holloway, '*Salome*: art or kitsch?', in Puffett (ed.), *Richard Strauss: Salome*, pp. 145–60. By leaving the dance to a post-composition stage, Strauss excised it from the texture of the opera. Alma Mahler caustically commented on the resulting inferior quality of the dance.

[74]   Wilde, 'Salomé', p. 574.

'Philistine', only created under the laws of musical contrast.[75] Thus, these contrasts are much more complicated than at first glance, for while the dissonant chromatic music in *Salome* may evoke the musical 'perversion' of the exotic Oriental court and its main heroine, Strauss describes Salome's music as an elevated 'sphere of human emotions'. In light of Strauss's comments, Jochanaan's 'religious, sublime' musical discourse could be read as a perverse diatonicism.[76] In a typically decadent reversal of values, Strauss renders Salome in sensuous chromaticisms, where her corrupt dissonant music of feminine emotions is valued, and humanized, against Jochanaan's bombastic ultra-masculine diatonic exaltations.

Yet Strauss further complicates the split between the spiritual Word and the sensuous musical voice as sheer timbre, as Jochanaan's voice itself splits in two. One pervasive orchestral motif seems to conjure up Jochanaan's disembodied voice – his 'voice–music', according to Carolyn Abbate – and engages with

Example 1.1   Richard Strauss, *Salome*, Opera in One Act (Melville, NY, n.d.)

Source: Reproduced by permission of Alfred Publishing.

---

[75]   See Strauss's letter to Stefan Zweig, 5 May 1935, in Willi Schuh (ed.), *A Confidential Matter: The Letters of Richard Strauss and Stefan Zweig, 1931–1935*, trans. Max Knight (Berkeley, CA, 1977), p. 90.

[76]   Morten Kristiansen, 'Strauss's road to operatic success: *Guntram, Feuersnot*, and *Salome*', in Charles Youmans (ed.), *The Cambridge Companion to Richard Strauss* (Cambridge and New York, 2010), pp. 105–18, p. 116.

Example 1.2   Richard Strauss, *Salome*, Opera in One Act (Melville, NY, n.d.)

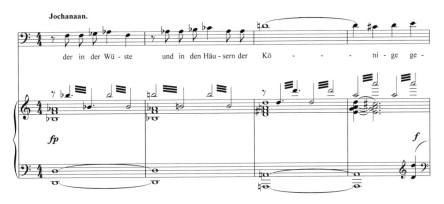

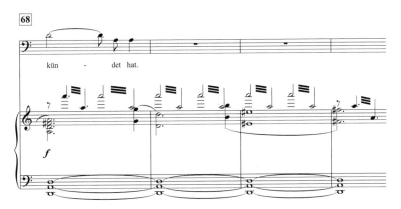

Source: Reproduced by permission of Alfred Publishing.

Jochanaan's embodied 'overpowering dark baritone'.[77] Associated with the presence and the prophecies of Jochanaan, this seven-note portentous theme delineates an ascending six-four chord. It is elaborated on by three descending fourths: two perfect fourths and one augmented fourth where the ominous dissonance resolves, only after a significant prolongation, to a perfect fourth. This motif acquires a spectral presence in the music permeating the orchestral texture by sounding across the brass, winds and strings. In its first fully fledged statement, the theme solemnly introduces Jochanaan's entrance on stage seven bars after Rehearsal Figure 61 (see Example 1.1). Jochanaan's prophetic singing on stage builds up to a *fortissimo* statement of his orchestral theme inaugurated

---

[77]   Carolyn Abbate, 'Opera; or, the Envoicing of Women', *Musicology and Difference: Gender and Sexuality in Music Scholarship* (Berkeley, CA, 1993), pp. 236–52.

by a perfect cadence into D major at Rehearsal Figure 68 (see Example 1.2). The associated tonality of D major signifies spirituality in the opera and reveals the prophetic nature of the motif as disembodied music. Like Jochanaan, his music here speaks from the heights of religious and prophetic exultation: with the spiritual tonality of D major, with Jochanaan's prophetic motif, and with the perfect authentic cadence as the 'divine rule' of Western music.

When Salome hears Jochanaan's double voice, she takes up and envoices his disembodied music. We can hear it resonating in Salome's theme as she sings, 'Er ist schrecklich' ['He is terrible'] at Rehearsal Figure 76. Like Jochanaan's orchestral theme, Salome's motif delineates a six-four chord, this time descending. It contains Jochanaan's signature descending perfect fourth, as if flirtatiously echoing the prophetic music without being able to sustain it (see Example 1.3). After taking up Jochanaan's theme first in the oboes and then in her melodic line, Salome further appropriates Jochanaan's sublime musical motif and sings it in his prophetic key of D major against the apocalyptic horns six bars after Rehearsal Figure 78: 'Wie abgezehrt er ist!' ['How wasted he is!'] The motif is right for a prophecy, and the key is right for a prophecy, yet the prophecy has turned into sensuous music, sung by a seductive soprano voice. To top it all, Salome perversely sings about the prophet's body with the theme of his disembodied voice.

When Jochanaan's disembodied voice–music is sung by Salome, the austere ascetic theme has already become sensuous. In this way, the manipulation of Strauss's orchestral motif continues to undermine the diametrical opposition of spirit and body. It now proliferates further ambiguities, in a similar vein to Wilde's subversion of Jokanaan's speaking voice as music, timbre and pure sonorousness.

As soon as Jochanaan hears Salome, he is audibly disconcerted by her womanhood, as a result adopts his otherwise sublime motif to question who she is. His voice, low in its range, trembles with stifled anger: 'Wer ist dies Weib, das mich ansieht?' ['Who is this woman who is looking at me?'] His rejection

Example 1.3 Richard Strauss, *Salome*, Opera in One Act (Melville, NY, n.d.)

Source: Reproduced by permission of Alfred Publishing.

comes as a visceral reaction distorting Jochanaan's disembodied voice–music, which Jochanaan sings here, clearly articulating it for the first time (at Rehearsal Figure 81).[78] The strings seem to harp on without direction, warping into religious perversity what would otherwise be a majestic conclusion of the Jochanaan music. In response, Salome proudly appropriates a diatonic language to introduce herself to the prophet (at Rehearsal Figure 83), but John the Baptist pushes her away acoustically with a shocking, *fortissimo*, jarringly dissonant augmented chord accompanying his words: 'Zurück, Tochter Babylons.' ['Stand back, Daughter of Babylon.']

The warped version of the motif at Rehearsal Figure 81 brings out the emotional corporeality of Jochanaan's voice and the real man, no longer a sublimated religious presence, as dotted rhythms, diminished triads and vertiginous chromatic ascents fuel his indignation. And it is during this moment of righteous anger that Jochanaan and Salome meet in the same physical space and tonal area of C♯, associated with the exotic Salome (at Rehearsal Figure 85). Just as the fascinated Salome dotes on Jochanaan's music by singing in the prophetic key of D major, so Jochanaan has come down out of his celestial tonal orbit and has landed in Salome's C♯ sphere of influence (of human emotions and affect). Indeed, as Wilde had foreseen, Jochanaan's spiritual voice becomes sensuous music in its chromatic C♯ undulations; both his corporeal (bass-baritone) voice and his disembodied voice (his orchestral motif, his 'voice–music') have been tainted by 'music'. When the prophet touches Salome musically, she responds by arpeggiating a C♯ major triad to accompany her most significant synaesthetic plea in Wilde's play: 'Sprich mehr, Jochanaan, deine Stimme ist wie Musik in meinen Ohren.' ['Speak again, Jochanaan, thy voice is like music to my ears.'] (see Example 1.4). What tautological irony: an operatic voice mellifluously sings that voice is music! It is precisely in the sphere of affect and sensuous music where Jochanaan and Salome meet.

In Wilde's phenomenology of the senses, the fatal gaze and the penetrating voice impact upon *Salomé*'s fictional world; they lethally enchain viewer (Narraboth) and viewed (Salome), the acoustically deflowered listener (Salome) and the prophetic speaker (Jokanaan). Likewise, sonic influence underlies Richard Strauss's music, as the characters vacillate between different tonalities, attracted or repelled, in a net of synaesthetic desires.[79] Self-reflexively, the opera informs the characters' music in terms of shifting power, domination and submission, as voices enter the spheres of influence of other characters. Just as Salome falls under the spell of Jochanaan's dark singing voice, Jochanaan cannot resist the princess's

---

[78]   The first fully fledged sung statement of the motif by Jochanaan appears in a rhythmically and contrapuntally distorted version when, outraged, Jochanaan denounces Herodias's incest and abominations at Rehearsal Figure 73. Orchestra and voice struggle torturously over the motif, trying to catch up with each other.

[79]   On transferable tonality, musical influence and domination in the opera, see Tethys Carpenter, 'Tonal and Dramatic Structure', in Puffett (ed.), *Richard Strauss: Salome*, pp. 93–106.

Example 1.4   Richard Strauss, *Salome*, Opera in One Act (Melville, NY, n.d.)

Source: Reproduced by permission of Alfred Publishing.

all-penetrating musical influence. Deeply disturbed by Salome's pleas to touch his body and kiss his mouth, the prophet curses her, singing again his sublimated orchestral voice–music in Salome's C♯ minor tonality at Rehearsal Figure 137, suggesting that his disembodied voice actually has a body that responds to sensory titillation, albeit negatively. Whereas Wilde's play is solipsistically created in the characters' subjective consciousness, the opera inevitably lays bare these same internal desires in transferable tonalities, motivic appropriations and tonal attractions. In a decisively modern coup d'état of irony, Strauss melds together the perverse diatonicism and exotic chromaticism of Jochanaan's and Salome's musical idioms, the prophet's sensuous abstinence reflected in the princess's synaesthetic desires as a negative double.[80]

Strauss actively reworks the interplay and power struggle between sensuous voice and spiritual Word suggested by Wilde's play. Thus, music in the opera acquires both a sensuous dimension in the singing voices of the baritone and the soprano, and a spiritual dimension in the orchestral motif associated with Jochanaan. Yet, neither orchestral music as spiritual disembodied voice, nor sensuous music remains unadulterated. We saw how Jochanaan corrupts his prophetic theme, but does Salome reach the heights of prophecy in Strauss's opera by spiritualizing and sublimating her supple luxuriant voice?

Indeed, in her final monologue, Salome synaesthetically conjoins body and spirit, vision and music, her embodied voice and Jochanaan's orchestral motif.[81] We witness the unification of the disembodied voice and the bodily mouth in Jochanaan's spectral visual and musical presences. His head on a silver platter emanates the musical motif of his disembodied voice. Mouth and voice, incense and taste, the coloured musical image of red fanfares and the taste and colour of the

---

[80]   In recent criticism, Strauss's Modernism is seen more in terms of his use of musical irony that rejects Wagnerian metaphysics, idealism, and the possibilities of redemption than in terms of technical innovations. Thus Charles Youmans identifies the perverse irony-informed overlap of Jochanaan's 'tonal grandiloquence and high-flown bombast' and Salome's 'cacophonous remix of Isolde's Liebestod', whereas Bryan Gilliam implies that the princess and the prophet gravitate toward one another in their narcissistic tendencies: 'sexual pathology' and 'extreme asceticism (inverted hedonism)'. On Strauss's irony, see Charles Youmans, 'Strauss and the nature of music', and Bryan Gilliam, 'Strauss and the sexual body: the erotics of humor, philosophy, and ego-assertion', in Charles Youmans (ed.), *The Cambridge Companion to Richard Strauss*, pp. 280–93, p. 292 and pp. 269–79, p. 277 (respectively). The perverse doubling of the characters goes back to Wilde's text, where Salome and Jokanaan share chastity and the whiteness of their bodies, as well as to Beardsley's drawings, where their profiles mirror each other as androgynous doubles in *John and Salome* and *The Climax* (see Figure 1.5).

[81]   While Carolyn Abbate aptly points out that Salome pursues 'a utopian quest' to transcend the separation of sound and sight, I disagree with her insistence on the acoustic delusion of the disembodied voice that disables the artistic attainment of synaesthetic, monistic, decadent union of spirit and body and the conflation of the senses in Salome's final monologue.

Example 1.5   Richard Strauss, *Salome*, Opera in One Act (Melville, NY, n.d.)

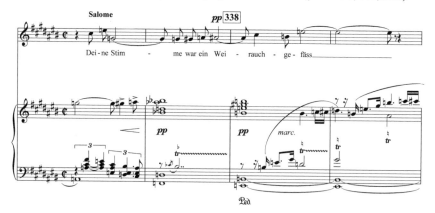

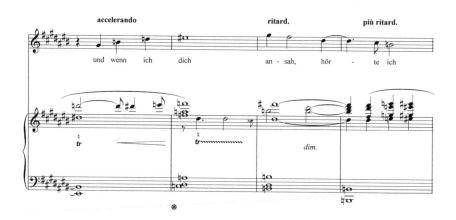

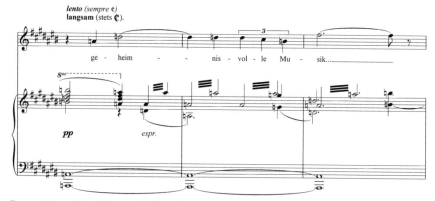

Source: Reproduced by permission of Alfred Publishing.

pomegranate from Salome's earlier attempts at enticing the prophet converge into a synaesthetic compound after his death: 'Deine Stimme war ein Weihrauchgefäss, und wenn ich dich ansah, hörte ich geheimnissvolle Musik.' ['Thy voice was an incense vessel and when I looked on thee I heard a strange music.'] (see Rehearsal Figure 337). Intoxicated by the recollected scent and sight of Jochanaan's strange voice, Salome reaches a cadential resolution in his prophetic tonality of D major. She meditates melodically on the prophet's strange 'music' until her line tapers off. At this point, Jochanaan's now synaesthetically embodied voice–music takes over against a D major backdrop, exuding incense, coloured red as the calls of fanfares, carrying the ethereal sound of the upper winds: cor anglais, oboes and flutes (see Example 1.5). Salome is musically cast as a mystic and a seer, as Wilde, too, saw his heroine. She is engrossed in contemplation of Jochanaan's head. Vision itself is spiritualized here, silencing the sensuous voice. Salome has internalized the prophet's disembodied music in her thoughts; she has made it her own and has synaesthetically become one with it. Thus, Salome enables Jochanaan's solemn prophetic theme to fulfil its synaesthetic potential in a mystical merger of spirit and the bodily senses. Jochanaan's 'strange music', both sensuous and mystic, issues from the violently severed head, conjured up across the decadent senses. In Salome's *Liebestod*, Jochanaan's music has attained the mystery of love and the mystery of death, thus opening up new synaesthetic horizons for Salome's creative afterlife across the arts.

The synaesthetic potential of the Salome myth fulfilled itself in Oscar Wilde's *Salomé*, and the legend's interartistic strivings reached their pinnacle in the play's intermedial transpositions. In the final analysis, I propose a transformative model based on the senses to explain the dissemination of Oscar Wilde's *Salomé* across the arts. Wilde's play stages a battle between language and the senses, which results in the decay or crumbling of language and the emancipation of the senses. While language's communicative potential is exhausted, vision and music prevail. Embodied in the play's leitmotivic structure, musical language reduces voices to timbre and words to sheer sound while the visual persists in desirous gazes and vividly descriptive similes.

Propelled by synaesthesia, the play's sensory expansion murders language as the tragedy's medium proper, empties out its essence, and catalyzes Salome's further transformations into Aubrey Beardsley's illustrations and Richard Strauss's opera. Playing with decadent notions of life, death and 'afterlife', this chapter delineates and demonstrates the workings of the decadent procedure of murdering and then reviving a dead language by engendering new extra-verbal, sensory life. Thus, the intermedial artwork appears as a new organism sprouting from the textual corpse of the questionable, in Wilde's case, original. In this sense, Wilde's *Salomé* not only self-consciously embodies and reflects on the Salome synaesthetic and interartistic tradition, but it also participates in a typically Modernist project by promoting its own aesthetic transformations across the arts.

Chapter 2

Visions of *Salome*, Visions of Wilde: Critical Readings of Oscar Wilde's *Salome* in Early Twentieth-Century Vienna

Sandra Mayer

Even if, by the end of the first decade of the twentieth century, Oscar Wilde's *Salome* on German-speaking stages had virtually been eclipsed in fame and popularity by Richard Strauss's operatic version, it may reasonably be argued that it was the Irish author's one-act tragedy that helped transform the Biblical theme into one of the most suggestive cultural myths of the *fin de siècle*. Portentously hinting at transgressive sexuality, morbid eroticism and blasphemous idolatry, which initially provoked the censor's ban on both sides of the Channel, the play touched the nerve of contemporary ideological concerns. Essentially, these consisted of 'the supremacy of artistic power in the face of political and religious authoritarianism; the assertion of female agency in the face of patriarchal authority; and the unapologetic expression of sexual desire in the face of cultural taboo and injunction'.[1] In its radical non-conformity, Wilde's tragedy represents a key moment in the formation of what Petra Dierkes-Thrun in her recent study *Salome's Modernity* has termed the 'modernist aesthetics of transgression', specifically understood as 'a replacement of traditional metaphysical, moral, and cultural belief systems with literary and artistic discourses that develop utopian erotic and aesthetic visions of individual transgression and agency'.[2] Indeed, Salome's transgressivity could not fail to make a profound impression on *fin-de-siècle* commentators, as Marie Luise Becker noted at the turn of the twentieth century in a richly illustrated survey entitled 'Salome in the Arts of the Last Millennium', and in relation to Hedwig Lachmann's recently published German translation of Wilde's play in the Viennese literary journal, *Wiener Rundschau*:

---

[1] Julie Townsend, 'Staking Salomé: The Literary Forefathers and Choreographic Daughters of Oscar Wilde's "Hysterical and Perverted Creature"', in Joseph Bristow (ed.), *Oscar Wilde and Modern Culture: The Making of a Legend* (Athens, OH, 2008), pp. 96–109, p. 156.

[2] Petra Dierkes-Thrun, *Salome's Modernity: Oscar Wilde and the Aesthetics of Transgression* (Ann Arbor, MI, 2011), p. 2.

Wilde's known hypersensitivity has brought forth a highly accomplished depiction of the severe malady of the age, which has given rise to such a character as Salome. There is sublime poetry and beauty in this play, but also something morbid and decadent. ... This is Salome, the king's daughter, the way she was reborn through art and human sensibility after one-and-a-half thousand years: sin and yet soul, woman and tigress, facing the abyss with a burning heart and pulsing veins.[3]

[Mit großer Feinheit hat Wildes bekannte Hypersensitivität die tiefe Erkrankung der Zeit zu schildern verstanden, aus der solche Naturen, wie die der Salome, erwachsen können. Es liegt eine unsagbare Poesie und Schönheit in diesem Stücke, aber auch etwas Krankes, Zerfallendes. ... Salome ist hier das Königskind, wie es Kunst und menschliches Empfinden in diesen anderthalb Jahrtausenden wiedergeboren haben, – Sünde und doch Seele, Weib und Tigerin, mit heißem Herzen und pochenden Pulsen an einen Abgrund gestellt.]

Conspicuously marked by the author's capability of merging dramatic convention with the outrageously suggestive avant-garde, Wilde's play was praised as a worthy addition to the annals of world literature by the German composer and music journalist Hugo Daffner. In his 1912 historical study of cultural representations of Salome, from the story's Scriptural origins to its salient presence in early twentieth-century art, Daffner places Wilde's extraordinary drama at the onset and centre of a seemingly ubiquitous, commercially exploited artistic fad: 'Thus, hardly ... a year goes by without some kind of literary adaptation of the tale of John the Baptist, or part of it, being presented to the reading and theatre-going public.'[4]

Indeed, the economically rewarding opportunities afforded by the 'Salome hype', observed by Theodor Antropp in the wake of the German and Austrian premieres of Wilde's play and Strauss's opera,[5] also made their mark on popular culture and vaudeville, attracting the attention of the Canadian-born dancer Maud Allan. Before successfully touring other European capitals between 1906 and 1908, Allan gave the first public performance of her legendary dance-act on 30 December 1906 at the Vienna Carltheater under the exotic title *The Vision*

---

[3]   Marie Luise Becker, 'Salome in der Kunst des letzten Jahrtausends', *Bühne und Welt*, 4/1 (1901/1902): pp. 201–9, p. 203. All English translations from German original sources are the author's.

[4]   'So vergeht denn nun nahezu ... kein Jahr, das nicht die Täuferepisode oder einen Ausschnitt daraus in irgendeiner dichterischen Fassung auf den Markt gebracht hätte', Hugo Daffner, *Salome, ihre Gestalt in Geschichte und Kunst: Dichtung – Bildende Kunst – Musik*, (Munich, 1912), p. 309.

[5]   'Salome–Rummel', in Theodor Antropp, 'Wiener Theater', *Österreichische Rundschau*, 33 (1912): pp. 478–9, p. 478.

of Salome: Balletic Tableau with Authentic Oriental Themes by Marcel Rémy.[6]
Even though the 15-minute presentation triggered some critical reflections on
'high' versus 'low' art and was primarily remarked upon by commentators due
to Allan's revealing costume, it appears to have failed to create a great sensation
among Viennese audiences, who, by all accounts, had become accustomed to
the inflationary phenomenon of scantily clad female dancers. A couple of weeks
earlier, Mata Hari had appeared in a similar act at the Vienna Secession Art Hall
and the Apollotheater,[7] and the reviewer for the *Neues Wiener Journal*, while duly
acknowledging Allan's undisputed allure, pronounced a remarkably unenthusiastic
verdict revealing a thoroughly dismissive opinion of modern dance as a form
of distinctly lowbrow entertainment: 'It surely would be a highly original and
promising occurrence if one day there was a female dancer who did not choose to
perform barefoot or more or less in the nude, was not wearing short skirts and was,
in fact, a skilled practitioner of her art.'[8]

Once Allan's act had been banned from the stage of the Viennese court opera
house by the authorities, who had also recently thwarted Gustav Mahler's keen
efforts to secure the first Austrian production of Strauss's *Salome*, it did not give
rise to further objections by the officials attending a private preview of the show,
as reported in the *Deutsches Volksblatt*. As will be explored in greater detail below,
the choice of theatrical venue not only constituted a crucial factor in the regulation
policy of contemporary theatre censorship, but actively determined public and
critical conceptions of art and aesthetic value judgements. Consequently, relegated
to the boulevard genres of operetta or variety theatre, and thus to the spheres of
light entertainment and popular culture, Maud Allan's Salome incarnation was
hardly to be classified as 'true, serious art' but was still 'sure to find its audience',
according to the *Deutsches Volksblatt* reviewer.[9] Similarly, the unnamed critic in
Reichspost opined:

> In the end, nobody will be convinced that naked dance performers constitute an
> artistic desideratum, especially when they have been banished from the "serious"
> opera stage and relocated to that of operetta, cabaret and vaudeville. The art
> lovers breathed hot air into their hands, which they had not been able to keep
> warm with an enthusiastic round of applause; those who took pleasure in Miss

---

[6] *Die Vision Salomes: Tanzgemälde mit original orientalischen Melodien von Marcel
Rémy*, Austrian Theatre Museum, playbills Carltheater 1906.

[7] Toni Bentley, *Sisters of Salome* (New Haven, 2002), p. 106.

[8] 'Es wäre sicherlich sehr originell und auch erfolgversprechend, wenn eines Tages
eine Tänzerin käme, die nicht barfuß oder sonst halb nackend aufträte, kurze Röcke anhätte
und wirklich tanzen könnte'. *Neues Wiener Journal*, 29 December 1906.

[9] 'Mit wahrer, echter Kunst hat die Produktion nichts gemein, aber sie wird dennoch
ihr Publikum finden', *Deutsches Volksblatt*, 29 December 1906.

Allan's performance needed their hands to hide their faces as they whispered into each other's ears.[10]

[Es ist eben niemand zu überzeugen, daß nackte Tänzerinnen wirklich ein Kunstbedürfnis seien, namentlich dann, wenn sie von der ernsten Bühne auf die der Operette und des Varietés verwiesen werden. Die Freunde der Kunst bliesen in die Hände, die sie nicht am Applaus wärmen konnten; die an Miß Allan Gefallen fanden, brauchten die Hände, um einander Mitteilungen zuzuflüstern.]

Defying traditional categories of genre and aesthetic evaluation, *The Vision of Salome* was received with a mixture of bemused condescension, lurid sensationalism and smug conservatism by Viennese critics, who had witnessed the local premiere of Wilde's theatrical novelty in 1903 and were then eagerly awaiting the first performance of Strauss's operatic adaptation in the Austrian capital, to be presented by a Breslau company on 25 May 1907 at the Deutsches Volkstheater. Yet Allan's act turned out to be the most popular Salome rendition in early twentieth-century England, where in 1908 it enjoyed a run of over 250 performances at London's Palace Theatre.[11] At the same time, and until its suspension in 1931, the censor's ban confined Wilde's play to a small number of private London productions, which were either boycotted, or, at best, largely indifferently received by the contemporary press.

Officially, the play had been refused a licence by the Lord Chamberlain in June 1892 on the basis of a traditional Protestant law which prohibited any stage representations of Biblical subjects.[12] However, Edward F. Smyth Pigott, the Lord Chamberlain's Examiner of Plays, indignantly dismissed by Wilde as a 'commonplace official ... who panders to the vulgarity and hypocrisy of the English people by licensing every low farce and vulgar drama',[13] appears to have had greater concerns about what he privately characterized as *Salomé*'s 'half Biblical, half pornographic' character.[14] Hence, according to William Archer, writing in May 1893, when *Salomé* was published in book form in the original French, 'its suppression by the Censor was perfectly ridiculous, and absolutely inevitable. The Censor is the official mouthpiece of Philistinism, and Philistinism

---

[10]   *Reichspost*, 1 January 1907.

[11]   Amy Koritz, 'Salomé: Exotic Woman and the Transcendent Dance', in Antony H. Harrison and Beverly Taylor (eds), *Gender and Discourse in Victorian Literature and Art* (DeKalb, IL, 1992), pp. 251–73, p. 262.

[12]   Richard Ellmann, *Oscar Wilde* (London, 1988), p. 351.

[13]   Oscar Wilde, *The Complete Letters of Oscar Wilde* (London, 2000), p. 531.

[14]   Pigott quoted in Joseph Donohue, 'Distance, Death and Desire in *Salome*', in Peter Raby (ed.), *The Cambridge Companion to Oscar Wilde* (Cambridge, 1997), pp. 118–42, p. 118.

would doubtless have been outraged had *Salomé* been represented on stage'.[15] Despite Wilde's vehement protests that the authorities' decision presented an assault on the 'artistic treatment of moral and elevating subjects' and evidently highlighted their generally low esteem of 'the stage as a form of art',[16] the play's depiction of moral and sexual transgression severely challenged English theatre audiences' tolerance of artistic licence. As Joseph Donohue speculates,

> *Salome* must have seemed to them almost a betrayal; the idiom was too unfamiliar, too threatening, and Wilde's models, dramaturgical and characterological, were too far afield from the West End repertoire of dramas and comedies of modern life and romantic costume plays, peopled by upper-class Londoners or their surrogates.[17]

Moreover, set remotely from the topicality and social milieu of Wilde's comedies, the author's exotic Symbolist tragedy allowed for diverse modes of biographical reading, since 'this very remoteness from late-nineteenth-century social mores gave Wilde the freedom to explore the concerns closest to his own life'.[18]

With regard to the subsequent analysis of the play's early twentieth-century Viennese reception, it seems relevant to note that in a 1905 letter to the editor of *The Saturday Review*, Robert Ross (Oscar Wilde's literary executor) refers to *Salomé* as 'the only drama which any English writer has been able to give to the répertoire [*sic*] of the modern European stage'. There, Ross claims, the play has been performed 'at constant intervals exactly as the author planned it, whereas even Shakespeare has to be doctored to suit the conventions of different countries'.[19] His mildly polemical allusion to reputedly superior Continental artistic tastes sets up a counter-image to the less than favourable critical reception of the play's 1905 English premiere, which had been organized as a private performance by the New Stage Club at the Bijou Theatre in London's Bayswater.[20]

Even if Wilde's Symbolist one-act tragedy may indeed have been the cornerstone of the author's restored literary acclaim 'wherever the English language is not spoken',[21] Ross's proposition turns out to be an overly confident appraisal, given the fact that the play was well-nigh universally perceived within a context of decadence, sexual perversion and a pathological condition of physical

---

[15]   William Archer, 'Mr. Oscar Wilde's New Play', in Karl Beckson (ed.), *Oscar Wilde: The Critical Heritage* (London, 1997), pp. 141–2, p. 142.

[16]   Oscar Wilde, 'The Censure and Salomé', in E.H. Mikhail (ed.), *Oscar Wilde: Interviews and Recollections* (2 vols, Basingstoke, 1979), vol. 1, pp. 186–9, p. 187.

[17]   Donohue, 'Distance, Death and Desire', p. 123.

[18]   Josephine Guy and Ian Small, *Studying Oscar Wilde: History, Criticism, and Myth* (Greensboro, NC, 2006), p. 146.

[19]   Robert Ross, 'Salomé', *The Saturday Review*, 27 May 1905.

[20]   William Tydeman and Steven Price, *Wilde: Salome* (Cambridge, 1996), p. 40.

[21]   Ross, quoted in Donohue, 'Distance, Death and Desire', p. 119.

and mental degeneration.[22] In the wake of the enforced public exposure of the most intimate details of its author's private life, *Salome* was increasingly interpreted as a striking testimony to what was seen as Wilde's morbid depravity and perverted poetic imagination, which is manifestly revealed by contemporary censorship records and press reviews of the play's 1903 Viennese premiere. In the capital of the Habsburg Monarchy, as elsewhere, only a very narrow set of commentators seemed to share Wilde's conviction that the artist was firmly positioned 'outside his subject' and consequently defied all attempts at moral categorization.[23]

Between Licence and Regulation:
Salome in the Light of Austrian Theatre Censorship

Serving an institutional agency invested with the governmental authority of determining hegemonic definitions of culture, the censor functions as a 'gate-keeper …, standing at crucial points of control, monitoring what comes in and what stays outside any given cultural or linguistic territory'.[24] Censorship, therefore, is deeply implicated in the dynamics of negotiating the preservation or transgression of established social, cultural and aesthetic norms and may be regarded as an institutionalized instrument of cultural regulation, as it fundamentally controls the selection, adaptation and subsequent reception of specific texts. Instituted by the state to secure the preservation of the established order and to forge a surface image of a homogeneous national culture, its need for coercive action arises from a clash of individual and collective identity, especially where it concerns the spheres of public life, religion, politics and moral convention.[25]

Hence, it appears inevitable that the statement issued by an Austrian police official in charge of theatre censorship in March 1903 should contain an extensive set of reservations with regard to *Salome*'s suitability for public performance. Foremost among these grave concerns were the offence potentially caused to public decency and religious sentiments and, most significantly, the play's – by all accounts – morally dubious author:

---

[22]　Sander L. Gilman, 'Strauss, the Pervert, and Avant Garde Opera of the Fin de Siècle', *New German Critique*, 43 (1988): pp. 35–68, p. 55.

[23]　Wilde, 'The Soul of Man under Socialism', in *Complete Works of Oscar Wilde* (London and Glasgow, 1948, reprinted 1977), pp. 1079–1104, p. 1093.

[24]　Michael Holman and Jean Boase-Beier, 'Introduction: Writing, Rewriting and Translation through Constraint to Creativity', in Boase-Beier and Holman (eds), *The Practices of Literary Translation: Constraints and Creativity* (Manchester, 1999), pp. 1–17, p. 11.

[25]　John A. McCarthy, 'Zensur und Kultur: "Autoren nicht Autoritäten!"', in John A. McCarthy and Werner von der Ohe (eds), *Zensur und Kultur, Censorship and Culture: Zwischen Weimarer Klassik und Weimarer Republik mit einem Ausblick bis heute* (Tübingen, 1995), pp. 1–13, p. 5.

It cannot be overlooked that in the play at hand the sensuous moment is glaringly accentuated, ... which, in a public performance, is likely to violate religious sentiments. In addition, ... the (already deceased) author, the Englishman [*sic*] Oscar Wilde, was publicly declared a sexual pervert, and therefore traces of his morbid disposition were looked for in his work also.[26]

[Gleichwohl wird man ... nicht übersehen können, dass in dem vorliegenden ... Stücke das sinnliche Moment grell in den Vordergrund tritt ... und dass desshalb [*sic*] durch die Aufführung eine Verletzung des religiösen Empfindens hervorgerufen werden könnte. Hiezu kommt noch, ... dass ferner der – bereits verstorbene Autor – der Engländer [*sic*] Oskar Wilde öffentlich als geschlechtlich pervers bezeichnet wurde und dass daher die Spuren dieser krankhaften Neigungen auch in seinem Werke ... gesucht würden.]

In fact, the repressive measures taken by the German state authorities in the case of Max Reinhardt's production of *Salome* in Berlin – subsequently privately premiered at the Kleines Theater on 15 November 1902 – had substantially contributed to creating a flurry of interest among the Viennese public.[27] Yet, in the eyes of the Austrian officials, the German example was one to be emulated rather than to be defied in an emancipatory act of cultural self-assertion. For as long as it remained in force, the German ban on *Salome* a priori precluded the permission of Wilde's controversial play in the Viennese theatre scene, as the relevant records imply. Therein, ample reference is made with regard to the suspension of the censor's ban and the subsequent first public staging of Reinhardt's production at Berlin's Neues Theater on 29 September 1903. However, the recommended licensing of the play by the Austrian censorship authorities remained conditionally tied to a compendium of suggested textual as well as dramaturgical modifications in order to alleviate the perceived offence to public moral and religious sensibilities.[28] In tune with James Joyce's assessment that *Salomé* was 'a polyphonic variation on the rapport of art and nature, but at the same time a revelation of ... [Wilde's] own psyche',[29] the play was regarded as a mirror image of its author's decadence, which called for the careful regulatory intermediation of the state authorities in the form of institutional censorship.

---

[26]   Archives of Lower Austria, St Pölten, censorship records 1582 ex 1903, 14 March 1903.

[27]   W. Eugene Davis, 'Oscar Wilde, *Salome*, and the German Press 1902–1905', *English Literature in Transition*, 44/2 (2001): pp. 149–80, p. 156.

[28]   Sandra Mayer and Barbara Pfeifer, 'The Reception of Oscar Wilde and Bernard Shaw in the Light of Early Twentieth-Century Austrian Censorship', *Platform*, 2/2 (2007): pp. 59–75, p. 65.

[29]   James Joyce, 'Oscar Wilde: The Poet of "Salomé"', in Ellsworth Mason and Richard Ellmann (eds), *The Critical Writings of James Joyce* (London, 1959), pp. 201–5, p. 205.

In principle, early twentieth-century stage censorship in the Habsburg Monarchy was bound to the provisions formulated by the Theatre Act of 1850, which prohibited the representation of anything that might be considered a breach of public order and penal law, or an offence to the imperial dynasty and commonly observed codes of moral and religious decorum. According to these regulations, theatres were required to obtain a licence for their planned productions from the governor of the respective crown land by submitting two copies of the script in advance, one of which was to be returned for subsequent revision and the consideration of recommended alterations. In order to prevent any violation of the law, representatives of the executive authority usually attended – and reported on – the dress rehearsals as well as the public performances of the approved theatre productions.[30] Following the powerful protest voiced by some of the most eminent figures of the Viennese literary and theatrical establishment of the 1890s, a reformed ordinance on the law's practical execution was released in 1903, generally allowing for a more liberal administration of the regulations in response to the far-reaching socio-economic and cultural transformations of the day.

Nevertheless, *Salome*'s 'fervent sensuality with its gruesome ending', considered likely to offend parts of the audience in their sense of decency, aroused the misgivings of censorship advisory board member, Carl Glossy.[31] In his report on the play's revised script, submitted by the Deutsches Volkstheater in October 1903, the widely esteemed literary historian and director of the Vienna City Library characteristically deems Wilde's drama a symptomatic literary expression of the author's legally established moral degeneracy:

> It is the work of a poet whose language is dazzling, whose imagination is fuelled by wild passion. Here, [in this play], the morbid, deviant disposition of the author is crudely revealed. For a reading audience, this product of a diseased mind might still be judged acceptable, but any physical realization of this play on stage appears problematic to me, to say the least. …[32]

> [es ist das Werk eines Dichters, dessen Sprache blendend, dessen Fantasie von wilder Leidenschaft erfüllt ist. Die krankhafte, widernatürliche Anlage des Verfassers kommt hier grell zum Ausdrucke. Als Lektüre mag man diese Ausgeburt eines kranken Geistes immerhin entgegen nehmen, aber eine Verkörperung dieses Stückes auf der Bühne scheint mir zum mindesten bedenklich. …]

---

[30]   Franz Spitaler, *Die Wiener Erstaufführung der Salome: Ein Beitrag zur Geschichte der Rezeption Oscar Wildes in Österreich* (Vienna, 1990), pp. 32–3; Djawid Carl Borower, *Struktur und Wandel der Wiener Theaterzensur im politischen und sozialen Kontext der Jahre 1893 bis 1914* (Vienna, 1986), pp. 91–3.

[31]   'glühende … Sinnlichkeit mit einem Grauen erregenden Schlusse'. Archives of Lower Austria, St Pölten, censorship records 1184 ex 1907, 18 October 1903.

[32]   Ibid.

Strikingly, Glossy's assessment attests to the suggestive force of the multidimensional, synaesthetic materiality of theatrical representation, acknowledged also by the authorities in their exceptionally strict directives for the play's stage production. These sentiments were no doubt shared by the anonymous reviewer of *Salomé*'s English premiere in *The Daily Telegraph*, who judged it 'a play to be read in the study – not to be seen on the boards'.[33]

Whereas Glossy's commentary primarily focused on the play's moral implications, the former Viennese First Crown Prosecutor, Franz Josef Ritter von Cischini, took a close look at its religious context, in particular its depiction of Biblical characters. More precisely, when it came to the theatrical portrayal of John the Baptist as an 'object and source of perverted sensuality', the legal board representative anticipated vigorous resistance from the Catholic clergy.[34] However, unless these reservations should be shared by the Governor, Cischini conceded that the imposition of a ban might be based on little justification, given the generally balanced treatment of the subject:

> For John the Baptist is portrayed in an entirely decent, dignified way. Salome's advances are rejected by him in a forceful manner that amounts to a sufficiently drastic depiction of the temptress's infamy. With his fictional representations of Salome, Herod and Herodias, the decadent author allows for a revealing glimpse into the corruption of the Roman Empire and the erotic parts do not appear likely to offend the sense of decency and to cause a public scandal since they are always attended by a moment of horror, which reaches its climax in the play's concluding scene.[35]

> [Denn die Figur des Johannes ist vollkommen correct, würdig. Die Zumutungen der Salome werden von ihm in energischer die Schändlichkeit der Verführerin genügend drastisch bezeichnender Weise zurückgewiesen. In den Figuren der Salome, des Herodes und der Herodias schildert der dekadente Autor in sehr anschaulicher Weise eine Scene aus der Dekadenz der Kaiserzeit und dürften die erotischen Stellen nicht geeignet sein die Sittlichkeit gröblich zu verletzen und öffentliches Aergerniß zu erregen, weil immer ein Moment des Grauens mitgeschildert wird, welches mit dem Schlusse seinen Gipfel erreicht.]

It is worth emphasizing that Cischini's recommendation explicitly took into account the play's prospective audience at the Deutsches Volkstheater, which was expected to be well acquainted with the challenging subject matter and aesthetics of modern drama. By then, the Deutsches Volkstheater had developed into a renowned theatrical venue, esteemed for its ambitious repertory of experimental

---

[33]   Quoted in Robert Tanitch, *Oscar Wilde on Stage and Screen* (London, 1999), p. 141.

[34]   'Objekt und Erreger perverser Sinnlichkeit'. Archives of Lower Austria, St Pölten, censorship records 1184 ex 1907, 1 November 1903.

[35]   Ibid.

contemporary European plays by such progressive authors as Frank Wedekind or Maxim Gorky, and had established close collaborative ties with other eminent German stages, particularly those based in the Prussian capital.[36]

Court Counsellor Ludwig Tils, government representative in the Lower Austrian parliament and administrative advisory board member, expressly pleaded in his evaluation in favour of the play's approval and took up a line of argument that echoed his colleague's judgement, quoted above. Despite John the Baptist's characterization as an object of 'lustful desire for a lewd woman',[37] Salome's aggressive erotic advances were deemed unlikely to give rise to charges of sacrilegious defamation, as the duly deferential depiction of the saint's acquiescent martyrdom restored the balance between poetic and moral justice. While it was accepted that any dramatic portrayal of Biblical figures might inevitably entail an unedifying account of their exposure to abuse, blasphemy and ill-usage, the censor remained sceptical about the play's 'atmosphere of sultry sensuality',[38] which he attributed to the author's homosexual orientation. However, the multiform ethical and aesthetic reservations about the granting of its public production licence appeared to be redeemed by its standards of artistic merit, as Tils qualified *Salome* as the work of a 'poet' and an outstanding example of contemporary drama. Ultimately, Tils benevolently concluded, the audience of the Deutsches Volkstheater ought not to be deprived of such an extraordinary play, since even its more objectionable parts, attesting to the author's 'poisoned imagination', could be regarded as the product of ulterior 'poetic motives'.[39] Accordingly, he merely advised a number of cuts and that the Baptist's severed head should be modestly concealed from the gaze of the audience.

Notwithstanding the contradictory, deliberately vague and inconclusive recommendations delivered by individual board members, *Salome* was cleared by governor's decree on 20 November 1903 and was premiered three weeks later, on 12 December, at the Deutsches Volkstheater. Quite in accord with its previous scandal-tainted history, its reception appears to have been divided evenly between clamorous protest and raving approval, as the police report on the premiere notes: 'The violent protest, which, immediately after the fall of the curtain, began with an intense chorus of hissing, was soon countered by roaring applause'.[40]

---

[36]   Clemens Höslinger, '*Salome* und ihr österreichisches Schicksal 1905 bis 1918', *Österreichische Musikzeitschrift*, 32 (1977): pp. 300–309, p. 300.

[37]   'Gegenstande des Begehrens eines lüsternen Weibes', Archives of Lower Austria, St Pölten, censorship records 1184 ex 1907, 18 November 1903.

[38]   'Atmosphäre schwüler Sinnlichkeit'. Ibid.

[39]   'Es geht wohl nicht an, dem Publikum ein Stück wie "Salome" vorzuenthalten, in dem selbst das Bedenklichste nicht als Spekulation auf die Sinnlichkeit sondern aus dichterischen Motiven (mag auch deren Quelle vergifteter Phantasie entstammen), niedergeschrieben wurde'. Ibid.

[40]   'Der starke Widerspruch, der sich unmittelbar nach dem Fallen des Vorhanges in lebhaftem Zischen äusserte, hatte bald mit lautem Beifalle zu kämpfen', Archives of Lower

Even if the absence of outright rejection and the ostensible appreciation of the aesthetic quality of Wilde's text in Hedwig Lachmann's German translation suggest a comparatively lenient execution of the authorities' censorship policy, the proposed cuts and amendments yet constitute an attempt to regulate and to carry out 'at least a partial transformation of cultural artefacts'.[41] Moreover, far from provoking an exemplary demonstration of Viennese literary liberalism in deliberate opposition to Berlin concepts of cultural modernity, the initial ban on the play's public performance in the Prussian capital and its eventual repeal set the guiding parameters of action for the Austrian officials. Notably, a comparative analysis of the theatrical systems in the two capitals, Berlin and Vienna, reveals a causal correlation between the commercialization of culture and the successful adoption of literary avant-garde tendencies.[42] While the increasingly competitive theatrical market in the German metropolis fostered a heightened susceptibility to capitalist mechanisms and thus engendered a quest for artistic innovation, Viennese stage repertories and their aesthetic norms remained principally determined by the affirmation of social distinction and representation sought by traditional local elites.[43] Accordingly, the censorship records highlight the fact that permissive notions of creative licence were contextually defined by the structural configuration of the Viennese theatrical landscape, as two of the three censorship board members, Cischini and Tils, specifically allude to what is perceived as the progressive core audience of the Deutsches Volkstheater. Therefore, it appears entirely in line with the artistic philosophy of the Deutsches Volkstheater that it should have housed the 1907 Viennese premiere of Richard Strauss's operatic setting of *Salome* as well, while the work was to remain barred from production at the Vienna court opera house until 1918.[44] As will be demonstrated, the extensive gamut of responses elicited by Wilde's vigorously debated tragedy from the Austrian theatre censors is paralleled by the contemporary press reviews of its premiere, summed up perhaps most aptly by the verdict offered in *Illustrirtes Wiener Extrablatt*: 'Their indignation over the play's gruesome ending may have made people purse their lips, but they soon changed their minds. It was instinctively felt that a poet was at work here'.[45]

Austria, St Pölten, censorship records 1184 ex 1907, 13 December 1903.

[41]   Mayer and Pfeifer, 'The Reception of Oscar Wilde', p. 70.

[42]   Peter Sprengel and Gregor Streim, *Berliner und Wiener Moderne: Vermittlungen und Abgrenzungen in Literatur, Theater, Publizistik* (Vienna, 1998), p. 28.

[43]   Ibid.

[44]   Höslinger, '*Salome* und ihr österreichisches Schicksal', p. 309.

[45]   'Die Entrüstung über das entsetzliche Ende mag die Münder gespitzt haben, aber gleich darauf besannen sich die Leute eines Besseren. Man fühlte es instinctiv, daß hier ein Dichter das Wort führte', *Illustrirtes Wiener Extrablatt*, 13 December 1903.

Sexual Pathology and Poetic Genius: Constructing the Image of the Author through the Critical Reception of *Salome*

'Like a dreadful, feverish dream this poem raced by us, lighting up in a hundred blood-soaked colours.'[46] This is how Siegfried Jacobsohn, the Berlin theatre correspondent for *Die Zeit*, strove to capture the resounding impression of the post-Naturalist theatrical sensation of Max Reinhardt's *Salome* production, premiered together with *The Importance of Being Earnest* in a private matinee performance at the Berlin Kleines Theater in November 1902. Praising the event as a 'paragon of taste, unity of style and magnificent individual performances',[47] and recording the attendance of such illustrious figures of the modern German art scene as Stefan George, Lovis Corinth and Richard Strauss, rapturous reviews by Jacobsohn and others were bound to shape the expectations of Viennese audiences. Undoubtedly, Reinhardt's holistic deployment of an atmospheric stage setting, musical elements and dance performance had made *Salome* the highlight of the theatrical season.[48] Hence, following its transfer to the Neues Theater in September 1903, the legendary theatre artist's 'first major experiment in symbolism' was widely remarked upon by the Viennese press,[49] and discernibly influenced the play's first Vienna production which was unfavourably reviewed by the Austrian critic Anton Lindner as an uninspired imitation of Reinhardt's *mise en scène*, and a 'badly stirred mixture of Nestroy and Krafft-Ebing'.[50]

In all probability, the enormous publicity the play received in Berlin and the controversy surrounding its initial stage ban ushered the Viennese premiere of *Salome* into the spotlight of public attention, where it rapidly reached the dimensions of a fervently disputed *cause célèbre*. 'Depending on one's point of view, a theatrical scandal was feared, anticipated or even hoped for', wrote the anonymous reviewer of the *Neues Wiener Journal*, subtly hinting at the sensationalist undercurrents of audience interest and adding dryly: 'All those who believe themselves to be particularly sensitive or robust will flock to the Volkstheater'.[51]

---

[46]   'Wie ein entsetzlicher Fiebertraum ist dieses Gedicht an uns vorübergejagt, aufglühend in hundert blutgetränkten Farben', Siegfried Jacobsohn, 'Oskar Wilde', *Die Zeit*, 19 November 1902.

[47]   'Die Aufführung der "Salome" war, scenisch wie schauspielerisch, ein Wunderwerk an Geschmack, an Stileinheit, an glänzenden Einzelleistungen', ibid.

[48]   Clair Rowden's chapter in this volume also briefly discusses Reinhardt's Berlin production of 1902.

[49]   Tydeman and Price, *Wilde: Salome*, p. 32.

[50]   'schlechtverrührte Mischung aus Nestroy und Krafft-Ebing', Anton Lindner, 'Von den Wiener Theatern 1903/04', *Bühne und Welt*, 6/1 (1903/1904): pp. 344–7, p. 344.

[51]   'Man fürchtete, erwartete oder erhoffte, je nach dem Standpunkte, einen Theaterscandal. ... Alle werden ins Volkstheater gehen wollen, die sehr schwach – oder sehr starknervig zu sein glauben', *Neues Wiener Journal*, 13 December 1903.

Essentially, the broad spectrum of critical responses on the occasion of *Salome*'s Vienna debut, directed by Richard Fellner, offers a striking panorama of diverse aesthetically and ideologically motivated assessments. In line with the official police report on its first night, the play – presented together with Erich Korn's one-act drama *Nachtmar* – sparked categorically divided audience reactions, alternating between surges of thunderous applause and fierce opposition. In contrast to the universally applauded Munich actress Lili Marberg in the Deutsches Volkstheater's 1906 revival of the original production, the 1903 performance delivered by Adele Hartwig from Berlin's Neues Theater – stepping in for the popular star actress Helene Odilon who had suffered a stroke – failed to find favour with Viennese critics. Speculating on the reasons for this lack of critical enthusiasm, it may be assumed that common expectations were indelibly shaped by the critical success of Gertrud Eysoldt's memorable interpretation of Salome in Max Reinhardt's production and her skilful realization of the part's subtle nuances, as characterized by Marie Luise Becker: 'Salome is an ancient nymph; in her case, adolescence is paired with the cunning of a brutal character'[52] (see Figure 2.1).

In the context of wide-ranging critical opinion, the *Neue Freie Presse* – the internationally most influential Austrian newspaper of the day and mouthpiece of upper-middle class liberalism – adopted an astonishingly invective and reactionary stance. In this case, a striking elective affinity with the far-right of the ideological spectrum of the contemporary media landscape may be traced, even if individual newspapers' motivations were diverse. Most notably, the rare occasion of seeing the clerical-conservative and Jewish-dominated liberal press united in their joint condemnation of 'perverted' artistic tastes incurred the eloquent mockery of Karl Kraus, one of the most eminent German-language satirists and cultural critics of his day: 'What a level of suggestive force must be inherent in a work of art that has succeeded in exposing such a pure and uniform manifestation of the philistine spirit!'[53]

In what amounts to a startling evocation of Max Nordau's degeneration theories in unison with suspicions of the play's veiled anti-Semitic bias, Friedrich Schütz's discussion of *Salome* in the *Neue Freie Presse* rehearsed the entire range of stereotypes and personal prejudice clinging to the author's reputation.[54] Portrayed

---

[52] 'Salome ist ein antikes Nixchen, das Halbreife paart sich hier mit der Raffiniertheit einer brutalen Natur', Becker, 'Salome-Darstellerinnen auf der modernen Bühne', *Bühne und Welt*, 9/1 (1906/1907): pp. 439–47, p. 439.

[53] 'Welche suggestive Kraft muß einem Kunstwerk innewohnen, das es vermocht hat, den Philistersinn … sich in Reinheit und Einheit offenbaren zu lassen!', Karl Kraus, '"Salome"', *Die Fackel*, 5/150 (1903): pp. 1–14, pp. 13–14.

[54] First published in German in 1892, *Entartung*, by the Hungarian-born Zionist activist, journalist and notorious cultural critic Max Nordau (1849–1923), lent a shrill voice to the angst-ridden imagination of the *fin-de-siècle* psyche, which conjured up apocalyptic spectres of political, socio-economic, cultural and racial decline. In Nordau's book, Wilde

Figure 2.1   Lili Marberg as Salome, Munich 1905
Source: Österreichische Nationalbibliothek (Austrian National Library), Bildarchiv und Grafiksammlung (Picture Archives and Graphics Department), Vienna.

as an inveterate plagiarist and insubstantial wit, prone to emulating Honoré de Balzac, Théophile Gautier and Charles Baudelaire in his hairstyle, clothing and drinking habits, Wilde was singled out for his ungainly physique, which was considered intimately reflective of his effete character:

> His appearance, a perfect target of caricature for all the satirical magazines, attracts people's attention even in the metropolitan bustle of London: the face with its limp and enervated features seems reminiscent of the bloated visage of Vitellius, a plump and awkward figure in eccentric dress with a green carnation in his buttonhole.[55]

> [Seine Erscheinung, ein Modell der Witzblätter, fällt selbst in dem Getriebe Londons auf: Ein Kopf mit schlaffen, früh entnervten Zügen, die an das schwammige Antlitz des Vitellius erinnern, eine plump-dicke Figur in Kleidern von absonderlichem Schnitt, mit einer grünen Nelke im Knopfloch.]

Devoting significant space to a vivid depiction of Wilde's legal case, the critic read *Salome* in the light of its author's alleged moral corruption, and prophesied its inevitable consignment to literary oblivion, since Wilde's 'mediocre talent was smothered in filth and disgrace'.[56]

Crucially, Schütz took vehement issue with what he perceived as the play's noticeably anti-Semitic subtext, resulting in the culturally inaccurate 'distortion of one of the greatest historical themes' and the caricature of its characters.[57] According to the critic, Herod is portrayed as a senile lecher and half-wit, and the prophet is reduced to a 'hypnotized somnambulist',[58] while the Salome character undergoes the most appalling transformation: 'Salome, the unconsciously sinful maiden of the Gospel, degenerates into a promiscuous harlot and killer for the sake of sexual excitement'.[59] Worst of all, in Schütz's estimation, was the offensive,

---

is explicitly singled out as an archetypal *pars pro toto*, epitomizing what Nordau considers as the sterile lethargy, mannered artificiality and moral aberration of decadent art, to which he dedicates an entire chapter. The remarkable public success of *Entartung*, whose English translation was published as *Degeneration* in February 1895, experienced a renewed upsurge in the wake of Wilde's conviction and imprisonment, which, in retrospect, Nordau's polemic seemed to have anticipated with such eerie foresight. Indeed, the inauspicious timing of Wilde's downfall lent an added layer of credibility to Nordau's elaborations, apparently substantiating his severe judgement of the author and subsequently exercising a prominent influence on the formation of Wilde's public image.

55   Friedrich Schütz, 'Oskar Wilde', *Neue Freie Presse*, 15 December 1903.

56   'seine mittelmäßige Begabung erstickte in Schmutz und Schande', ibid.

57   'Verzerrung eines der größten historischen Stoffe', ibid.

58   'hypnotisierter Nachtwandler', ibid.

59   'Salome, das unbewußt sündige "Mägdlein" des Evangeliums, sinkt zur mannstollen Dirne und Lustmörderin herab', ibid.

farcical representation of the Pharisees as a 'quintet of swaying Jews of repugnant demeanour'.[60] Moreover, their stereotypical gestural patterns are parodistically underscored by the calculated use of local Jewish jargon, which by then had come to be associated with the late-nineteenth-century influx of unacculturated Eastern European Jews, giving rise to anti-Jewish tensions in the capital of the Habsburg Monarchy. As an opponent of Theodor Herzl's Zionism and fervent propagator of Jewish assimilationism, Kraus, to a certain extent, shared Schütz's objections, as he considered the linguistic marker of Jewish 'otherness' the basis of anti-Semitic sentiment. However, Kraus identified its usage as an unfortunate dramaturgical device introduced by the director and a mildly polemical attempt to exploit local racist prejudice for the sake of dramatic effect.[61] Challenging Schütz on his paranoid suspicions of a covert anti-Semitic attack embedded in any depiction of Jewish characters, Kraus ironically hinted at the unacknowledged motives of Schütz's exceptionally fierce diatribe against Wilde's homosexuality: 'Oscar Wilde of course was a paederast and Friedrich Schütz is not. Good for him! ... As long as a writer does not take a clear stance against homosexuality, it apparently remains doubtful whether he should not be regarded as "one of them" after all'.[62]

In the event, Schütz's anxious concern to dissociate the Jewish self-image from the 'perverted' discourse of a 'degenerate' author appears not unfounded when read alongside the openly hostile and condemning review which appeared in the *Reichspost*, the Christian–Social press organ supporting the anti-Semitic politics of Karl Lueger, mayor of Vienna from 1897 to 1910. For the unnamed *Reichspost* critic, the nature of Wilde's 'tragedy of gaol or madhouse poetry', whose characters were deemed 'dream-like visions of a morbidly excited brain',[63] could be explained with regard to its legally convicted author. Insinuating a correlation between Jewishness, sexual perversion and avant-garde literature,[64] the reviewer offered a blatantly anti-Semitic assessment: 'The entire play is explained by the fact that it was written by an individual who was sent to prison on account

---

[60] 'Quintett wackelnder Juden mit häßlichen Gebärden', Ibid. This comment refers to the opening scene of *Salome*, which contains the following lines: 'FIRST SOLDIER: What an uproar! Who are those wild beasts howling! SECOND SOLDIER: The Jews. They are always like that. They are disputing about their religion.' Wilde, 'Salomé', in *Complete Works*, pp. 552–75, p. 552. On Richard Strauss's musical rendering of the quintet of Jews, and their *mise en scène* by Atom Egoyan, see Caryl Clark's chapter in this volume.

[61] Kraus, '"Salome"', p. 9.

[62] 'Oscar Wilde war nämlich ein Päderast, und Friedrich Schütz ist keiner. Wohl ihm! ... Solange ein Schriftsteller gegen den Homosexualismus nicht ausdrücklich Stellung genommen hat, kann man eben immer noch zweifeln, ob er nicht auch am Ende "einer von ihnen" ist', ibid., p. 2.

[63] 'Tragödie der Zuchthaus- oder Irrenhausdichtung'; 'Traumgestalten eines krankhaft erhitzten Gehirnes', *Reichspost*, 15 December 1903.

[64] For a more thorough treatment of the subject, specifically see Sander L. Gilman's essay 'Strauss, the Pervert, and Avant Garde Opera of the Fin de Siècle'.

of his sexual aberrations. Yet, there were people in the audience, mostly Jews, who fell into a veritable frenzy of ecstasy over Wilde's tragedy.'[65] After reporting a general outbreak of mirth among the audience upon the appearance of the group of clamouring Jews in the first scene, the anonymous commentator of the aristocratic–clerical newspaper *Das Vaterland* made a similarly snide remark:

> The audience, which had filled the theatre to capacity and among which, this time, more than the usual proportion of Semitic physiognomies were to be detected, received the play with roaring applause; at the same time, a not insignificant amount of opposition was to be noted.[66]

> [Das Publikum, welches das Theater bis auf das letzte Plätzchen besetzt hatte, und in welchem diesmal mehr als gewöhnlich semitische Physiognomien bemerkt werden konnten, spendete am Schlusse lärmenden Beifall, doch machte sich auch eine nicht unbedeutende Opposition geltend.]

Against the normative background of *fin-de-siècle* categories of sexual behaviour, abounding with sinister images of female hysteria, sadistic debauchery and morbid erotomania,[67] *Salome*'s orgiastic sensuality and obsessive eroticism inevitably came to signify an allegory of the author's illicit desires. Thus, the unsigned review in the *Deutsches Volksblatt* attributed a substantial degree of the enormous audience interest in the play to Wilde's widely publicized social ostracism:

> We feel inclined to call this play a tragedy of sensuality, but not the kind of wholesome sensuality that has an invigorating and fertilizing effect and that actually sustains the world; rather, it is the kind of sensuality that is the product of a diseased brain and that defiles and destroys everything with its perverted appetites.[68]

> [Wir möchten dieses Stück am liebsten die Tragödie der Sinnlichkeit nennen, aber nicht jener gesunden Sinnlichkeit, die belebend und befruchtend wirkt und die Welt erhält, sondern einer Sinnlichkeit, die dem kranken Gehirn entspringt, die mit ihren perversen Trieben alles schändet und alles zerstört.]

---

[65] 'Das ganze Drama hat freilich eine wichtige Erklärung: Es stammt von einem Individuum, das wegen sexueller Verirrungen ins Zuchthaus kam. Trotzdem fanden sich Leute, zumeist Juden, die vor Entzücken über diese Tragödie rasten', ibid.

[66] *Das Vaterland*, 13 December 1903.

[67] Richard A. Kaye, 'Sexual Identity at the fin de siècle', in Gail Marshall (ed.), *The Cambridge Companion to the Fin de Siècle* (Cambridge, 2007), pp. 53–72, p. 53.

[68] *Deutsches Volksblatt*, 13 December 1903.

In a different rhetorical strategy, the critic in the *Neues Wiener Tagblatt* opened his discussion of *Salome* with an extensive reference to the seemingly autobiographical account of Wilde's homoerotic sympathies in *The Picture of Dorian Gray*. Yet in *Salome*, the writer identified the pathological condition of Wilde's 'poetic character' as erupting with even greater suggestive force:

> The subject of this tragedy, in which Wilde indulges with voluptuous pleasure, may be highly repulsive, but still we remain under the enchanting spell of a poetic energy which provides us with a fiery-coloured vision of a historical period that marks the birth of Christianity – the dawn of salvation, rising out of wild and savage passions, deepest despair and the political and social turmoil of the Jewish people.[69]

> [Aber so abstoßend auch der Stoff dieser Tragödie ist, in dem Wilde mit wollüstigem Behagen wühlt, wir stehen doch unter dem Zauberbanne einer dichterischen Kraft, die ein in glühende Farben getauchtes welthistorisches Zeitbild an uns vorüberrauschen läßt, in dem neben wilden, wüsten Leidenschaften, neben verruchten Instinkten aus dem tiefen Jammer, aus der politischen und sozialen Verworrenheit des jüdischen Volkes die Morgenröte der Erlösungsidee emporsteigt.]

Not unlike the previously quoted members of the censor's advisory board, a sizeable number of Viennese reviewers articulated genuine praise for the impressionistic wealth of imagery, the sensuous power and incantatory rhythm of Wilde's dialogue. For instance, the *Neues Wiener Journal* critic ranked Wilde, together with Maurice Maeterlinck and Gustav Klimt, among the most notable representatives of modern art, which was perceived to be geared towards unmasking the core of modern civilization in all its crude savagery; for him, Wilde's tragedy appeared as an 'orgy of unbridled hedonism' and kept its spellbound audience firmly clasped within the 'predator's claws' of suspense and nervous excitement.[70]

The ambivalent critical responses occasioned by the Vienna premiere of *Salome*, placing greater emphasis on the play's author than the particulars of its stage production, are fed by a dense amalgam of moral, aesthetic and ethical criteria and betray a sense of indecision about an appropriate critical approach, necessitated by the work's potential for controversy. Otto Pohl, for example, vaguely hinted at the dilemma underlying the majority of critical judgements of Wilde's remarkable drama in his *Arbeiter-Zeitung* review: 'Poetic works like *Salome* may not be considered particularly edifying by sane and healthy individuals, but one cannot deny that Wilde's tragedy possesses the kind of beauty that often comes with illness

---

[69]   *Neues Wiener Tagblatt*, 13 December 1903.

[70]   'Orgie des schrankenlosen Genußtriebes', *Neues Wiener Journal*, 13 December 1903.

and softens the invalid's features'.[71] Max Burckhard's verdict, however, was more to the point and directly in accordance with the position taken by the censors, when he proposed that 'Wilde's *Salome* is a tragedy of necrophilia. Indeed, it is more than that: it is the work of a poet – maybe it is not the work of a poet for the masses, but the work of a poet it is nonetheless.'[72]

Despite the theatrical furore it caused, Wilde's Biblical tragedy was more or less ousted from Viennese stages in the wake of the worldwide success of Richard Strauss's opera, which nevertheless 'ensured Wilde's permanent entry into the mainstream of German culture'.[73] It was generally perceived that the crass theatrical effects of Wilde's play had found their complementary counterpart, and thus consummate expression, in Strauss's music, which added substance to the characters and thus, according to Hugo Daffner, could be likened to 'garments required to clothe Wilde's fictional creations'.[74] Just as Wilde himself appears to have been conscious of the 'refrains whose recurring *motifs* make *Salome* so like a piece of music and bind it together as a ballad',[75] the musical quality of the play – highlighted by the repetitive patterns of its stylized dialogue and the 'distinctly monological and formally integrated narrative texture' of its one-act structure – was widely registered by contemporary critics.[76] As Rainer Kohlmayer has shown, Lachmann's German translation is largely based on the English version of the play and is therefore 'rougher and more solemn than the French'.[77] At the same

---

[71]   'Dichtungen wie "Salome" mögen allerdings Gesunden nicht erquicklich sein, aber man darf dem Drama Wildes jene Schönheit nicht absprechen, mit der oft die Krankheit die Züge der Menschen überhaucht', Otto Pohl, 'Feuilleton', *Arbeiter-Zeitung*, 19 December 1903.

[72]   'Wildes "Salome" ist die Tragödie der Leichenschändung. Sie ist freilich außerdem noch etwas: sie ist das Werk eines Dichters. Nicht eines Dichters für die Menge vielleicht, aber doch das Werk eines Dichters', Max Burckhard, 'Wilde's "Salome" im Volkstheater', *Die Zeit*, 13 December 1903.

[73]   Robert Blackburn, '"The unutterable and the dream": Aspects of Wilde's Reception in Central Europe 1900–1922', *Irish Studies Review*, 11 (1995): pp. 30–35, p. 32. A 1906 revival of the original run of the play was followed by two smaller-scale productions at the Deutsches Volkstheater and the Neue Wiener Bühne in 1913, as well as a widely reported guest performance of Alexander Tairov's Moscow Chamber Theatre in 1925. Subsequently, it was to take 65 years for Wilde's *Salome* to be revived on the Viennese stage.

[74]   'Er [Strauss] ... wob die Gewande, wie sie den Gestalten Wildes nötig waren', Daffner, *Salome, ihre Gestalt in Geschichte und Kunst*, p. 379.

[75]   Wilde, 'De Profundis', in *Complete Works*, pp. 873–957, p. 922.

[76]   David Wayne Thomas, 'The "Strange Music" of *Salome*: Oscar Wilde's Rhetoric of Verbal Musicality', *Mosaic*, 33/1 (2000): pp. 15–38, p. 20.

[77]   Rainer Kohlmayer, 'From Saint to Sinner: The Demonization of Oscar Wilde's *Salomé* in Hedwig Lachmann's German Translation and Richard Strauss's Opera', in Mary Snell-Hornby, Zuzana Jettmarová and Klaus Kaindl (eds), *Translation as Intercultural Communication: Selected Papers from the EST Congress, Prague 1995* (Amsterdam and Philadelphia, PA, 1997), pp. 111–22, p. 114.

time, however, it 'chooses an elevated form of contemporary spoken German that is dramatically intensified through variation, compounding and a dynamic rhythm'.[78] For instance, Ludwig Hevesi, commenting on the 1903 premiere of *Salome*, noted that 'these dialogues have their own rhythm, a concealed underlying stanza structure marked by refrains, echoing lines, and accompanied by the minor characters as if they were playing musical instruments'.[79] Similarly, the Viennese literary scholar and theatre critic Helene Richter observed in her 1912 study of Oscar Wilde's literary career: 'The stylized characters themselves are matched by their magnificently stylized diction, Jokanaan's hymnic intensity, the flourishing opulence of Salome's speech, the refrain-like repetitions, which have an utterly mesmerizing effect on the soul, like some kind of magnetic force'.[80]

Instead of commissioning a libretto for his opera, Richard Strauss undertook the musical setting of a shortened version of Hedwig Lachmann's German translation of *Salome*, whose 'dynamic style [...] thus constituted a verbal programme that inevitably influenced the creative process of composing'.[81] When reviewing the first performance of Strauss's *Salome* in Vienna in May 1907,[82] which was celebrated as a first-rate social event by the members of the local cultural elite, some critics were genuinely impressed by the symbiotic alliance of Wilde's drama and Strauss's music, while others turned out to be unsettled by the musical dissonance and its harsh accentuation of the gruesome action on stage. For Robert Hirschfeld, writing in the *Wiener Abendpost*, it was precisely the musical structure of Wilde's text which rendered it essentially incompatible with its operatic setting: 'Wilde's poetic drama ... contains such gentle music ... and it is cruel to kill music with music'.[83]

For similar reasons, the Austrian poet, composer and visual artist Gerhard Rühm – whose 1983 German 'poetic adaptation' of Wilde's play may well be

---

[78]   Ibid., p. 115.

[79]   'Diese Gespräche haben alle eine eigene Rhythmik. Einen heimlichen Strophenbau, der sich durch Refrains gliedert, ein Echo-sprechen gleichsam, und von Nebenfiguren wie auf Instrumenten begleitet wird', Ludwig Hevesi, '"Salome"', *Fremden-Blatt*, 15 December 1903.

[80]   'Den stilisierten gestalten entspricht die prachtvolle stilisiertheit der diktion, die refrainartigen wiederholungen, die wie magnetische einflüsse die seele hypnotisieren, der hymnenartige schwung Jokanaans, die blühende üppigkeit der sprache Salomes', Helene Richter, 'Oscar Wildes künstlerische Persönlichkeit', *Englische Studien*, 45 (1912): pp. 201–57, p. 240.

[81]   Kohlmayer, 'From Saint to Sinner', p. 119.

[82]   For a thorough analysis of the critical reception of Strauss's opera in early twentieth-century Germany and Austria, see the second chapter in Dierkes-Thrun, *Salome's Modernity*, pp. 56–82.

[83]   'Die Wildesche Dichtung ... hat die zarteste Musik in sich ... Es ist grausam, Musik mit Musik zu erschlagen', Robert Hirschfeld, '"Salome" von Richard Strauß', *Wiener Abendpost*, 27 May 1907.

regarded as the decisive factor in prompting the (short-lived) renaissance of Wilde's *fin-de-siècle succès de scandale* after a 65-year local stage absence – laments the fact that, in terms of stage presence, Wilde's drama cannot compete with Richard Strauss's frequently performed opera, adding:

> This seems particularly unfortunate, since the opera cannot replace the stage play. ... Poetic works which, like Wilde's *Salome*, are characterized by such distinct musical qualities will only forfeit some of their expressive force through a musical setting, which naturally distorts the melody and rhythm of speech valued so highly by Wilde.[84]

> [das ist vor allem darum bedauerlich, weil sie das sprechstück nicht ersetzen kann. ... dichtungen, die – wie wildes "salome" – an sich schon so ausgeprägte musikalische qualitäten haben, können durch eine vertonung an eigensubstanz nur verlieren; sie verzerrt naturgemäß sprachmelodie und sprachrhythmus, auf welche wilde doch so großen wert legte.]

Even if *Salome* may not have generated substantial interest beyond its turn-of-the-century cultural hype, the play's controversial Viennese premiere set the scene for the introduction of Wilde's society comedies and their author's breakthrough on the Viennese stages. More than any other of Wilde's works, *Salome* became instantly embroiled in an impenetrable web of journalistic sensationalism, biographical myth-making and ideological instrumentalization, which rendered its evaluation virtually inseparable from the author's much-publicized history of moral 'misconduct'. In Vienna, as in other major European centres, contemporary literary and theatre critics were faced with a precarious balancing act, in which they usually failed to unravel the intricate entanglement of the aesthetic, ethical and ideological criteria employed in the discussion of the Irish author's literary output. Ultimately, this obscuring conflation of life and work, art and legend – pushed to extremes in the case of the reception of Wilde's risqué Biblical tragedy – may be considered as instrumental in the configuration of the author's elusive, chameleon-like image and, to some extent, still remains a significant factor in his works' enduring appeal to critics, theatre practitioners, translators and audiences.

---

[84] Gerhard Rühm, 'oscar wildes "salome" und meine deutsche nachdichtung', *Protokolle*, 4 (1982): pp. 141–52, p. 141. Thus Rühm, as well as Robert Hirschfeld in 1907, does not appreciate the propensity of Wilde's text to engender synaesthetic and intermedial reinterpretations of the Salome story by the very music of the text, as described by Polina Dimova.

Chapter 3

Whose/Who's Salome?
Natalia Trouhanowa, a Dancing Diva

Clair Rowden

No one will dispute that the dance scene in Paris in the 1890s and early 1900s was incredibly rich. Despite the supposed decadence of the form on the stage of the Opéra,[1] American and Russian dancers were pouring into Paris where ballet and pantomime spectacles in the music hall theatres were going from strength to strength.[2] Here mimes, dancers and actors together performed spectacles that crossed traditional notions of genre, boundaries between art forms and 'high' and 'low' art.[3] If dance was decadent, it was also diverse. Post-Wagnerian, post-Nietzschean, post-Mallarméan aesthetics cried out for stage spectacles in which all elements were truly integrated,[4] artists, musicians, painters and dancers strictly collaborating to provide synthetic and synaesthetic spectacles, where each medium worked in harmony to provide an ultimate aesthetic experience.[5] In dance terms, Romantic balletic technique was seen as a worn out, uncommunicative language, while gesture from the pantomime tradition, reinvigorated through Russian practice, came to the fore.[6] Moreover, choreographer and dancer Mikhail Fokine

---

[1]   Ivor Guest, *Le Ballet de l'Opéra de Paris: trois siècles d'histoire et de tradition*, trans. Paul Alexandre (Paris, 1976).

[2]   Sarah Gutsche-Miller, 'Le ballet-pantomime sur la scène des Folies-Bergère: *Fleur de lotus* (1893) et les conventions du ballet populaire', in Jean-Christophe Branger (ed.), *Musique et chorégraphie en France de Léo Delibes à Florent Schmitt* (Saint-Etienne, 2010), pp. 123–49.

[3]   Lynn Garafola, *Legacies of Twentieth-Century Dance* (Middletown, 2005), p. 162.

[4]   Stéphane Mallarmé, 'Les Fonds dans le ballet', in Henri Mondor and G. Jean-Aubry (eds), *Stéphane Mallarmé, Œuvres complètes* (Paris, 1945), pp. 307–9. See also Felicia McCarren, 'Stéphane Mallarmé, Loie Fuller, and the Theater of Femininity', in Ellen W. Goellner and Jacqueline Shea Murphy (eds), *Bodies of the Text: Dance as Theory, Literature as Dance* (New Brunswick, 1995), pp. 217–30.

[5]   Timothée Picard, 'Modèle de la danse et synthèse des arts chez les artistes ayant collaboré avec Ida Rubinstein', in Pascal Lécroart (ed.), *Ida Rubinstein: une utopie de la synthèse des arts à l'épreuve de la scène* (Besançon, 2008), pp. 19–30.

[6]   Davinia Caddy, 'On Ballet at the Opéra, 1909–1914, and *La Fête chez Thérèse*', *Journal of the Royal Musical Association*, 133/2 (2008): pp. 220–69, p. 223. This article is incorporated as a chapter in her *The Ballets Russes and Beyond: Music and Dance in Belle-Epoque Paris* (Cambridge and New York, 2012).

referred to balletic movement – as opposed to balletic technique or mime, both associated with Romantic ballet – as an ideal for the communication of dramatic expression.[7]

The Salome story and associated cult, stimulated by literature and the fine arts, came into its own in this period at the birth of modern dance. An iconic story of a dancer, allied to a fashionable exoticist location, meant that creators and interpreters of both highbrow and more popular forms of culture turned their attention to the Jewish princess, and the possibilities her story offered for synthetic spectacle. Paris had seen the rise of stars of modern dance, such as Loïe Fuller, Isadora Duncan and the extreme media coverage of certain *étoiles* such as Régina Badet, Liane de Pougy or Cléo de Mérode. Richard Strauss's opera *Salome* was premiered in the French capital in 1907, another based on a similar text by French composer Antoine Mariotte in 1910. Also in 1907, Maud Allan arrived in Paris with her reputedly scandalous dance interpretation of Salome, closely followed by the Russians Natalia Trouhanowa, Tamara Karsavina and Ida Rubinstein who danced Salome to a number of different scores.

A little less 'spiritual' but more practical than some of her contemporaries, Natalia Trouhanowa was a strong actress and character dancer, as well as master of stage craft, with great entrepreneurial spirit in artistic endeavour. In step with the aesthetic concerns of her era, she was allied to the post-Naturalist movement which strove to create synthetic theatrical experience. She debunked Romantic balletic technique, and advocated a renewal of dance through modern choreographic gesture. This chapter offers a detailed examination of Trouhanowa's different embodiments of Salome, and in particular, her dancing in 1912 of *La Tragédie de Salomé* with a scenario by Robert d'Humières and music by Florent Schmitt. The extant material relating to this production in Parisian archives demonstrates how Trouhanowa set about 'authoring' the role, and reception materials relating to her performances allow us to perceive how her work was situated in the wider cultural and aesthetic climate of *belle-époque* Paris, particularly in relation to the Salomes danced by Loïe Fuller and Ida Rubinstein.[8]

A telegram sent by Richard Strauss to the Parisian impresario Gabriel Astruc on 19 May 1907 read: 'FRONHANOVVA IMPOSSIBLE'.[9] 'Mission impossible'? Or just Natalia Trouhanowa? Strauss had a difficult relationship with the Russian star that danced the 'Dance of the Seven Veils' (for the Czech soprano Emmy Destinn)

---

[7]   Deborah Mawer, *The Ballets of Maurice Ravel: Creation and Interpretation* (Aldershot, 2006), p. 8.

[8]   While no article on danced Salomes during the period 1907–1912 can completely overlook the performances of Wilde's *Salomé* by Ida Rubinstein who danced the 'Seven Veils' to music by Alexander Glazunov, full consideration of these performances is beyond the scope of this current chapter, as is the proliferation of Salomes in Parisian boulevard theatres.

[9]   Read 'Trouhanowa impossible'. Bibliothèque-Musée de l'Opéra, Bibliothèque nationale de France, Archives, Carton 2240, II (11). [Hereafter BnF Opéra.]

during the Parisian premiere of his opera in May 1907. Trouhanowa reported, 'I came to take a curtain call, he [Strauss] stopped me and, preventing me from going on stage, he said it was his place to take a bow, for dance was but an inferior art.'[10] On the other hand, Romain Rolland recounted how Strauss 'is charmed by all the French, except by Mademoiselle Troukhanova [*sic*] and he drinks to all the French, except Mademoiselle Troukhanova [*sic*]'.[11] The collaborative process of creation that was to motivate both Trouhanowa and Strauss at other points in their careers (and with other people) was absent in what can be read as a pure clash of personalities. Strauss's reported remark can be only disingenuous as Wayne Heisler Jnr.'s recent study of Strauss's ballets has shown,[12] and his ire purely directed at the dancer herself. And yet ballet was still seen as a 'minor art', and only with the 1910 performances of the Ballets Russes which comprised only dance did 'ballet' really come of age in the modern era, revealing the intrinsic value of modern dance.[13]

Trouhanowa seemingly reported to the press the most horrific insult she could muster, for her own beliefs in the power of dance to communicate powerful emotions, and ones at least as powerful as music and opera, were unequivocal. And yet, with regard to *Salome*, Trouhanowa did not seem overly concerned with the Parisian production (apart from ensuring that her costumes were an exact replica of those worn by the singer Emmy Destinn), expecting to arrive from Monte Carlo (where she was paid by the day) two days before the dress rehearsal, step into the role and dance the nine minutes of Strauss's music as she saw fit (see Figure 3.1).[14]

The press tells us very little about what she actually did on stage – many describing Trouhanowa as merely cautiously voluptuous and languorous – although one critic was struck by a kneeling Trouhanowa who leant backwards, touching the nape of her neck to the ground.[15] Whatever she did do, however, was seen as

---

[10]   'Je venais saluer, il m'arrêta et, m'empêchant de rentrer en scène, me dit que c'était à lui de saluer, car la danse n'était qu'un art inférieur.' 'Leurs Confidences: Natacha Trouhanowa', *Fantasio*, 1908, Département des Arts du Spectacle, Bibliothèque nationale de France, RO–12776 (2). [Hereafter BnF Arts du Spectacle.]

[11]   *Richard Strauss & Romain Rolland: Correspondence*, ed. Rollo Myers (London, 1968) p. 157, Rolland's diary for 28 May 1907.

[12]   Wayne Heisler Jnr., *The Ballet Collaborations of Richard Strauss* (Rochester, 2009).

[13]   Aurore Després, 'Place et fonction de la danse dans la synthèse des arts sur la scène', in Lécroart (ed.), *Ida Rubinstein*, pp. 31–46, p. 32.

[14]   BnF Opéra, Archives, Carton 2240, III, contains 7 items of correspondence between Trouhanowa and Astruc, including a note presenting her excuses to Strauss for arriving late to rehearsal on 3 May 1907, as well as her written resignation (undated) from the production. According to the press, Trouhanowa danced for four performances before her resignation, and was replaced by Aïda Boni, who had danced the role for the singer Mariette Mazarin in Brussels in March and April of the same year.

[15]   Nozière [Fernand Weil], 'Le Théâtre', *Gil Blas*, 9 May 1907.

Figure 3.1   Natalia Trouhanowa in Strauss's *Salome*
Source: Photograph published in *Le Théâtre*, 202 (May 1907), p. 7. Private Collection.

relatively chaste in comparison to the more lascivious and shocking performance given by Maud Allan at the Théâtre des Variétés the previous evening.[16]

Three years later, in April and May 1910, both Strauss's *Salomé* (in French translation) and the opera *Salomé*, by Frenchman Antoine Mariotte, were given in Paris within a fortnight of each other, and Trouhanowa was once again back on the scene, dancing for singer Lucienne Bréval in the performances of Mariotte's opera. At the same time as Strauss had conceived his opera, Mariotte also had begun to write an opera based directly on Oscar Wilde's French play. Strauss's publisher had acquired the rights to Wilde's text and Strauss was approached by Mariotte seeking permission for his opera to be performed. A much-publicized controversy ensued, and the fascinating correspondence and negotiations between Mariotte, Strauss and an inflexible Adolph Fürstner are well-documented in the Parisian archives and musical press.[17] Only through the intervention of the diplomatic Rolland was Mariotte free to perform his *Salomé* in Paris, and the opera was mounted by the Frères Isola at the Théâtre de la Gaîté in April 1910, two weeks prior to the Opéra premiere of Strauss's work. Thus the spring of 1910 in Paris became an artistic battle ground for the French versus the German Salome, the reception of Mariotte's work being intimately bound to that of Strauss in a press predisposed towards Mariotte, the underdog, and his opera after the hand they had been dealt. Mariotte's opera became a nationalist cause, defended not only by artists and those involved in mounting the opera but also by the critical press in general.

At the Opéra, Mary Garden had been cast as Salome. She chose to dance herself and while some critics were scathing of her melodramatic gesticulation and constant movement,[18] they still conceded that her composition of the character

---

[16] It is unclear to what music Maud Allan danced *La Vision de Salomé*, but it is generally believed that she danced to an arrangement of Strauss's 'Dance of the Seven Veils' by the Belgian musician and critic Marcel Rémy. Earlier in this volume, Sandra Mayer noted the original title of the show (in translation) in Vienna in 1906 as *The Vision of Salome: Balletic Tableau with Authentic Oriental Themes by Marcel Rémy*, which does not suggest the involvement of Strauss's music. In her autobiography *My Life and Dancing* (London, 1908), Allan refers to Rémy as a musician and Greek scholar who helped her research Greek poses, but she says nothing about her music for *La Vision de Salomé*, nor Rémy's part in it. For a recent discussion of Allan's Salome, see Petra Dierkes-Thrun, *Salome's Modernity: Oscar Wilde and the Aesthetics of Transgression* (Ann Arbor, 2011), pp. 83–100.

[17] See my chapter '*Salome* and modern opera: a Parisian perspective', in Günter Brosche and Jürgen May (eds), *Richard Strauss–Jahrbuch 2011*, herausgegeben von der Internationalen Richard Strauss–Gesellschaft in Wien und dem Richard Strauss–Institut in Garmisch-Partenkirchen (Tutzing, 2011), pp. 163–76.

[18] For example, Adolphe Aderer, 'Premières Représentations', *Le Petit Parisien*, 7 May 1910, p. 2.

was remarkable and exemplary.[19] Many openly praised her stage presence, Henry Gauthier-Villars suggesting that Garden had conceived Salome as a dancer and seduced with her body from the start.[20] To ensure the critical success of Mariotte's opera, the Frères Isola had cast the *doyenne* of the opera stage Lucienne Bréval as Salome. At 40, Bréval should have been at the height of her art, but press reports suggest a consummate but rather stately actress with a voice of already declining brilliance. Fifteen years her junior, Natalia Trouhanowa was thus cast to interpret the 'Dance of the Seven Veils', the dancer seizing the opportunity to deploy her Salome 'box of tricks', and apparently succeeding in taking erotic voyeurism (of the audience) to a new level. Wearing as little as possible, Trouhanowa was considered opulent, lascivious and infinitely troubling.[21] Many critics evoked or even cited Flaubert's highly charged description of Salome's dance from *Hérodias* (1877) in order to avoid relating their own erotic experience.[22]

But Trouhanowa came into her own in April 1912 with the mounting of a dance spectacle, in association with Jacques Rouché, comprising four symphonic works: *Istar* by Vincent d'Indy, *La Tragédie de Salomé* by Schmitt, *Adélaïde, ou le langage des fleurs* (an orchestration of the *Valses nobles et sentimentales*) by Maurice Ravel, and *La Péri* by Paul Dukas.[23] Each work was given in a different set, designed and painted by a different reputed French designer. In these 'Concerts de danse', each composer conducted his own work at the head of the Orchestre Lamoureux. By reuniting four works by the elite of French compositional talent, by rejuvenating ballet through the use of evocative French symphonic music and the talents of French stage designers, Trouhanowa was seen to achieve a perfection of collaboration between the arts. Louis Schneider referred to Greek drama with regard to the works' communion of sound, colour and gesture,[24] and synaesthesia

---

[19]   See Victor Debay, 'La "Salomé" de Richard Strauss à L'Opéra', *Le Courrier musicale*, 15 May 1910, pp. 392–3; Adolphe Jullien, 'Revue musicale', Feuilleton du *Journal des Débats*, *Le Journal des Débats*, 15 May 1910, pp. 1–2.

[20]   Henry Gauthier-Villars, Louis Schneider and Louis Handler, 'Théâtre national de l'Opéra. Salomé', *Comœdia*, 7 May 1910, pp. 1–2. Handler suggests that Garden 'dances like Trouhanowa herself' (p. 2).

[21]   Louis Vuillemin, 'Théâtre municipal de la Gaité-Lyrique. Salomé', *Comœdia*, 23 April 1910.

[22]   See, for example, Robert Brussel, 'Les Théâtres', *Le Figaro*, 23 April 1910.

[23]   In the context of these dance spectacles by Natalia Trouhanowa, *La Péri* by Dukas and *Adélaïde* by Ravel have been treated (respectively) by Helen Julia Minors and Deborah Mawer. Helen Julia Minors, 'Paul Dukas's *La Péri* (1911–12): A Problematic Creative–Collaboration', *Dance Research*, 27 (2009): pp. 227–52; Mawer, *The Ballets of Maurice Ravel*.

[24]   Louis Schneider, 'Au Théâtre municipal du Châtelet. Les Concerts de Danse de Mlle Trouhanowa. La mise en scène et les décors', *Comœdia*, 24 April 1912, p. 2.

was evoked with regard to the scenery, the movement of colours being a direct corollary of the surging of the sound wave.[25]

As the only premiere of the evening, *La Péri* was an important yardstick by which to measure the collaborators' collective achievements in the renewal of French dance.[26] Synchronization between the arts where each medium retained its distinctive value but worked together to create a cohesive whole was an aesthetic aim for Dukas,[27] but Trouhanowa's artistry was crucial in achieving this synthesis, as she concerned herself with all aspects of the production. Indeed, Helen Minors has demonstrated how, for *La Péri*, Trouhanowa interpreted the scenario, commented on the lighting, stage location, and characterization, and incorporated the precise text–music relationships into her score, effectively reading the narrative structure of the poem and music into her dance, thus making sure that the aural and visual dimensions formed a tight mimetic relationship.[28] For the critics, the perceived fusion of symphonic poem and modern dance in Dukas's 'poème dansé' demonstrated that 'ballet' was capable of conveying pathetic emotions,[29] and this new expressive genre was termed a 'lyric form'. Ballet was thus undergoing a renaissance through the power of music: critics saw that more expressive and evocative choreography could be born of music liberated from traditional constraints of dance, and which would conserve, despite its physical commentary, the freedom of symphonic development.[30]

But this evening of 'art dance' also contained another Salome, one originally conceived for Loïe Fuller by Robert d'Humières and Florent Schmitt in November 1907. Thus in the wake of Strauss's *Salome* in Paris, Fuller luxuriously mounted the extravaganza *La Tragédie de Salomé*, its fashionably aestheticized Orientalism

---

[25]　Henry Gauthier-Villars, 'Musique', *Le Mercure de France*, 16 May 1912, pp. 411–16.

[26]　Both *La Péri* and *La Tragédie de Salomé* were conceived as dance music. On the Ballets Russes's appropriation of pre-existing, non-dance music for choreographic interpretation and its negative reception, as also performed by Trouhanowa, see Caddy, *The Ballets Russes and Beyond*, pp. 147–59, who cites Victor Debay's extended article published in the wake of Trouhanowa's 'Concerts de danse', 'Vers l'erreur', *Le Courrier musical*, 15 May 1912, pp. 290–93.

[27]　Minors ('Paul Dukas's *La Péri*', p. 228) makes a distinction between Dukas's idea of synchronization and a Wagnerian fusion of the arts, as Dukas outlined in 'La déception scénique', *Chroniques musicales sur deux siècles 1892–1932* (Paris, 1980), pp. 186–9. Originally published in October 1896.

[28]　Minors, 'Paul Dukas's *La Péri*', p. 244.

[29]　Robert Brussel, 'De la Musique et de la danse. Les concerts de Mlle Trouhanowa', *La Revue musicale S.I.M.*, 15 May 1912, pp. 56–60.

[30]　Ibid.; Marcel Galbat, 'Les Concerts de danse de Mlle Trouhanowa', *Comœdia*, 19 April 1912, pp. 1–2. Only the traditionalist Henri de Curzon saw dance's new direction as false, declaring modern dance the antithesis of art which, by definition, was convention-bound. Henri de Curzon, 'La Semaine. Paris. Concert de danse de Mlle Trouhanowa', *Le Guide musical*, 23 April 1912, p. 334.

and excess pushing her spectacle firmly into the realms of the camp and the kitsch.[31] This 'mute drama' was the second Salome that Fuller had interpreted,[32] and was atypical in her output. Not only did Fuller appear without her enveloping costumes made from huge volumes of silk and concealed batons with which to manipulate the cloth, but also *La Tragédie de Salomé* comprised a commissioned libretto and score, thus presenting a literary and musical narrative unlike her usual music hall shows which consisted of individual numbers danced to a *pot pourri* of often pre-existing musical excerpts. *La Tragédie de Salomé*, therefore, combined technically innovative lighting effects and Fuller's 'light dances' (in the style of her greatest triumphs) with mimed scenes, bringing these spectacles much closer to traditional ballet and the popular theatre of the boulevards than had been her previous successes.

In 1910, Schmitt's original music, scored for 20 musicians and lasting an hour, was reworked into a symphonic poem, for full orchestra lasting less than half an hour.[33] The symphonic poem's vivid imagery and the lure of Salome for modern dancers meant, however, that the score was swiftly transposed back to the theatre, Trouhanowa being the first of the Russians to perform *La Tragédie de Salomé*. But Humières's libretto differed to Wilde's play. Indeed, it was not a libretto as such: characters were not given sequential and consequential actions in the way they were in Romantic ballet libretti which were printed much in the same way as a play. Rather, Humières provided a scenario which described characters and onstage events. This transfer to a narrative form meant that while Humières's scenario was written in a heady decadent style, it dismissed much of the sophisticated symbolism of Wilde's text, particularly the reflexive obsession with the gaze (and thus representation), presenting a more straightforward interpretation of the classic story.

Of particular importance to this chapter are the differences in Humières's scenario from the 'Dance of the Seven Veils' onwards. The dance forms the start of the final section and all action is seen only in flashes of lightning as Salome

---

[31]   Susan Sontag, 'Notes on Camp', in *Against Interpretation and Other Essays* (London, 2009), pp. 275–92.

[32]   Fuller first danced a 'lyric pantomime' *Salomé* to a libretto by Armand Silvestre and C.H. Meltzer, and a score by Gabriel Pierné at the Comédie-Parisienne in March 1895, the same theatre that saw the premiere of Wilde's play (staged by the Théâtre de L'Œuvre) just 11 months later. Pierné's score was evocative and suggestive but it was hastily written, and there seems to have been little collaboration between the artists with regard to an aesthetic vision, and little musical translation of gesture, or correspondence between the libretto and the score which contains very few stage directions. For further details, see my 'Loïe Fuller et Salomé: les drames mimés de Gabriel Pierné et de Florent Schmitt', in Branger (ed.), *Musique et chorégraphie en France*, pp. 215–59.

[33]   The symphonic poem was given its premiere by the Orchestre Colonne, on 8 January 1911, conducted by Pierné. See Yves Hucher, *Florent Schmitt* (Paris, 1983), p. 157. The score was published by Durand in 1912.

dances and an aroused Herod rips off her veils. Salome thus appears momentarily nude in silhouette, before an onstage John the Baptist comes out of the shadows to cover her with his cowl.[34] Herod is furious and Herodias orders John's execution. Salome is presented with the Baptist's head on a platter and dances, before casting the platter over the parapet into the Dead Sea which begins to smoke on contact with the Precursor's blood. Half unconscious, Salome falls against the abandoned throne before seeing John's head on the parapet. She cannot meet the gaze and turns her head away. Multiple heads then appear at different points of the stage, as if Salome's deranged mind was hallucinating, before she completely loses her senses in a frenzied final 'dance of terror': the sky turns blood-red, a storm descends, trees are uprooted and architectural stone displaced in an apocalyptic and moralizing finale.

Trouhanowa collaborated with Schmitt and Humières to create a consummate spectacle, and many of her preparatory papers and letters to various collaborators are conserved in Parisian archives. Thus, some attempt at a genetic analysis of her performance can be made, examination of Trouhanowa's creative choices allowing today's audiences/readers a better understanding of her own aesthetic beliefs and statements, and how she went about creating them.[35] Trouhanowa asked Schmitt for any specific advice he could give her,[36] and wrote long letters to Humières regarding her vision of the scenario.[37]

She also paid great attention to the costumes (see Figure 3.2), scenography, lighting and scenery (by Maxime Dethomas, see Plate 2), desiring a lightweight solution suitable for a touring production and evoking a recent production by Gordon Craig as a model of simple yet modern effective stage design and craft[38] (see Figure 3.3).

Trouhanowa was especially concerned with the mimetic aspects of her dance and their correspondence to the published libretto in order to keep the majority of her public – which, in an intimate way between *artistes*, she qualified as 'ignorant and foolish' – enthralled.[39] She asked Humières for small modifications to the

---

[34]   Dancers would have worn a full-body, flesh-coloured leotard, similar to those worn for the obligatory nude scene in *ballets–pantomimes* presented at the Folies-Bergère.

[35]   Josette Féral, 'Introduction: Towards a Genetic Study of Performance – Take 2', *Theatre Research International*, 35 (2008): pp. 223–33.

[36]   Département de la Musique, Bibliothèque nationale de France, LAS Trouhanowa à Schmitt, 1. [Hereafter, BnF Musique.]

[37]   See BnF Opéra, Fonds Rouché Pièce 74 (2), 30 January 1912.

[38]   Ibid. It is not clear to which Gordon Craig production Trouhanowa is referring in this letter. See also BnF Opéra, Fonds Rouché Pièce 74 (4) and (5), the latter wrongly catalogued as Pièce 75 (5). BnF Opéra, Fonds Rouché Pièce 74 (13) is a bill from Muelle the costume maker, which shows that 27 costumes were bought for *La Tragédie de Salomé* (including two for Trouhanowa, as opposed to 14 for *Adelaïde*, of which only one was for Trouhanowa) at a cost of 5,600 Francs (only 2,900 Francs were spent for *Adelaïde*).

[39]   BnF Opéra, Fonds Rouché Pièce 74 (2), 30 January 1912.

Figure 3.2   Natalia Trouhanowa in Schmitt's *La Tragédie de Salomé*
Source: Photograph published in *Comœdia Illustré*, 15 May 1912, p. 638. Private Collection.

Figure 3.3   *La Tragédie de Salomé*
Source: Photograph published in *Comœdia Illustré*, 15 May 1912, p. 638. Private Collection.

scenario to be reproduced in the published programme,[40] 'so as not to be caught out by the press or public opinion that might find the text and the execution ill-matched'.[41] But the second section of the scenario, entitled 'Les enchantements sur la Mer', remained of particular concern to Trouhanowa. Here, Herod and Herodias remain seated, pensive, lost in decadent, fearful erotic reverie as mysterious lights modulate on the sea, revealing a lost city in which the royal couple's former (sexual) exploits and crimes are played out. Then a voice rises from the depths, accompanied by lascivious forms from which Salome appears to dance the 'Seven Veils'. Trouhanowa feared that her dance could do little to translate the poetic text which also made reference to different lighting effects that were the speciality of

---

[40]   *Concerts de Danse. N. Trouhanowa* (Paris, 1912). The same scenario (with one extra sentence) was later published in Robert d'Humières, *Théâtre II: Pièces orientales* (Paris, 1924), pp. 301–4. This version of the scenario is a slightly shorter one than was published by Durand at the front of the full score of the symphonic poem (Paris, 1912). Humières's longer scenario for Loïe Fuller in 1907 was printed in the published programme, *La Tragédie de Salomé*, Programme du Théâtre des Arts, BnF Opéra, PRO. B. 25, pp. 9, 12, and is reproduced in Appendix 2 of my 'Loïe Fuller et Salomé', pp. 257–60.

[41]   'afin de ne pas être attrappé par la presse ou l'opinion des gens qui trouverait disparate le texte et l'exécution!' BnF Opéra, Fonds Rouché Pièce 74 (2), 30 January 1912.

Loïe Fuller: 'without special equipment we won't know how to communicate the precision [of the text] to the public without rendering ourselves ridiculous!'[42] She therefore resorted to lighting changes which accompanied dances symbolizing elements of that text, suggesting an 'incense dance' to symbolize the sea, as a way to skirt round the tricky relationship between text and stage gesture which was nevertheless important to Trouhanowa in an era when the place and function of the dance libretto or narrative was increasingly called into question by both performers and audiences. Indeed, for certain ballets such as *Le Sacre du Printemps* in 1913, the Ballets Russes did away with librettists altogether, Igor Stravinsky, Vaslav Nijinsky and Nicolas Roerich – the composer, the choreographer and the designer – participating in a newly reconfigured collaborative process of creation more suited to their aesthetic project.[43] Thus, in modern dance, the general impression created by the dance, music and scenery, particularly of the Ballets Russes, was more important than musical mimeticisms.[44] Yet as Annegret Fauser has shown, despite the arrival of the Modernist era in music and the arts, French audiences' long experience of ballet and pantomime endowed them with sophisticated capabilities in matching music to meaning without the aid of text, the latter becoming an unnecessary interference, even misleading audiences by upsetting their horizons of expectation and reception.[45] Trouhanowa meant to avoid this at all costs by using all strategies available to her.

The last section of *La Tragédie de Salomé*, comprising the 'lightning dance' – effectively the 'Dance of the Seven Veils' – and the 'dance of terror' are perhaps the most revealing of Trouhanowa's artistry. The music and stage action for these two dances is little changed from Schmitt's and Humières's original version of 1907, as danced by Loïe Fuller. Humières had provided a detailed version of his scenario for Fuller's programme, and the autograph full score comprises detailed stage directions, synchronized with the music, which give a good idea of the pantomime and sometimes of the dances themselves. Yet while Fuller's Salome had been the product of Humières and her prodigious technical capabilities, Trouhanowa's Salome was her own creation, as her various versions and visions

---

[42]   'Je crois que malgrès [*sic*] la beauté poétique du texte, sans outillage spécial, nous ne saurons sans risquer d'être ridicules pouvoir en faire comprendre la précision au public!', Ibid.

[43]   Després, 'Place et fonction de la danse', p. 43.

[44]   Caddy discusses the question of mimeticism and how it has been treated in musicology in the last 20 years in the introduction to her *The Ballets Russes and Beyond*.

[45]   Annegret Fauser, 'Visual Pleasures, Musical Signs: Dance at the Paris Opéra', in Bryan Gilliam (ed.), *Music, Image, Gesture, The South Atlantic Quarterly*, 104/1 (Winter 2005): pp. 99–124, p. 114. Mismatch between the published libretto, the music and the stage gesture was particularly prevalent in the reception of the Ballet Russes's Parisian premiere of Richard Strauss's score *La Légende de Joseph* (Berlin and Paris, 1914), which was accompanied by the publication of an overly long symbolist scenario by Hugo von Hofmannsthal and Harry Kessler.

for the libretto attest,[46] and her own, as well as Salome's subjectivity was at the centre of her portrayal.

While Lawrence Kramer and Linda and Michael Hutcheon have interpreted the 'Dance of the Seven Veils' as empowering Salome,[47] Kramer insists that it is only by kissing John the Baptist's silenced head that Salome acceeds to the male power of speech and writing, and it is precisely her appropriation of the phallic language that provokes Herod – and Wilde – to order her death.[48] In Wilde's *Salomé*, on Herod's orders the slaves put out the torches, and the stars and the moon disappear, but only after Salome has kissed the head. Lina Munte, the first Salome in the premiere of Wilde's play by the Théâtre de L'Œuvre in February 1896, was seen to take the head by the ears in order to passionately, even savagely kiss it.[49] Gertrud Eysoldt, Salome in Max Reinhardt's famous 1902 and 1903 Berlin productions of Wilde's play, was seen to repeatedly stroke and kiss the bloodstained head,[50] almost all the critics agreeing that she brought out the anarchic and animalistic traits of Salome to great effect.[51] Her dynamic acting style was seen to contribute greatly to the overall and synaesthetic impression of Reinhardt's production which demonstrated his post-Naturalist theatre aesthetics (also influenced by Gordon

---

[46] See also BnF Opéra, Fonds Rouché Pièce 113 (1, 8, 10, 11, 12). Despite Trouhanowa's controlling hand in this spectacle, she still worked with her regular choreographer Ivan Clustine, as she had done for her dance in Strauss's opera in 1907. See Garafola, *Legacies of Twentieth-Century Dance*, p. 154.

[47] Both Kramer's and the Hutcheon's texts were discussed briefly in the introduction to this volume. Linda and Michael Hutcheon, *Bodily Charm: Living Opera* (Lincoln and London, 2000); Lawrence Kramer, 'Culture and musical hermeneutics: the Salome complex', *Cambridge Opera Journal*, 2/3 (1990): pp. 269–94.

[48] Kramer, 'Culture and musical hermeneutics', p. 280.

[49] See for example, Henry Bauer, 'Les Premières Représentations', *L'Echo de Paris*, 13 February 1896. Many Parisian reviews of this performance are collected together in a 'Recueil factice du Théâtre de l'Œuvre', BnF Arts du Spectacle, RE 10889 (Microfilm 102070).

[50] After the private performance in Berlin in November 1902, the production of Wilde's *Salome* was transferred to the larger and better appointed Neues Theater in September 1903, where it enjoyed a successful run of performances. See William Tydeman and Steven Price, *Wilde: Salome*, Plays in Production (Cambridge and New York, 1996), p. 38, citing from the *Breslauer Nachrichten* of 17 November 1902. Tydeman and Price discuss Reinhardt's use of a spotlight to portray moonlight but suggest, according to press accounts of the 1903 performances, that the clouds did indeed cover the moon as Salome addressed the head, obscuring the kiss from full view. This may have constituted a conservative change between the 1902 and 1903 performances.

[51] Rainer Kohlmayer, 'From Saint to Sinner: The Demonization of Oscar Wilde's *Salomé* in Hedwig Lachmann's German Translation and in Richard Strauss's Opera', in Mary Snell-Hornby, Zuzana Jettmarová and Klaus Kaindl (eds), *Translation as Intercultural Communication. Selected Papers from the EST Congress – Prague 1995* (Amsterdam and Philadelphia, PA, 1997), pp. 111–22.

Craig and Adolphe Appia),[52] his own search for a synthesis between the arts resulting in an atmospheric blend of mood, music and visual theatre, 'a harmony of words, sounds, gestures, colours and forms which Berlin has not experienced before and which will remain unforgettable'.[53]

In Strauss's opera in 1907, following established performance traditions, it appears that Emmy Destinn carried the dismembered head down to the proscenium arch and laid on the floor in a spotlight in order to speak directly to it and kiss it.[54] Lucienne Bréval, heralded by the press as a moving, sober, proud, noble and pathetic Salome, more discreetly had the head placed on the edge of the cistern and sat or stretched out next to it, with her head at the same level as the Baptist's head (see Figure 3.4). In the scenario of *La Tragédie de Salomé*, the kiss does not exist. Trouhanowa, however, wished to stage the kissing of the head, unlike Fuller who appears to have just danced with it on the platter. Moreover, Trouhanowa decided to occult the head from full view, covering it with one of her discarded veils before kissing it, then lifting it over her head and casting it spectacularly and ritualistically into the sea[55] (see Figure 3.5). 'It will be almost hieratic, religious, I don't know how to describe it! A little like the way in which we cover the symbols of Christ's body in the Orthodox religion!'[56] Thus, in a similar way to decadent literature, Trouhanowa appropriated religious symbolism and ritual while jettisoning Christian morality.[57] The covered head rendered the kiss less explicit, less fleshy, but its veil – Salome's veil – heightened a certain, rather traditional Orientalist eroticism.[58] In addition, Trouhanowa/Salome remained the subject, the head, the object of now both desire and veneration.

---

[52]   See Hugo von Hofmannsthal's essay 'Reinhardt as an International Force', reproduced in translation by Sidney Howard in Oliver M. Sayler, *Max Reinhardt and his Theatre* (New York and London, 1968), pp. 16–27. For a short discussion of the work of Adolph Appia, see Hedda Høgåsen-Hallesby's chapter later in this volume.

[53]   Quotation by Siegfried Jacobsohn, given in Rainer Kohlmayer and Lucia Krämer, '*Bunbury* in Germany: Alive and Kicking', in Stefano Evangelista (ed.), *The Reception of Oscar Wilde in Europe*, The Athlone Critical Traditions Series: The Reception of British and Irish Authors in Europe (London, 2010), pp. 189–202, p. 191. Gertrud Eysoldt portrayed a brutal Salome of predatory sexual appetites, and Kohlmayer discerns the culmination of this bestial portayal of Salome in Strauss's opera, the success of which eclipsed Wilde's text, but also assured its appropriation in German culture, as discussed by Sandra Mayer earlier in this volume. Maud Allan's portrayal of Salome is also said to have been influenced by Reinhardt's productions. See Tydeman and Price, *Wilde: Salome*, p. 140.

[54]   Louis Schneider, 'Salomé', *Le Théâtre*, 202 (May 1907), pp. 3–8, p. 8.

[55]   BnF Opéra, Fonds Rouché Pièce, 74 (4), n.d.

[56]   'Ce serait une chose presque hiératique, réligieuse, je ne sais vous dire comment! Un peu comme dans la religion orthodoxe comme on couvre les symboles du corps du Christ!' See BnF Opéra, Fonds Rouché Pièce, 74 (2), 30 January 1912.

[57]   Jean Pierrot, *L'Imaginaire décadent 1880–1900* (Paris, 1977), pp. 110–12.

[58]   See Annabelle d'Huart and Nadia Tazi, *Harems* (Paris, 1980), p. 60; Malek Alloula, *Le Harem Colonial: images d'un sous-étorisme* (Paris, 1981), p. 14.

Figure 3.4   Lucienne Bréval in Mariotte's *Salomé*
Source: Photograph published in *Le Théâtre*, 1 June 1910, p. 12. Private Collection.

The result of the 'Dance of the Seven Veils' seen only intermittently through flashes of lightning, however, intensifies the objectivity of the dancer, the lightning creating fixed, stylized poses of certain actions; tableaux, snap shots, silhouettes of the progress of Salome's dance are presented for the in-house audience, in a similar way to Strauss's later prescription for the dance in his opera.[59] But in Humières's scenario, the head has its revenge, coming back to haunt Salome, fixing her once again as the subject of the male (yet now disembodied) gaze. Yet the appearance of multiple heads was abhorrent to Trouhanowa, who wrote: 'Whatever we do with the head will be idiotic, dead, amateurish or ridiculous, such as projections, wax heads, etc.'[60] Thus Trouhanowa wished to translate Salome's hallucination purely through expressive mimed action. She preferred also to repeat the opening dramatic 'motif' of John slowly crossing the stage, this time trailing one of Salome's veils, presumably the one through which she had kissed his head. She believed both actions would better render Salome's true fear and despair, for they would symbolize the indestructible and the immortal. As with her analogy to the

---

[59]   This text is briefly discussed in the introduction to this volume and is reproduced as an appendix in Derrick Puffett (ed.), *Richard Strauss: Salome*, Cambridge Opera Handbooks (Cambridge, 1989), pp. 165–7.

[60]   'Tout ce qu'on va faire avec la tête va être idiot, mort, saltimbanque ou ridicule, c'est à dire projection, tête en cire etc'. BnF Opéra, Fonds Rouché Pièce 74 (4), n.d.

Figure 3.5   Production drawing of *La Tragédie de Salomé*
Source: By Maxime Dethomas, reproduced in *Concerts de danse. N. Trouhanowa* (Paris, 1912). Private Collection.

body and blood of Christ, Trouhanowa equated John the Baptist with his cousin and chose to reincarnate, to resurrect, to bring back to life a whole John who does not gaze on anyone, but just passes through as a mystical symbol of time immemorial, or even as a Christian symbol of eternal life. In this way, Trouhanowa established a grandiose narrative frame – one might say patriarchal frame – yet subverted the notion of the Baptist's gaze and Salome's objectivity once more.

Kramer stressed how Salome is crushed as a direct result of the kiss: Humières's Salome is not killed by male actors, but patriarchal order is still enforced in other ways. Rather than have the palace collapse in the final storm, which Trouhanowa qualified as 'Sampsonesque', Trouhanowa preferred to have a cypress tree uprooted and fall across the terrace as a symbol of the insurmountable, and which would provoke Salome's final attack.[61] Thus Trouhanowa's internalized, subjectified drama – acted out through gesture – allied with the forces of nature would provoke 'the hystero-epilepto-desperate fury which would make her collapse in an "infernal delirium"'.[62] Yet while Trouhanowa managed to detract attention away from the gaze of the Baptist on Salome, she neatly slipped into the position in modern realist theatre of the hysteric to be gazed upon by all and sundry.[63]

But does Schmitt's score have any insights to offer? The 'lightning dance' is a frenzied, heaving battle of wills between Herod and Salome, that with its jerky rhythms – alternating two bars of $3\frac{1}{2}/4$ with sections in 2/4, 3/4, 4/4 and 3/8 – loses all notion of seduction that traditionally characterizes the 'Dance of the Seven Veils'. The 'dance of terror' peroration is a tense mixture of static anticipatory passages as John's head appears, followed by a vivid, surging, howling storm. As in his other Orientalist compositions, Schmitt used erotic dancing and hysteria as occasions for musical innovation.[64] In Constantinople in 1903, the composer had seen dervishes praying, scourging and dancing in extreme ecstatic states.[65] Thus Schmitt exploited rhythmic syncopation, polyrhythms, bitonality

---

[61]   Ibid.

[62]   'C'est là que je voudrais ce dechainement histero-épilepto-desesperé qui la ferait s'écrouler dans un "delir infernal".' BnF Opéra, Fonds Rouché Pièce 74 (2), 30 January 1912.

[63]   As Elin Diamond affirms, in psychological realist theatre – highly influenced by the acting style of the Italian star Eleonora Duse – 'hysteria in effect created the performance text for dramatic modernism. Spectators were offered the physician/analyst's point of view, invited to scrutinize the performer's body for the signifiers of psychic trauma'. See Elin Diamond, 'The Shudder of Catharsis in Twentieth-Century Performance', in Andrew Parker and Eve Kosofsky Sedgwick (eds), *Performativity and Performance* (London and New York, 1995), pp. 152–72, p. 158.

[64]   See Jann Pasler, 'Florent Schmitt', in Stanley Sadie (ed.), John Tyrrell (exec. ed.), *The New Grove Dictionary of Music and Musicians*, second edition, 29 vols (London, 2001), vol. 22, pp. 542–5.

[65]   Catherine Lorent, 'Florent Schmitt et l'Orient', *Salammbô: Un film de Pierre Marodon d'après Flaubert. Musique de Florent Schmitt*, Eté Florent Schmitt. Avignon,

and percussively treated chords – all redolent of Stravinsky's *The Rite of Spring* – to portray an atmosphere of exotic violence and frenzy, passion and arousal in these last two dances.[66] The score is therefore highly evocative, suggestive of the action even, with occasional gestures – such as a musically-rendered hurried exit, or Salome repeatedly turning her head away from her visions of John the Baptist's dismembered head – that would not be out of place in Romantic ballet pantomime.[67] Despite these mimetic passages, the storm and hallucination were obviously more difficult to render in dance. The critic Jacques Pillois chided Trouhanowa for movements to Schmitt's score which were not synchronized with the music – its duration, intensity and cohesion – believing Schmitt's supple rhythms to remain dead on stage. He wrote evocatively of triple metres and passages in 5/4 in both the final dances which were animated by at once vehement yet breathless crescendos, interspersed with tragic silences. Moreover, he condemned the mimed action accompanying this music which 'does not manage to translate in gestures of an equal expressive strength, which does not follow the hallucinatory progression, which lessens or betrays the rare vigour' of the music.[68] Thus despite all Trouhanowa's efforts and concern for the mimetic relationship between music and dance, it seems that the results did not always provoke a comforting consensus of opinion.

When Schmitt's score was first performed in 1907, it was paid only cursory critical attention due to Loïe Fuller's domination of the stage. Equally, no critic thought to compare Schmitt's music to that of at least the 'Dance of the Seven Veils' from Strauss's score.[69] Schmitt had attended the Parisian premiere of Strauss's opera in May 1907, before heading for his home in the Pyrenees, where he wrote his score between August and October.[70] But it was only with performances of the symphonic poem by the Concerts Colonne in January 1911, and Natalia Trouhanowa's dance interpretation of the symphonic poem in April 1912, that

---

Opéra de Paris Garnier, Montpellier, La Roque d'Anthéron (Paris, July 1991), special edition, pp. 13–15.

[66] Schmitt dedicated the score of his symphonic poem (1912) to Stravinsky who was highly delighted with it and who was instrumental in gaining Diaghilev's interest in the work. Nevertheless, Robert Craft suggests that Stravinsky expressed an entirely different opinion in private correspondence with Diaghilev, qualifying his true opinion as 'unprintable'. See Robert Craft (ed.), *Stravinsky: Selected Correspondence, Volume II* (London and Boston, MA, 1984), pp. 104–14.

[67] At rehearsal figures 59 and 60 in the full score of *La Tragédie de Salomé* (Paris, 1912), pp. 118–21.

[68] 'ne parvient pas à transposer en gestes d'une égale puissance expressive, dont elle [la figuration] ne suit pas l'hallucinante progression, dont elle [la figuration] amoindrit ou trahit la rare vigueur.' Jacques Pillois, 'A Propos d'un Concert de Danse', *Le Courrier musicale*, 1 May 1912, pp. 266–8, p. 267.

[69] Nozière ('Le Théâtre', *Gil Blas*, 10 November 1907) simply noted that both composers had been 'painfully moved by the sadness of oriental sensual pleasure'.

[70] My thanks to Catherine Lorent for this information.

critics began to take more notice of the expressive power of Schmitt's score, its brightness of colour, its stifling atmosphere of lust, blood and madness,[71] its sad and feverish voluptuousness or wild and whimpering despair.[72] Georges Pioch in *Gil Blas* in April 1912 was one of the first critics to compare the two composers' interpretations of Salome. For him, Schmitt, like Strauss portrayed a pure soul going mad, becoming desperate, through unconsciousness and monstrosity, which violated listeners' sensitivities in an orgy of invention and timbre. Schmitt's score was seen as less miraculous than Strauss's,[73] but was deemed to avoid the 'disconcerting vulgarity' that saturated Strauss's genius. What that 'disconcerting vulgarity' is, is open to interpretation: Pioch may have had the 'Dance of the Seven Veils' – with its eclectic mix of traditional Orientalisms and Viennese waltz – in mind, or, more credibly, he may have been referring to a widely perceived 'vulgarity' born of Strauss's compositional virtuosity itself.

In 1907, Schmitt's supple and vibrant score did not escape the notice of Henry Gauthier-Villars who found it both imposing and impressive:

> Visibly, the Queen of Fire does not dominate the sumptuous symphony that sparkles around her. … Florent Schmitt's score is not one whose movements and inflections can be easily expressed externally. Quivering with internal energy and contained ardour, the composer's idea … has something tense, concentrated and profound about it that does not give itself away all at once and which does not immediately translate into physical lines and shapes.[74]

> [Visiblement, la Reine-du-Feu ne domine pas la somptueuse symphonie qui chatoie autour d'elle. … La partition de Florent Schmitt n'est pas de celles dont on peut aisément extérioriser les mouvements et les inflexions. Toute frémissante de vie intérieure et d'ardeur contenue, la pensée de ce compositeur … a quelque chose de tendu, de concentré et de profond qui ne se livre pas tout de suite et ne se traduit pas immédiatement en lignes et en formes plastiques.]

While conceived as music to accompany dance and mimed action, Schmitt's symphonic score was easily tamed by neither Fuller, nor Trouhanowa for that matter. What Fuller failed to achieve through dance, however, Gauthier-Villars saw realized through her breathtaking technological lighting effects which, in synaesthetic vein, he compared to Schmitt's symphonic procedures; according to

---

[71]   Alfred Bruneau, 'Au Théâtre', drawn from 'Recueils factices d'articles de presse de critique dramatique par divers auteurs, réunis et classés par Edmond Stoullig', *dit* 'Cahiers Stoullig', BnF Arts du Spectacle, SR 95/713 (1912), p. 372.

[72]   Henry Malherbe, 'La Renaissance du ballet français', *Musica*, 140 (May 1914): pp. 94–5.

[73]   Strauss's compositional talents were equated with supernatural powers in the French reception of *Salome*. See my chapter '*Salome* and modern opera'.

[74]   Henry Gauthier-Villars, *Comœdia*, 10 November 1907, p. 2.

Gauthier-Villars, Fuller was destined to become the dance interpreter who would transpose for the eye, the nuanced dream of contemporary symphonists. But Natalia Trouhanowa possessed a very different, far more balletic idea about how dance should relate to modern symphonic music.

Four days before the premiere of her 1912 'Concerts de danse',[75] Trouhanowa spoke of her motivation for this show in *Le Gaulois*:

> I wonder if a musician can make himself understood purely by the language of sounds; I ask myself also if an idea has an absolute equivalent in the world of beautiful harmonies. That which would surprise you even further, is that I have also often asked myself if dance itself, free from convention, can directly translate diverse moods and sentiments. These troubling questions have often haunted me, and I arrived at the conclusion that these two arts owe each other the fullest aid and that, in ballet, the music should step beyond the choreography. Yes, the gesture must be supported by musical development; dance must be as the sung phrase in relation to the symphonic fabric.[76]

> [je me pose ce problème de savoir si un musicien peut arriver à faire comprendre par le seul langage des sons; je me demande aussi si une idée a son équivalent absolu dans le monde des belles harmonies. Ce qui vous étonnera encore davantage, c'est que je me suis souvent demandé [*sic*] aussi si la danse elle-même peut traduire directement, sans aucune part de convention, les divers états de l'âme. Ces questions troublantes m'ont souvent hantée [*sic*], et je suis arrivé [*sic*] à cette conclusion que ces deux arts se doivent l'aide la plus complète et que, dans le ballet, la musique doit même avoir le pas sur la chorégraphie. Oui, le geste doit être soutenu par le développement musical; la danse doit être ce qu'est la phrase chantée par rapport à l'étoffe symphonique par exemple.]

Trouhanowa had previously expressed her opinions on the aesthetic bankruptcy of conventional balletic technique,[77] but here voiced her belief in modern dance which, free from worn-out balletic convention, could replace the human voice as a communicator of powerful emotions.[78] Thus all Trouhanowa's Salomes,

---

[75]   Two performances were scheduled; two extra ones were added due to popular demand.

[76]   Tout-Paris, 'Bloc-Notes Parisien. Les Concerts de danse de Mlle Trouhanowa', *Le Gaulois*, 18 April 1912.

[77]   Pierre Mortier, 'Mademoiselle Natacha Trouhanowa', *Le Théâtre*, 1 July 1909.

[78]   Indeed, as one critic wrote with a few years hindsight in 1919: 'Our composers have learnt from Wagner to treat voices like instruments. Effectively, Wagner's lyric dramas are but symphonies with chorus. From there, to relegate the voices to the background in order to give precedence to mime, there is but a small step.' ['Nos compositeurs ont appris de Wagner à traiter les voix comme les instruments. En somme, les drames lyriques de Wagner ne sont que des symphonies avec chœurs. De là, à reléguer la voix au second plan

danced to symphonically conceived music by Strauss, Mariotte or Schmitt,[79] were meant to be as expressive as their sung counterparts; in possession of a 'voice', Trouhanowa could slip more easily into the active, subject position than the dancer who traditionally only existed in the visual realm.[80] All Trouhanowa's artistic choices attest to this in *La Tragédie de Salomé*, for apart from her final appearance as Charcotesque hysteric, she constantly tried to shift her Salome from the object to the subject position, and through expressive balletic movement to produce a 'voice' which might participate in the music drama. Indeed, even Trouhanowa's objectified hysteric at the end of *La Tragédie de Salomé* could be redeemed in a 1980s feminist reading that might see her final hysterical seizure as a manifestation of the self, a breaking out of patriarchal norms of behaviour, a mode of resistance to the dominant order, as the ultimate pre-symbolic expression of her persona.[81]

The predominance of modern dance during the first decade of the twentieth century was borne on a wave of aesthetic experience which craved a synthesis of the arts, a breaking down of the traditional barriers and conventions that had kept each art relatively separate for at least the previous century. Late-nineteenth century traditional balletic and operatic forms were seen by many as decadent, over-used, to have become conventional signifiers of an art which had run its course, which no longer had anything to say, which could no longer 'speak' to audiences. Ballet music was identified as one of the worst examples of this, the outspoken and radical Isadora Duncan affirming that apart from Edouard Lalo's *Namouna*,[82] there was not one French ballet score from the last 100 years which was not mediocre.[83] With the rise of Austro–German symphonism and Wagner's music drama through the course of the nineteenth century, the traditional French genres of ballet and opera were increasingly put under pressure, with composers as

---

pour donner la préséance à la mimique, il n'y a qu'un pas.'] Max Carrère, 'La critique musicale', *Bonsoir*, 8 April 1919.

[79]   While Strauss's and Mariotte's scores are symphonically conceived, the 'Dance of the Seven Veils' nevertheless remains clearly 'dance music'.

[80]   See Carolyn Abbate, 'Opera; or, the Envoicing of Women', in Ruth A. Solie (ed.), *Musicology and Difference* (Berkeley, CA, 1992), pp. 225–58, pp. 253–4. See also Caddy's discussion of the Ballets Russes production of Rimsky-Korsakov's opera *Le Coq d'Or* (1914) in her *The Ballets Russes and Beyond*, pp. 160–83 where she presents the ascendancy of modern dance in relation to the 'demise' of opera.

[81]   See Mary Ann Smart's discussion of *Lucia di Lammermoor* and her examination of this Foucault-influenced view of insanity and its adoption in the 1980s by feminist literary critics. Mary Ann Smart, 'The Silencing of Lucia', *Cambridge Opera Journal*, 4/2 (July 1992): pp. 119–41.

[82]   On the reception of Lalo's *Namouna* and its place as a forerunner for modern dance music, see Marie-Hélène Coudroy-Saghaï, 'L'infortunée *Namouna* d'Edouard Lalo: une œuvre de précurseur', in Branger (ed.), *Musique et chorégraphie en France*, pp. 73–87.

[83]   Duncan's opinions were published just weeks before Trouhanowa's 'Concerts de danse', although they likely date from earlier than 1912. Isadora Duncan, 'Les Idées d'Isadora Duncan sur la Danse', *La Revue musicale S.I.M.*, 15 March 1912, pp. 8–11.

diverse as Jules Massenet, Dukas, Alfred Bruneau, Gustave Charpentier and Claude Debussy experimenting with new forms and languages (both poetic and musical) in order to synthesize French tradition, to create innovative musical discourse and stage technique. First Debussy's opera *Pelléas et Mélisande*, then Strauss's *Salome* provided opportunities for wide-ranging and complex press debate over the future of modern opera, the Parisian critical mass presenting factions that were difficult to reconcile.[84] Conservatives often regarded the replacement of operatic conventions by symphonic convention (still perceived as Germanic) as 'cultural invasion'. This was much less the case, however, with the conventions of dance music, as if there was indeed a consensus that ballet music needed reinvigorating and dynamic change.[85]

That renewal received new impetus with the arrival in Paris of the Ballets Russes and the general aesthetic quest for synthetic and synaesthetic spectacle, although the metaphor of cultural invasion and an anxiety over the influence of the Russian ballet on national traditions was still present.[86] Nevertheless, the vibrancy of the creations of those who collaborated to produce the Russian spectacles directly encouraged – not least through commissions – the young generation of French composers to write ballet scores, and ballet came to be seen as *the* genre or vehicle for modern music. The influence was reciprocal: modern dance was seen to spawn musical innovation and new music was seen as an impetus to innovative balletic movement and gesture.[87]

In August and September of 1909, Ida Rubinstein performed in a Parisian variety spectacle dancing the 'Seven Veils' to music by Alexander Glazunov. While Trouhanowa worked with the relatively conservative choreographer Ivan Clustine,[88] Rubinstein worked with Mikhail Fokine and danced on sets created by Léon Bakst. Previously given in Saint-Petersburg in December 1908, Rubinstein's mimed Salome slipped past much mainstream 'respectable' Parisian critical attention as it was performed in a musical hall theatre – the Olympia – and during the summer when most of Parisian society was out of the city. Rubinstein's

---

[84]   In relation to the reception of *Pelléas et Mélisande*, see Jann Pasler, '*Pelléas* and Power: Forces Behind the Reception of Debussy's Opera', *Nineteenth-Century Music*, X/3 (Spring 1987): pp. 243–64, reprinted in Jann Pasler, *Writing Through Music: Essays on Music, Culture, and Politics* (Oxford, 2008), pp. 181–212.

[85]   Nevertheless, as late as 1924, Strauss was condemned by the Viennese press for having violated the art of ballet by importing qualities of symphonic development and motivic elaboration into the score of *Schlagobers*. See Wayne Heisler Jnr., 'Kitsch and the Ballet *Schlagobers*', *The Opera Quarterly: Sound Moves*, 22/1 (Winter 2006): pp. 38–64, p. 49.

[86]   Caddy, *The Ballets Russes and Beyond*, pp. 122–52.

[87]   Malherbe, 'La Renaissance du ballet français'.

[88]   Caddy remarks that despite the appointment of Ivan Clustine as ballet master at the Opéra from 1909 onwards, there was no massive overhaul of the ballet and its repertoire. Caddy, 'On Ballet at the Opéra', p. 225.

movements on stage, however, influenced by new theories of 'plastic motion' that Vsevolod Meyerhold (who directed the play) began to explore from 1905 onwards,[89] were lost on some critics who believed her art to be only within the realm of comprehension of the elite.[90] Others believed it comprehensible only because of the quality of the artists – Rubinstein and Fokine – qualifying the choreography itself as 'elusive'.[91] Robert de Montesquiou, who became a close friend to Rubinstein during this period and went repeatedly to see the show, however, was one of the rare critics who wrote a full-length article on Rubinstein's performance, which he saw as heightened by the surrounding musical hall acts.[92] He described Rubinstein's Salome in terms such as 'hieratic majesty', 'intense poetry', 'sustained piety' and 'haughty pride', and invoked Flaubert's description of the dance as the general inspiration. He also described in detail how Rubinstein's whole body was wrapped in seven gauzy scarves of different colours that restricted her movements, but which were unravelled one by one as the music progressed and the choreography accelerated.[93] No comment was made on how gesture corresponded to music, and Glazunov's seven and a half minutes of evocative music slipped by most critics with little comment. However, the first half comprises a long static pedal which supports Orientalist arabesques – both in terms of harmonic and instrumental colour – only followed in the last three minutes by an augmentation and acceleration towards a thrilling climax.[94] The stasis which lasts for over half of Glazunov's score would correspond well with Rubinstein's restricted movement and symbolic representation, before the final unveiling.

A little more than a month after Trouhanowa's 'Concerts de danse' on the stage of the Théâtre du Châtelet in June 1912, Rubinstein gave a performance of the whole of Wilde's *Salomé*, once again with Glazunov's music, in the same theatre as part of the Ballets Russes's season. Press coverage was dominated by

---

[89]   Garafola, *Legacies of Twentieth-Century Dance*, pp. 157–8.

[90]   Anon., 'Spectacles & Concerts. La Réouverture de l'Olympia', *Le Figaro*, 23 August 1909, p. 5.

[91]   Strapontin, 'Paris la Nuit', *Gil Blas*, 23 August 1909, p. 3. Fokine recounts in his memoirs how he simultaneously taught Rubinstein how to dance and choreographed the 'Seven Veils', deciding to 'do something unusual with her in the style of Botticelli'. Michel Fokine, *Fokine: Memoirs of a Ballet Master*, trans. Vitale Fokine, ed. Anatole Chujoy (Boston, Toronto, 1961), p. 137.

[92]   Garafola, *Legacies of Twentieth-Century Dance*, pp. 158–9. Garafola examines the personal correspondence between Rubinstein and Montesquiou during this period.

[93]   Bakst's costumes for the Saint-Petersburg performance are described in Tydeman and Price, *Wilde: Salome*, p. 146.

[94]   Glazunov wrote an 'Introduction' and 'La Danse de Salomé' for the 1908 Saint-Petersburg performances of *Salomé* (published in piano score by M.P. Belaïeff of Leipzig in 1912). The musical language betrays a certain classicism, looking back to *Scheherazade* of Rimsky-Korsakov.

reviews of other works – such as *Hélène de Sparte*, a tragedy by Emile Verhaeren with music by Déodat de Séverac – and once again, Rubinstein's Salome slipped past many critics.[95] Neverthless, she split the opinion of those who commented on her performance between those who could appreciate the 'ambiguities and irrationalities' of her acting techniques and her intense and audacious mime during the dance,[96] and those for whom her voice, accent and mannered delivery were as tedious and pretentious as her dance.[97] An inherent tension in these synthetic, post-Naturalist productions of Wilde's play was diagnosed by Isadora Duncan when she saw a production of *Salomé* at the Kamerny Theatre in Moscow after the Russian Revolution. She was struck by the contradiction between, on the one hand, the actors' symbolic gestures and on the other, the extreme realism at certain points of the drama (such as the dance and all action with the dismembered head).[98] These contradictions are of course present also in Wilde's written text, but their embodiment on stage highlights this tension, and visibly, both Trouhanowa, with her realistic final hysterical seizure, and Ida Rubinstein were plagued by differences in critical opinion about how these tensions might best be handled.

At the same time as Trouhanowa's and Rubinstein's 1912 Salome performances, Strauss's opera was revived at the Opéra with Marie Kousnezoff in the title role. Kousnezoff, a highly skilled actor and dancer (who had studied with Fokine) as well as lyric soprano, danced the 'Seven Veils' herself, and was considered incomparable as a singer/dancer.[99] In the following season, *La Tragédie de Salomé* was given by the Ballets Russes with Tamara Karsavina in the title role,[100] but

---

[95]   Serge Grigoriev, stage manager for the Ballets Russes, did not mention *Salomé* in his memoires of the 1912 season. See his *The Diaghilev Ballet 1909–1929*, trans. Vera Bowen (London, 1953).

[96]   In relation to the reception of the Ballets Russes's performances of *L'Après-midi d'un faune* in May 1912, Caddy discusses the emergence of a Modernist form of spectatorship which valued embodiment and aesthetic response. Caddy, *The Ballets Russes and Beyond*, p. 102

[97]   A number of reviews for this performance are collected together in the 'Cahiers Stoullig', BnF Arts du Spectacle, SR95/713 (1912), pp. 521–4.

[98]   Opinions expressed in a letter from Russia to her brother Augustin Duncan, reprinted (in French translation by Sonia Schoonejans) in Isadora Duncan, *La Danse de l'avenir* (Bruxelles, 2003), pp. 85–6.

[99]   See BnF Opéra, Dossier d'artiste. Kousnezoff danced Potiphar's wife, a role originally conceived for Rubinstein, in the Ballets Russes's Parisian premiere of Strauss's ballet *La Légende de Joseph* in May 1914.

[100]   Three photographs of Karsavina in this role are available at the BnF Opéra, microfilm-2090. See also Georges Linor, 'Les Ballets Russes au Théâtre des Champs-Elysées', *Comœdia*, 14 June 1913, p. 2; Richard Bizot, 'The Turn-of-the-Century Salome Era: High- and Pop-Culture Variations on the Dance of the Seven Veils', *Choreography and Dance*, 2 (1992): pp. 71–87, pp. 83–4; Tydeman and Price, *Wilde: Salome*, pp. 148–50. The tenth autograph letter from Humières to Schmitt from a group of 11 letters held at the BnF Musique (Bobine 21332) is concerned with this show, and mentions Diaghilev's conception

this extravagant performance was overshadowed by Rubinstein's premiere the following day of Gabriele d'Annunzio's *La Pisanelle ou la Mort parfumée*.[101] In the post-war era, Rubinstein danced to Schmitt's score herself, with choreography by Nicolas Guerra at the Opéra (April 1919), in what seems to have been another slightly reworked version of Humières's scenario. In a reversion to balletic technique, Rubinstein supplemented her usual symbolic mimed style with point work, much to the surprise of the critics who, while unanimous in praise of Schmitt's score, were divided over Rubinstein's success as well as that of the show in general. This production equally aimed at a synthesis of the arts but seems to have missed the mark, being described as 'totally incomprehensible',[102] and comprising an overloaded staging,[103] which dominated the musical material and suppressed any attempted fusion of the physical and musical expression.[104] Three months later, Mariotte's opera was revived on the same stage, using scenery originally designed for Strauss's opera, given a facelift by the original designer of Trouhanowa's *La Tragédie de Salomé*, Maxime Dethomas. Lucienne Bréval reprised the role, but was once again replaced by a dancer, Jeanne Delsaux, for the 'Dance of the Seven Veils'.

In 1907, Natalia Trouhanowa inherited the Parisian high-art lyric and dance stage traditions of representing Salome. Neither the scenario conceived by Paul Milliet and Georges Hartmann for Massenet's 1881 opera *Hérodiade*, nor that by Armand Silvestre and C.H. Meltzer for Gabriel Pierné's score *Salomé*, danced by Loïe Fuller at the Comédie-Parisienne in 1895, actually contained a 'Dance of the Seven Veils'. In an unusual strategy for grand opera where ballet and dance *divertissement* was an important part of the spectacle, the iconic dance in *Hérodiade* is subsumed into the virtuosic, bravura aria for Herod, 'Vision fugitive'. The gaze of the court and the audience is subverted and channelled through Herod as he imagines the dance in an onanistic dream. Only he is allowed to 'see' Salome's dance, it is the creation of his own drugged mind and the rest of 'us' must relive it through his retelling.[105] In Fuller's 1895 'lyric pantomime' *Salomé*, the 'Dance

---

of the scenario. This letter is partially reproduced with errors in Hucher, *Florent Schmitt*, pp. 161–2. The study of this production is beyond the scope of this chapter.

[101] *La Pisanelle ou la Mort parfumée*, play by Gabriele d'Annunzio, scenery by Léon Bakst, directed by Vsevolod Meyerhold, first performed 13 June 1913, Théâtre du Châtelet, Paris.

[102] Louis d'Hurcourt, 'Soirées parisiennes', *La Patrie*, 8 July 1919.

[103] Pierre Lalo, 'La Musique', Feuilleton du *Temps*, *Le Temps*, 9 April 1919.

[104] Adolphe Boschot, 'La Musique', *L'Echo de Paris*, 7 April 1919.

[105] In terms of operatic precedents, Massenet's opera *Hérodiade* (1881) had come in the wake of Flaubert's *Salammbô* and 'Hérodias' from his *Trois Contes*, Mallarmé's *Hérodiade* and Gustave Moreau's series of Salome painting from the late 1870s. In Massenet's opera, with a libretto by Paul Milliet and Henri Grémont (alias Georges Hartmann), Salome does not actually dance. See my *Republican Morality and Catholic Tradition at the Opera: Massenet's* Hérodiade *and* Thaïs (Weinsberg, 2004), pp. 165–73.

of the Seven Veils' is replaced by one symbolizing Salome's internal dilemma, torn between fear, her mother's will and her growing religious sentiment, but which nevertheless arouses Herod's desire for Salome. Trouhanowa's strength in character dance meant that, with her choreographer Ivan Clustine, she had no trouble stepping into the exotic role of Salome in 1907, and despite her constant repositioning of her heroine as subject rather than object in *La Tragédie de Salomé* in 1912, Trouhanowa's interpretations remained more within the classical, nineteenth-century norms of the *femme fatale*, aided and abetted by Humières's dance scenario which was less decadent and more conventional than Wilde's audacious play.

Ida Rubinstein, on the other hand, cast off the mantle of Flaubert, Moreau and Huysmans to drag Wilde's *Salomé* kicking and screaming into the twentieth century, giving this symbolist and ironic text the full expressionist and *über-camp* works of exotic dance spectacle, dealing with the many different interpretative layers which that implied.[106] Petra Dierkes-Thrun has recently argued, along with other scholars, that Wilde's *Salomé* should be read as a forward-looking Modernist text, and that it is its 'aesthetics of transgression and its continuation of modernist investments in the ecstatic, subversive, individual body that have made the Salome theme so popular in the twentieth century.'[107] Rubinstein, who was openly bisexual, may well have been drawn to Wilde's Salome due to the transgressive sexualities presented in the play and its fashionably aestheticized Orientalism – to which world many of her heroines, danced for the Ballets Russes, belonged – and which, by this time, had become a cipher for queer eroticism.[108] The Jewish American feminist conceptual artist Eleanor Antin problematized the notions of race, dance and sexuality in the 1970s in her portrayal of the fictitious Russian ballerina Eleanora Antinova, 'forced' into performing stereotypical,

---

[106]   Susan Sontag's ground-breaking categorization of camp in 1964 has been the subject of heavy rebuttal, especially from the gay community who accused Sontag of taking away the homosexual referent of camp, minimizing its homosexual connotations and making it acceptable and inoffensive to bourgeois culture. For brief discussion of Sontag's text, see the introduction to this volume.

[107]   Dierkes-Thrun, *Salome's Modernity*, p. 8.

[108]   Emily Apter, 'Acting Out Orientalism: Sapphic Theatricality in Turn-of-the-Century Paris', in Elin Diamond (ed.), *Performance and Cultural Politics* (New York and London, 1996), pp. 15–34, at pp. 19–20. Rubinstein had, of course, commissioned *Le Martyre de saint Sébastien* from Gabriele d'Annunzio and Claude Debussy (working along with Fokine and Bakst) in 1910, the hero's 'perverse sexuality' and 'extreme religious mysticism', set against an Orientalist backdrop, providing another familiar vehicle for Rubinstein's talents. Debussy's score contained overt musical allusion to Strauss's *Salome*, and was followed in 1912 by a commission from another 'Salome dancer', Maud Allan, for the exotic ballet *Khamma*. See Ralph P. Locke, 'Unacknowledged Exoticism in Debussy: The Incidental Music for *Le martyre de saint Sébastien* (1911)', *Musical Quarterly*, 90/3–4 (2007): pp. 371–415.

exoticized and eroticized roles in European Modernist ballet.[109] Antin's detection of marginalization of black and Jewish women in this way cannot be applied to the upper class, non-practicising Jewess, society star and patron that Rubinstein was, but it does lead us once again to the question of subjectivity and how Rubinstein and (the heterosexual) Trouhanowa set about interpreting their various roles. Suzanne Cusick has described the lesbian aesthetic response as a preference for artistic choices which invite and allow participation as one chooses, with which one may experience a continuous circulation of power.[110] And one cannot deny that both Trouhanowa and Rubinstein, despite collaborating with choreographers, did not script the narratives of their productions as fully as any soloist or choreographer. But as Lynn Garafola points out, these two dancers were experimenting at the frontier of Modernism, helping to shape its multivarious forms and striking diversity.[111]

Trouhanowa was, nevertheless, much more a French establishment figure than Rubinstein. Despite her horrific relationship with Strauss, Trouhanowa owed him and his Salome her entry into the 'Tout-Paris', for just one month after Strauss's opera in Paris in 1907, Trouhanowa was engaged at the Opéra and fêted by society.[112] Trouhanowa's aspirations could be read as somewhat bourgeois and her choices limited to a certain extent within the boundaries of traditional conventions, and despite her outspoken aesthetic statements, her presence and artistic influence never solicited a response tinged with cultural anxiety. Yet this era represents an intense period of stage experimentation, and opera and ballet – along with their composers, designers, choreographers and interpreters – were drawn into a defining search for the ultimate theatrical experience. Moreover, as the traditional role of the voice and cantabile melody was increasingly disputed in modern taut orchestral music drama, comparison between operatic and danced Salomes became inevitable.[113] In this context, Natalia Trouhanowa moved from the opera to the ballet stage, modulating her performance of Salome to different scores, and constantly refined and affirmed her dynamic and individual aesthetic vision and artistic personality.

---

[109]   Lisa Bloom, 'Contest for meaning in body politics and feminist conceptual art: revisioning the 1970s through the work of Eleanor Antin', in Amelia Jones and Andrew Stephensons (eds), *Performing the Body/Performing the Text* (London and New York, 1999), pp. 153–69.

[110]   Suzanne G. Cusick, 'On a Lesbian Relation with Music: A Serious Effort Not to Think Straight', in Philip Brett, Elizabeth Wood and Gary C. Thomas (eds), *Queering the Pitch: New Gay and Lesbian Musicology* (New York and London, 1994), pp. 67–84.

[111]   Garafola, *Legacies of Twentieth-Century Dance*, pp. 161–2.

[112]   Ibid., p. 152.

[113]   Trouhanowa wrote to Vincent d'Indy on 10 April 1911: 'The art of dance is life itself ... it's a song without words'. ['L'art de la danse, c'est la vie ... le chant sans paroles'.] BnF Arts du Spectacle, RO-12776 (1), p. 1.

Chapter 4

Salome's Slow Dance with the Lord Chamberlain, London 1909–10

Anne Sivuoja-Kauppala

Richard Strauss's opera *Salome* had its world premiere in Dresden on 9 December 1905. By the end of 1906 it had been given in 16 theatres in Germany as well as in Turin and Milan.[1] Salome was not permitted to step into the Vienna Opera before 1918, but the Viennese audiences did enjoy their share of Straussian decadence in May 1907 when the Breslau State Theatre toured their production to the Deutsches Volkstheater, with their local prima donna, Fanchette Verhunk (1874–1944) singing and dancing the title role.[2] In the Anglophone world, Salome travelled even less smoothly. In 1907, the Metropolitan Opera in New York was able to give a public rehearsal and the premiere of the work, before the other three sold-out performances – with Olive Fremstad (Salome) and Carl Burrian (Herod) – were banned due to the moral disapproval of the Metropolitan Opera Board, the magnate J.P. Morgan's daughter Mrs. Satterlee at its head.[3] And yet the competing Manhattan Opera House, run by Oscar Hammerstein, mounted the French *Salomé* with Mary Garden singing and dancing the title role in January 1909 and in February, Hammerstein took the production (with Mary Garden) to his Philadelphia Opera Company where it was nevertheless followed by public disapproval, notably voiced by local church leaders. During the first Chicago Grand Opera Company's production of *Salome*, in November 1910, the police interfered with performances, and Mary Garden ran into public dispute about the alleged immorality of her performance. As a result, Baltimore refused to stage *Salome* in December 1910, whereas Milwaukee welcomed it and the box-office

---

[1]   Günther Lesnig, '100 Jahre *Salome*: die ersten 50 Jahre', *Richard Strauss–Blätter*, 54 (2005): p. 52.

[2]   Ibid., p. 53. See also Sandra Mayer's chapter for discussion of Viennese censorship.

[3]   Ibid. On this occasion, 'The Dance of the Seven Veils' was not performed by Olive Fremstad herself, but by Bianca Froelich. See Michael T.R.B. Turnbull, *Mary Garden* (Portland, OR, 1997), p. 66.

success that came with it for a performance on 9 December 1910.[4] The difficulties with the American *Salome* performances were keenly reported in the British press.[5]

Salome's path to London was more successful but no less laborious. Oscar Wilde's play *Salomé* had been banned in 1892 by the Lord Chamberlain, whose ban also had jurisdiction over Strauss's opera whose libretto was based directly on Wilde's play. Performing *Salome* required the Lord Chamberlain's earlier decision to be revoked, an event that eventually took place, and Aino Ackté (1876–1944), the Finnish prima donna, achieved a colossal victory in the title role of Strauss's opera under the baton of Thomas Beecham (1879–1861) at Covent Garden in December 1910.[6] By bringing together for the first time the Lord Chamberlain's *Salome* correspondence,[7] and Aino Ackté's personal letters,[8] this chapter focuses on the process of licensing *Salome*, the societal anxieties involved and their consequences for performance. It also discloses the active role adopted by Aino Ackté, how she challenged the Lord Chamberlain on and offstage in shaping the details of her Salome performance under the surveillance of censorship. On the operatic stage, it is conventionally Salome who, during her dance, casts off her seven veils. In the frame of this chapter, it is the Lord Chamberlain who becomes unveiled as he is drawn from the wings of the theatrical world into the limelight.

This chapter contributes to the reception history of Richard Strauss's *Salome* but instead of focussing on Strauss's intentions or a 'definitive' *Salome*, it concentrates on the making of a particular *Salome* performance, in London in 1910, and the people involved in that process. Inevitably, the censor's role emerges as pivotal. Thanks to surviving documents, a microhistorical frame of analysis becomes a

---

[4]   Mary Garden and Louis Biancolli, *Mary Garden's Story* (New York, 1951), pp. 126–7 and 209–15; Turnbull, *Mary Garden*, pp. 67 and 83–4; John Pennino, 'Mary Garden and the American Press', *The Opera Quarterly*, 6/4 (1989): pp. 70–71; Lesnig, '100 Jahre *Salome*', pp. 57–8.

[5]   See for instance *The Daily Telegraph*, 3 December 1910; *The Lady's Pretorial,* 10 December 1910; *The Evening Standard,* 9 December 1910; *The Onlooker*, 10 December 1910.

[6]   Aino Ackté was born Aino Achté but changed the spelling of her surname to Ackté in 1896 while still studying at the Paris Conservatoire. The pronunciation of her surname sounds similar to the French 'acheté(e)' [bought] about which she was frequently teased by her solfège teacher Paul Vidal who used to ask in their lessons if she had already been 'achetée'. See Aino Ackté, *Muistojeni kirja* (Helsinki, 1925), p. 51. By the end of 1895 she had started signing her private letters as Aïno. The umlaut added an exotic touch to her name for those who spoke Finnish and Swedish, but also aided others with the pronunciation of her name.

[7]   British Library, Lord Chamberlain's Salome Correspondence, 1910/815; henceforth BL LCP CORR – Salome – 1910/ 815 T. I would like to express my gratitude to Roberta Montemorra Marvin who advised me of the existence of the Lord Chamberlain's *Salome* papers.

[8]   Aino Ackté–Jalander Archive, National Library of Finland, Coll. 4 as well as Heikki Renvall Archive, National Archives of Finland.

possible methodological option, revealing the people active behind the walls of a public censorship institution.[9] Attention paid to individuals – the censor's officials, Thomas Beecham, Alfred Kalisch and Aino Ackté – and their relationships in this specific historical and cultural situation offers a local modulation to the performance history of *Salome*.

The 1909 Application

Despite the Lord Chamberlain's earlier ban, Thomas Beecham had developed the desire to stage Richard Strauss's *Salome* on British soil. In December 1909, he submitted his first application for *Salome* performances at Covent Garden. His application followed by mere weeks a report of the Joint Select Committee, nominated by the Prime Minister Sir Henry Campbell-Bannerman, which investigated the Lord Chamberlain's activities. The publication of the Select Committee's report in November 1909 increased political and public pressure against censorship, but did not lead to its suppression. Among other things, it was suggested that the ban on Scriptural characters on stage should be lifted. This, and many other suggestions, remained at the discretion of the Lord Chamberlain.[10] Nevertheless, the social and political climate was ripe for an attempt to revoke the Lord Chamberlain's earlier refusal to allow performances of *Salome*. According to John Lucas, Beecham had planned to give *Salome* as a part of his first 1910 opera season (19 February to 19 March) at Covent Garden alongside Strauss's *Elektra*.[11] This fact may be inferred also from a letter by Ethel Smyth, sent to Lord Althorp (1857–1922), the then Lord Chamberlain, a few days after Beecham's application in which she pleaded for a swift and positive decision:

> Also, as the terrible business of selecting artists has to be done very long before hand, & if Salome (about which Beecham is at this moment arranging in Berlin on tentative lines only, pending the decision ab. [about] the license [*sic*]) is not to be done, quite other arrangements have to be made, I shall be most grateful if the thing could be decided with the greatest possible expedition.[12]

---

[9]   Jacques Revel, 'Micro-analyse et construction du social', and 'L'institution et le social', in Jacques Revel, *Un parcours critique. Douze exercises d'histoire sociale* (Paris, 2006), pp. 56–84 and 85–110 (respectively).

[10]   John Johnston, *The Lord Chamberlain's Blue Pencil* (London, 1990), pp. 58–65; Richard Findlater, *Banned! A Review of Theatrical Censorship in Britain* (London, 1967), pp. 111–12.

[11]   Charles Reid, *Thomas Beecham: An Independent Biography* (London, 1962), p. 97; John Lucas, *Thomas Beecham. An Obsession with Music* (Woodbridge, 2008), p. 53.

[12]   Ethel Smyth to Lord Chamberlain (Lord Althorp), 7 December 1909, BL LCP CORR – Salome – 1910/ 815 T. Part of this letter is quoted also in Lucas, *Thomas Beecham*, p. 54. Smyth's action in the licensing of *Salome* may be explained not only by her liberal

Her letter also reveals that the 'sore points' in the libretto were well anticipated: '... The idea of suppressing passages calculated to give offence (biblical [*sic*] allusions mainly) was mine. ... his [Beecham's] one wish is to keep the acting of the last scene such as shall not make the sort of sensation Fremstad's performance did in America.' Lord Althorp's answer to Ethel Smyth two days later was without much hope for the *Salome* performances:

> My dear Miss Smyth. You may rely on my giving every consideration to the work that you mention, but I am doubtful as to its prospects, for the same story has already been discussed and decided upon.[13]

In the space of a few days, the application went round the Lord Chamberlain's Office. Both the Comptroller Douglas Dawson (1854–1933) and the Examiner of Plays, George Alexander Redford (186[?]–1916) read the submitted German libretto for *Salome*, and Dawson negotiated the situation with the Lord Chamberlain. They all unanimously decided that the libretto could not be licensed. On the basis of their correspondence, it appears that Dawson played a leading role in this process, although he was not nominated as the Examiner but as the Comptroller. However, according to Steve Nicholson, Dawson was the actual source of power, even in relation to the Lord Chamberlain himself.[14] Earlier that year, Redford had received a note from Lord Althorp who had been displeased with his approval of the play *The Sins of London*, because some of its scenes were later judged to represent 'the worst possible taste'.[15] And in spring 1909, the Examiner had licensed a play on his own authority, without referring it to the Lord Chamberlain at all.[16] Furthermore, the external parliamentary Joint Select Committee of 1909 had inspected Redford's activities with keenness.[17] As a result, within the Lord Chamberlain's Office, it was the Examiner himself who was under surveillance. In this potentially high-risk affair, it must have seemed advisable to keep the Examiner in the background, as his judgement was seen as somewhat

---

values but perhaps more by her personal relation to Thomas Beecham who earlier in 1909 had conducted her opera *The Wreckers*. Curiously, Ethel Smyth remains silent on this subject in her book *Beecham and Pharaoh* (London, 1935). On the other hand, censorship was still in force at the time her book was published.

[13]   Lord Althorp's letter to Ethel Smyth, 9 December 1909, BL LCP CORR – Salome – 1910/ 815 T.

[14]   Steve Nicholson, *The Censorship of British Drama 1900–1968*, vol. I: 1900–1932, (Exeter, 2003), p. 76.

[15]   Ibid., p. 72.

[16]   Johnston, *The Lord Chamberlain's Blue Pencil*, pp. 60–62, 265–7.

[17]   Nicholson, *The Censorship of British Drama*, vol. I, p. 72; Dominic Shellard and Steve Nicholson with Miriam Handley, *The Lord Chamberlain Regrets ... A History of British Theatre Censorship* (London, 2004), p. 63.

unreliable.[18] These measures may explain why Redford was careful and fast in handling the *Salome* application, his anticipation of action to be taken in the event of an appeal, and his discussion of the wording of the letter by which he informed Thomas Beecham of the refusal of his licence to perform *Salome*:

> … in accordance with your [Douglas Dawson's] instructions I propose to send Mr. Beecham the usual intimation, copy of which I enclose. Hitherto, I have generally found that an intimation in this form is regarded as a refusal of the License [*sic*]; avoids giving the reasons for the refusal, and keeps the <u>personality</u> of the Lord Chamberlain out of the matter. In this case if an appeal is made to the Lord Chamberlain; an official confirmation might then be sent, and if deemed desirable the reasons for the Lordship's decision might be given.[19]

The 1910 Application

Neither Beecham, nor anyone from his opera company made any immediate appeal against the 1909 refusal, and for about a year, there is no correspondence regarding the *Salome* affair in the Lord Chamberlain's registers. But *Salome* was far from a closed book for Thomas Beecham, and he made a new attempt to have *Salome* staged during his second 1910 Covent Garden season (from 3 October to 31 December).[20] Albert Archdeacon, the manager of the Thomas Beecham Opera Company, re-opened the licensing case in a letter to the Lord Chamberlain of 24 October 1910. Lucas credibly suggests that Beecham considered *Salome* a potential box-office magnet which was desperately needed to rescue Beecham's Covent Garden Season, both artistically and economically.[21] However, the timing of Archdeacon's letter also points to one other motive: the presence of a celebrated Salome performer in London.

Aino Ackté had arrived in London around 20 October to give a concert, organized by the company Concert Direction Daniel Mayer.[22] Immediately upon

---

[18]   Shellard and Nicholson with Handley, *The Lord Chamberlain Regrets…*, pp. 61–4.

[19]   G.A. Redford's letter to Douglas Dawson, 10 December 1909. See also Douglas Dawson's letters to G.A. Redford, 9 and 10 December 1909. All in BL LCP CORR – Salome – 1910/ 815 T.

[20]   The start of this season had been postponed twice due to illness. See Harold Rosenthal, *Two Centuries of Opera at Covent Garden* (London, 1958), p. 355.

[21]   Lucas, *Thomas Beecham*, pp. 65–6.

[22]   Ackté, 'The Celebrated Continental Prima Donna', appeared as a soloist with The New Symphony Orchestra (conducted by Landon Ronald) along with the pianist Vassily Sapellnikoff, at the Royal Albert Hall Sunday Concerts, on 23 October 1910. Ackté's programme included Ophelia's mad scene from Ambroise Thomas's *Hamlet*, 'Ariette' by Paul Vidal, and the 'Valse' from *Mme. Chrysanthème* by André Messager. She gave another concert in Liverpool on 25 October 1910.

her arrival, she made it known that she was prepared to perform Salome in London. One of her trusted friends was a certain Papa Hartl who, judging by Ackté's letters to her husband Heikki Renvall, was well acquainted with the press and important people in the music business in London. Ackté also met the baritone Clarence Whitehill (1871–1932) who was already engaged to perform at Covent Garden. He let Ackté know that he carried considerable influence in London and asked if Ackté was interested in appearing with him in Massenet's *Thaïs*, one of Ackté's favourite roles. Ackté naturally replied in the affirmative, although she considered the role Salome as the ultimate prize.[23] Through Hartl, Ackté was contacted by the Thomas Beecham Opera Company on 22 October, and immediately after her concert of 23 October, Hartl relayed to Ackté that Beecham was highly interested in the prospect of having her perform *Salome*, for which he was going to apply for a 'censorship licence'.[24] An audition was initially arranged for 28 October, but Beecham postponed their meeting to the next day, much to Ackté's annoyance.[25] Hope of a successful outcome prompted Ackté's British agent Daniel Mayer to remind her of her obligation to pay him 10 per cent of any possible engagement fee with Beecham, which Ackté seems to have humbly accepted.[26] This settlement was extremely profitable to Mayer as Ackté was eventually asked to prepare to appear as Senta, Elsa and Elisabeth, as well as Salome. John Lucas suggests that Ackté had come to London in order to appear as Senta in Beecham's Covent Garden Season,[27] and she did sing Senta before Salome, but on the basis of Actké's correspondence it is more likely that performance of the role of Senta was negotiated and agreed with Beecham only after Ackté had come to London and given her concert organized by Daniel Mayer.[28]

Beecham's second Covent Garden season had begun at the start of October 1910 without a performance licence for *Salome*, and moreover, without any application for such a licence having been submitted. But on the day following Ackté's concert, Archdeacon wrote a strongly worded appeal to the Lord Chamberlain, protesting against his refusal to license *Salome* which, of course, had taken place the previous year. Archdeacon indeed painted *Salome* as a much-needed box-office draw which

---

[23]   Aino Ackté's letter to Heikki Renvall, London, 22 October 1910, National Archives of Finland, Heikki Renvall Archive, carton 4 (henceforth NA HR 4).

[24]   Aino Ackté's letters to Heikki Renvall, London, 22 and 23 October 1910, NA HR 4.

[25]   Aino Ackté's letters to Heikki Renvall, London, 22, 23, 26 and 27 October 1910, NA HR 4; Albert Archdeacon's letter (The Thomas Beecham Opera Company) to Aino Ackté, London, 27 October 1911, National Library of Finland, Aino Ackté–Jalander Archive, Coll. 4.16, henceforth NL AAJ, Coll. 4.16.

[26]   A letter from Concert Direction Daniel Mayer to Aino Ackté, London, 26 October 1910, NL AAJ, Coll. 4.16; Aino Ackté's draft letter to Concert Direction Daniel Mayer, NL AAJ, Coll. 4.17.

[27]   Lucas, *Thomas Beecham*, pp. 66–7.

[28]   Albert Archdeacon's letter to Aino Ackté, Covent Garden, 9 November 1910, NL AAJ, Coll. 4.16.

could rescue Thomas Beecham from bankruptcy due to the expensive business of producing operas, adding 'there is no doubt whatever that this will be Mr. Beecham's last attempt to give opera in London, as no one, however rich he may be, can stand so huge a drain upon his purse'.[29] Archdeacon also claimed: 'there is shown in all classes and all sides a widespread desire to hear this advanced musical work and it cannot be that musical England alone in the world should be deprived of the opportunity of hearing the finest opera of modern days.' Archdeacon, like Ethyl Smyth, was well aware of the sensitivities of staging *Salome*: 'To all who have seen and heard the opera in question, there is nothing in it to shock or affect the morals or beliefs of the public, and I venture to say, My Lord, that you yourself after seeing the opera would hold the same opinion. *The only episode likely to give offence, the head of John the Baptist, can easily be eliminated.*'[30]

Steps Towards Licensing

Archdeacon was answered not by the Lord Chamberlain himself but by the Comptroller from the same office, Sir Douglas Dawson who, after negotiating with his superior, opened a breach for a conditional licensing:

> The presentation on the Stage of St. John the Baptist could not be permitted, while some of the expressions regarding St. John the Baptist used by Salome in the dance scene and the introduction of the Head of the Saint are both indecent and objectionable.

---

[29]   This quotation and the following (given with my emphases), are from Albert Archdeacon's letter (The Thomas Beecham Opera Company) to the Lord Chamberlain, London, 24 October 1910, BL LCP CORR – Salome – 1910/ 815 T.

[30]   The presentation of the decapitated head was prohibited also in Russia (1908), and posed all sorts of problems. At the premiere of Wilde's play at the Comédie-Parisienne in 1896, the wax head, on loan from Paris's waxwork museum, had been broken in the last rehearsal and the pieces glued back together for the actual performances. The head used in the London Bijou Theatre's private performances in 1905 had been too unrealistic (painted cardboard) causing an anti-climax. See William Tydeman and Steven Price, *Wilde: Salome* (Cambridge, 1996), pp. 27–8, 43–4 and 61–2. The decapitated head continued to be a problem also in 1918 when a licence was sought from the Lord Chamberlain for Wilde's play *Salomé*, the Examiner being George Street at that time. The licence was not granted for political reasons, as there was a public campaign spearheaded by Noel Pemberton Billing (M.P.) against Maud Allan's alleged immorality (including lesbianism), Allan suing Billing for libel. The play was nevertheless produced, with Maud Allan in the title role, at the Royal Court Theatre on 12 April 1918 as a private performance, thus out of the reach of the long arm of the Lord Chamberlain. See Philip Hoare, *Wilde's Last Stand: Decadence, Conspiracy & The First World War* (Trowbridge, 1997), pp. 61–3, 97–8 and 222–3; Tydeman and Price, *Wilde: Salome*, pp. 81–5.

> Were it possible to present the Opera without the appearance of the Prophet on Stage, and if the portions of the libretto which are offensive were eliminated, the Lord Chamberlain would be very happy to reconsider the whole question of producing the Opera.[31]

Beecham had (correctly) predicted that a single appeal from his company might not be sufficient to persuade the Lord Chamberlain to reconsider his earlier refusal. Therefore, he contacted also the Prime Minister, Herbert H. Asquith (1858–1928). Through Mrs. Asquith (1864–1945), Beecham received an invitation to meet the Prime Minister, first at 10 Downing Street, and later at the Asquith's place of retreat at Stroud Valley. Margot Asquith was well known for her liberal tastes and Maud Allan, the infamous Salome dancer of huge popularity in London, had become a family friend of the Asquiths.[32] Therefore, it may be assumed that the Prime Minister was personally amenable to the notions of decadence inherent in the representation of *Salome*. Beecham put his case for *Salome* to Asquith, probably in the hope of creating more political pressure against the Lord Chamberlain's policy. Therefore, in Beecham's strategy, it was important to convince the Prime Minister of the urgent reasons for having *Salome* performed:

> I explained to him the nature of the *contretemps* over *Salome*. Strauss was the most famous and in common opinion the greatest of living composers; this was his most popular work; it was to be played for the first time to a few thousand enthusiasts who wanted to hear it; it did not concern, so far as I could see, those that did not want to hear it; being given in German, it would be comprehended by few; and lastly, I could not envisage the moral foundation of the Empire endangered by a handful of operatic performances. Would it not be more judicious to give the piece a chance? Otherwise we might run the risk of making ourselves slightly ridiculous in the eyes of the rest of the world by taking an exceptional attitude towards a celebrated work of art, as we had done so often in the past before the advent to power of the present enlightened government.[33]

A week after Douglas Dawson had given some hope for the licensing of *Salome* with revisions, Vaughan Nash (1861–1923) from the office of 10 Downing Street wrote to Sir Douglas informing him that Beecham had been in contact with the Prime Minister, and had requested permission for private performances of *Salome*,

---

[31]   Douglas Dawson's letter to Albert Archdeacon, 31 October 1910, BL LCP CORR – Salome – 1910/ 815 T.

[32]   Felix Cherniavsky, *The Salome Dancer. The Life and Times of Maud Allan* (Toronto, 1991), pp. 175–81. The Asquiths became embroiled in Noel Pemberton Billing's campaign against Maud Allan in 1918, tainting Margot Asquith's reputation as Allan lost her case and Billing was cleared of libel. See Hoare, *Wilde's Last Stand*, pp. 89–189.

[33]   Sir Thomas Beecham, *A Mingled Chime. An Autobiography* (London, 1961 [1944]), p. 142.

regardless of the official refusal.[34] The Lord Chamberlain, who had received the title of Lord Spencer after the death of his half-brother, responded to Douglas Dawson the next day, and his letter illustrates a changed attitude:

> It is all capital about Beecham and Salomé, – with St John the Baptist altogether out of the scenes, and the filthy allocation to the head also omitted. I think all will be well. –

> As you have told Nash that a bowdlerized form of the opera will be licensed, he could so inform the Prime Minister.[35]

On the basis of archival material, it seems that Nash's letter and the response from the Lord Chamberlain's office immediately set the wheels of a rapid procedure in motion during which all the elements deemed improper were removed from the *Salome* libretto so that it could be licensed. Most interesting is the prominent role taken by the Lord Chamberlain's office, and particularly Douglas Dawson (and not the Examiner G.A. Redford) in the 'grooming process' of *Salome*. However, this was not entirely against normal practice, because the Examiner was instructed to co-operate with theatre managers in such cases, suggesting changes so that a licence could be granted.[36] However, this time the co-executor was not the Examiner, but the Comptroller.

Aino Ackté was immediately informed that she needed to get ready for *Salome*.[37] She sensed, however, that the matter was not yet settled because in the rehearsal for *The Flying Dutchman* (sung in German), Beecham had told his orchestra and soloists that the announcement of *Salome* was to be withheld from the press.[38] On 18 November, Beecham had one more discussion with the censors, as Church officials had requested more changes in the wording. Ackté commented to her husband:

---

[34]   Vaughan Nash's letter to Douglas Dawson, London, 7 November 1911, BL LCP CORR – Salome – 1910/ 815 T. As well as music-hall shows, private performances were beyond the grip of the Lord Chamberlain; see also Johnston, *The Lord Chamberlain's Blue Pencil*, p. 59.

[35]   Lord Spencer's letter to Douglas Dawson, Wallington, 8 November 1910, BL LCP CORR – Salome – 1910/ 815 T.

[36]   Johnston, *The Lord Chamberlain's Blue Pencil*, pp. 60, 267.

[37]   Aino Ackté's letter to Heikki Renvall, Berlin, Hotel 'Der Kaiserhof', 11 November 1910, NA HR 4.

[38]   Aino Ackté's letter to Heikki Renvall, London, [14] November 1910, NA HR 4.

Quelle blague – as if some word would be the most sinful thing and issue here. In any case we are having our first Salome rehearsal today. What luck as otherwise I was desperate from this hanging around. [39]

[Quelle blague – niinkuin jokin sana olisi se syntisin kohta ja puoli! Kaikissa tapauksissa on meillä nyt tänään ensimmäinen Salomeharjoituksemme. Se on onni, sillä muuten olin förtviflad tästä roikkumisesta.]

The next day, *The Daily Telegraph* printed a rumour according to which *Salome* would be given at a series of private Sunday evening performances such as Beecham had requested from the Prime Minister at the beginning of November.[40] But happily, *The Daily Telegraph*, along with many other newspapers, was able to print the news about the official licensing of *Salome* on 23 November. However, from the point of view of the official records of the Lord Chamberlain, this news was premature because the Lord Chamberlain's daybooks state that *Salome* was only licensed six days later, on 29 November 1910, nine days before the actual premiere.[41] It was also announced that Aino Ackté would sing and dance the title role. She immediately hastened to telegraph this good news home, although she was puzzled as to why the premiere could not take place before parliamentary elections on 6 December 1910![42]

The Capital Problem

Although not stated in the intimation sent by Redford to Beecham (in December 1909), the main reason for refusing performances of *Salome* was its depiction of Biblical persons and events, as in general, the Lord Chamberlain's office would

---

[39]   Aino Ackté's letter to Heikki Renvall, London, 18 November 1910, NA HR 4. Aino Ackté's mother tongue was Swedish but she used Finnish with her husband. Ackté's Finnish was not only highly personal, but also often comprised words borrowed from French and Swedish. Here, for instance, the word 'förtviflad' ['desperate'] is Swedish of the early twentieth century.

[40]   *The Daily Telegraph*, 19 November 1910.

[41]   The Register of Lord Chamberlain's Plays, vol. VIII, 1904–1910, British Library, Add. 61952. Salomé, p. 214. *No. License*. 815. *Title of Stage Play*. Salomé. *Nature of Play*. Opera. (in German). *Theatre*. Royal Opera. Covent Garden. *Acts*. 4 [*sic*]. *Date of Licence*. 29:11'10. *Date of Entry*. 1:12'10. *Words and Passages to be omitted in Representation*. 'Licensed by the Lord Chamberlain on the understanding that the revised version of the libretto as placed on record is the only one produced.' This register entry was one of the few tasks given to the Examiner Redford in the actual licensing process of *Salome* in 1910; undated letter, BL LCP CORR – Salome – 1910/ 815 T.

[42]   *The Daily Telegraph, Evening Standard, The Times, The Evening News*, 23 November 1910. Aino Ackté's letter to Heikki Renvall, London, 22 November 1910, NA HR 4.

not allow references to the Scriptures.[43] But Scriptural references, particularly the names of people and places, could be removed from the text. For instance, in the middle of the nineteenth century in London, Verdi's *Nabucco* was allowed a licence only after its Hebrews became Babylonians, and the events were removed from Old Testament Jerusalem and Babylon to Assyria and Niniveh. God was renamed Isis, and the hero Nabucco appeared as Nino or Anato.[44] Nevertheless, the original storyline was often preserved (even in libretti or plays based on Scriptural texts), as was the case for *Nabucco*, as well as for the play *Juditha* which drew upon the Apocryphal story of Judith and Holofernes.[45] As Roberta Marvin concludes: 'an Examiner might easily be swayed to grant a licence to a biblical story if the plot were simply "unscripturalized"'.[46]

Mere 'unscripturalization' was not enough to permit the licensing of *Salome*, as evidenced in Douglas Dawson's letter to the Advisory Board;[47] the head posed insurmountable problems:

> Dear Sir,
> The Lord Chamberlain has been appealed to on several occasions by Mr. Beecham, who is now producing Operas at Covent Garden Theatre, to reconsider his decision against the performance of Strauss's Opera "Salome," and bearing in mind the expressed desire of lovers of music to hear this Opera, the Lord Chamberlain has consented to reconsider his decision under certain conditions. After considerable discussions at several interviews between the Lord Chamberlain, Mr. Beecham and myself, the original libretto, a translation into German from the French, has been reconstructed and submitted for the Lord Chamberlain's approval.
> The Opera is to be performed in German.
> There is to be no allusion whatever to John the Baptist, his place being taken by a fictitious person styled "The Prophet."
> His Head does not come upon the Stage, but it is replaced by a blood stained sword to which Salome sings.

---

[43]   Johnston, *The Lord Chamberlain's Blue Pencil*, p. 61.

[44]   Roberta Montemorra Marvin, 'The Censorship of Verdi's Operas in Victorian London', *Music & Letters*, 82/4 (2001): pp. 582–610, pp. 590–91.

[45]   Marvin affirms that *Juditha* was in fact Paolo Giacometti's tragedy *Giuditta*, licensed in 1858. Ibid., p. 592.

[46]   Ibid.

[47]   An Advisory Board was set up in 1910 by Douglas Dawson and nominated by the Lord Chamberlain to assist in delicate licensing decisions. Its members were Sir Edward Carson, Sir Squire Bancroft, Sir John Hare, Professor Walter Raleigh and S.O. Buckmaster, the *ex officio* member being Douglas Dawson. See Johnston, *The Lord Chamberlain's Blue Pencil*, pp. 66–9; and Nicholson, *The Censorship of British Drama*, vol. 1, pp. 77–9. The Advisory Board did not participate in the licensing process of *Salome*, it was only informed about it by Dawson.

All biblical allusions have been eliminated.

In the above circumstances the Lord Chamberlain feels that he cannot now refuse to allow the production, and as time presses he proposes to license the Opera on Monday next.[48]

These guidelines imposed many alterations on the libretto,[49] executed by Alfred Kalisch (1863–1933), a German-born music journalist and translator who particularly championed Richard Strauss's music.[50] Indeed, several days after the licence for *Salome* was announced in the press, Kalisch gave a talk at the Concert-Goer's Club at the Royal Academy of Music entitled 'What attitude should be adopted towards the music of Richard Strauss?'[51] Moreover, Kalisch knew Strauss personally and had contributed a biographical chapter to Ernest Newman's book on Strauss.[52] Besides bowdlerizing *Salome*, Kalisch also translated into English Strauss's *Elektra, Der Rosenkavalier* and *Ariadne auf Naxos*. Thus, the execution of textual changes to the *Salome* libretto was in professional, caring hands. According to some newspapers, Beecham also helped in revising the libretto; however, I have not been able to find letters or any other documents concerning Beecham's participation.[53]

In less than two weeks, Kalisch sent a new version of the libretto to Douglas Dawson who recommended its acceptance, after minor adjustments.[54] The changes were made to the German libretto and no English libretto was provided, neither for the Lord Chamberlain nor for the Covent Garden audience.[55] However, Kalisch's published an article on the textual revisions in *The World* so that the press and public alike could read what had been changed and how.[56] Curiously,

---

[48] Dougals Dawson's letter to the members of the Advisory Board, London, 23 November 1910, BL LCP CORR – Salome – 1910/ 815 T. This is also the date that news of the licensing appeared in the newspapers.

[49] British Library, Lord Chamberlain's Plays, Salome 1910, henceforth BL LCP 1910/31 (Salome) T.

[50] Raymond Holden, *Richard Strauss. A Musical Life* (New Haven, 2011), p. 131.

[51] 'Music and Musicians. Dr Strauss's "Salome"', *The Morning Post*, 28 November 1910.

[52] See the chapter 'Richard Strauss: the man' by Alfred Kalisch in Ernest Newman, *Richard Strauss* (London and New York, 1908), ix–xxi.

[53] See for instance, *The Evening News*, 23 November 1910; *Illustrated Sporting and Dramatic News*, 3 December 1910; *The Manchester Guardian*, 9 December 1910.

[54] Alfred Kalisch's letter to Douglas Dawson, London 19 November 1910, BL LCP CORR – Salome – 1910/ 815 T.

[55] BL LCP CORR – Salome – 1910/ 815 T; BL LCP 1910/31 (Salome) T; Alan Jefferson, *The Operas of Richard Strauss in Britain 1910–1963* (London, 1963), p. 47.

[56] Alfred Kalisch asked in his letter to Douglas Dawson (London, 4 December 1910, BL LCP CORR – Salome – 1910/ 815 T) for Dawson's approval for his article: 'I have been asked by the Editor of the World to write an article on the modifications of the text of Salome, to be published on Tuesday. Mr. Beecham thinks it desirable that it should be

Ernest Newman erroneously claimed G.A. Redford as responsible for the textual changes, despite being aware of Alfred Kalisch's role in drafting them.[57] Nothing in his article, however, suggests that he was aware of the role played by the Comptroller Douglas Dawson in bowdlerizing *Salome*, and the only official of the Lord Chamberlain's office he mentions – several times in a sardonic tone – is the Examiner G.A. Redford, who, as stated previously before, was kept out of this procedure.

Table 4.1   Modifications of direct Scriptural references to people and places

The original libretto	The bowdlerized libretto*
Jochanaan	der Prophet [The Prophet]
5 Juden (aus Jerusalem) [Five Jews (from Jerusalem)]	5 Gelehrte (aus der Ferne) [5 learned men (from afar)]
Palästina [Palestine]	Land der Sündigen [Land of sinners]
Samaria	Gebirge [Mountains]
Die Bergen [*sic*] Judäas [Judaean Mountains]	Die Bergen [*sic*] des Nordens [Northern Mountains]
Die Gärten von Tyrus [Gardens of Tyre]	Die Gärten von Corinth [Corinthian Gardens]
der Gott [God]	die Götter [Gods]
Assyrien [Assyrians]	Persien [Persians]
Tochter Babylons [Daughter of Babylon]	Kind der Unzucht [Adulterous child]

Note: * All English translations of the bowdlerized libretto are by the author.

submitted to you before publication & I accordingly send you a copy of it. I should be putting [*sic*] obliged to you if would kindly look at it & let me know if you approve. As the paper goes to press on Monday afternoon I should be grateful if you would be so very kind as to ring me up before 1 o'clock, so that I can work the needful alterations (if any) in time.' Neither I, nor Raymond Holden have been able to locate the article in question, although sources such as Rosenthal, *Two Centuries of Opera*, p. 357, indicate that such an article was indeed printed.

57   'It is true that the new words are Mr. Kalisch's, but, as they must have been written at the Censor's hint, and are evidently agreeable to this gentleman, we can regard them as virtually his own.' Ernest Newman, 'Strauss's "Salome"', *The Nation*, 17 December 1910.

The textual modifications were very much in line with the Lord Chamberlain's existing policy regarding the suppression of Scriptural references, as applied to theatrical plays as well as to the libretti of Verdi's operas.[58] Therefore, the Christian 'God' was more or less routinely modified; it may have become heaven ('Dio' became 'cielo'), some other foreign deity (such as Isis), or was pluralized as in the licensed version of *Salome*. Even angels were not allowed to appear, but were transformed into Fates.[59] In *Salome*, avoiding Scriptural names and subjects caused systematic modifications in the comical scene with the learned Jews, where the theological debate about whether Elias had truly seen God had to be de-Christianized.[60] Nevertheless, the Scriptural names Herod and Herodias were preserved in the censored version; the name Salome was not a problem in this regard as it is not a Scriptural name at all.[61]

Although not stated in Dawson's letter to the Advisory Board, the whole crux of the drama was changed. In the uncensored version, the young Salome's unbridled sexual desire of Jochanaan is key. The censored Salome is stripped of sexual inclinations but not of passion, as she desperately wants to be blessed by the Prophet and follow him, even to death. Reminiscent of the libretto of Massenet's *Hérodiade* (1881), this ingenious modification marked the depth of Salome's passion, as death could also be interpreted in this decadent, *fin-de-siècle* context as erotic bliss or *jouissance*. Furthermore, as Roberta Marvin notes, religious fervour was an acceptable outlet for the passions of Victorian women.[62] Thus Kalisch's solutions preserved Salome's fanaticism, converting it, however, from the realm of the sexual to the religious.

For example, Salome's confession of being in love with the Prophet's body ('Ich bin verliebt in deinen Leib, Jochanaan!' ['I am amorous of thy body, Jokanaan!'])

---

[58] Johnston, *The Lord Chamberlain's Blue Pencil*, p. 60; Marvin, 'The Censorship of Verdi's Operas', p. 591.

[59] Jochanaan's 'Ich höre die Flügel des Todesengels im Palaste rauschen …' ['I hear in the palace the beating of the wings of the angel of death …'] became 'Ich höre die Parzen, die im Palaste deinen Lebensfaden zerreisen …' ['I hear in the palace the Fates tearing your thread of life …']. All quotations of Wilde's *Salomé* are drawn from the *Complete Works of Oscar Wilde* (London and Glasgow, 1948, rpt. 1977), pp. 552–75.

[60] Zweiter Jude, 'In Wahrheit weiss niemand, ob Elias in der Tat Gott gesehen hat. Möglicherweise war es nur der Schatten Gottes, was er sah.' ['Verily, no man knoweth if Elias the prophet did indeed see God. Peradventure it was but the shadow of God that he saw.'] became Zweiter Gelehrte: 'In Wahrheit weiss niemand, ob ein Mensch je Götter gesehen hat. Möglicherweise war es nur der Schatten der Götter, was man sah.' ['Verily, no man knoweth if any man did indeed ever see Gods. Peradventure it was but the shadow of Gods that one saw.']

[61] The names Herod and Herodias appear for instance in Matthew 14: 1–11 and Mark 6: 14–28, the Biblical sources for the Salome story. The name Salome is not given in the Bible, where she appears as the unnamed daughter of Herodias. One of the earliest sources that names her is Flavius Josephus's *Jewish Antiquities* (first century AD).

[62] Marvin, 'The Censorship of Verdi's Opera', p. 596.

is transformed into a dependence of a different sort ('Ich kann nicht leben ohne Dich, O du Prophet' ['I cannot live without thee, O Prophet']), thus preserving her passion but rechanneling it into a societally more acceptable mode. Consequently, Salome's original and famous desire-filled exclamations about kissing Jokanaan's mouth had to be altered too: 'Lass mich deinen Mund küssen, Jochanaan!', ['Let me kiss thy mouth, Jokanaan'] / Ich will deinen Mund küssen, Jochanaan' ['I will kiss thy mouth, Jokanaan'], became 'Ich will dir zum Tod folgen, O du Prophet' ['I will follow thee to death, oh Prophet'].[63]

These were probably the most audible textual modifications not only because these lines are set to music in a distinctive way but also because they are repeated several times by Salome in a highly advantageous register for the soprano voice. However, there are many more modifications intended to veil the Scriptural prophecies voiced by the Prophet. For instance, the following Old Testament prophecy had to go:

> Jauchze nicht, du Land Palästina, weil der Stab dessen, der dich schlug, gebrochen ist. Denn aus dem Samen der Schlange wird ein Basilisk kommen, und seine Brut wird die Vögel verschlingen.[64]

> [Rejoice not thou, land of Palestine, because the rod of him who smote thee is broken. For from the seed of the serpent shall come forth a basilisk, and that which is born of it shall devour the birds.][65]

In the bowdlerized version, it became:

> Jauchze nicht, du Land der Sündigen, weil die Kraft dessen, der dich quält, gebrochen ist. Denn aus dem Samen des Königs wird ein Wüterich kommen, und seine Wut wird Menschen verschlingen.[66]

> [Rejoice not thou, land of Sinners, because the power of him who tortures you is broken. For from the seed of the king shall come forth a madman and his madness will devour the people.]

In this way, the prophecy was removed from its Biblical context and became a warning against political agitation under a mad ruler who will bring disaster.

Another prophecy about the One who comes after John was heavily modified also:[67]

---

[63]   BL LCP 1910/31 (Salome) T.

[64]   Richard Strauss, *Salome*, Richard Strauss Edition, Complete Stage Works, full score (Vienna, 1996), Rehearsal Figure 39.

[65]   Wilde, 'Salomé', in *Complete Works*, p. 556, based on Isaiah 14: 29.

[66]   BL LCP 1910/31 (Salome) T, p. 6 (die Stimme des Propheten).

[67]   Drawn from Luke 3: 16 and John 1: 26–7.

Nach mir wird Einer kommen, der ist stärker als ich. Ich bin nicht wert, ihm zu lösen den Riemen an seinen Schuh'n. Wenn er kommt, werden die verödeten Stätten frohlocken. Wenn er kommt, werden die Augen der Blinden den Tag sehn. Wenn er kommt, die Ohren der Tauben geöffnet.[68]

[After me shall come another mightier than I. I am not worthy so much as to unloose the latchet of his shoes. When he cometh, the solitary places shall be glad. When he cometh the eyes of the blind shall see the day. When he cometh, the ears of the deaf shall be opened.][69]

The bowdlerized version reads:

Der Tag kommt wo die Königsreiche befreit werden. Die neuen Herrscher werden die Völker der Erde glücklich machen. Wenn sie kommen werden die Gefangenen frohlocken. Wenn sie kommen werden die Ernten der Felder schöner blühen. Wenn sie kommen wird das Sonnenlicht heller scheinen.[70]

[The day will come when the kingdom will be relieved. The new rulers will make the people of Earth happier. When they cometh the prisoners shall be glad. When they cometh the fields shall produce better harvests. When they cometh the sun shall shine brighter.]

Instead of preaching the coming of the Messiah, the Prophet in the censored version talks of a kingdom's liberation from its current oppressors: these new earthly rulers would make all happy, and even the sun would shine more brightly. What the people were waiting for in the bowdlerized *Salome* was not the Son of Man, but an unnamed (pluralized) agent or ruler. This modification again preserves the emotional attitude of expectancy, but its object has been modified to avoid the literal Scriptural reference.

Only one longer passage was entirely omitted: the discussion between the two Nazarenes, Herod and Herodias. This is probably because the Nazarenes recount the miracles performed by Jesus, His turning water into wine at the Canaan wedding, His restoring sight to the blind and the resurrection of the daughter of Jairus. Herod's comments about the waking of the dead were also removed.[71] As I have not been able to locate the score of the censored version it is impossible to

---

68   Strauss, *Salome*, Rehearsal Figure 11.
69   Adapted from Wilde, 'Salomé', pp. 553–4.
70   BL LCP 1910/31 (Salome) T, p. 3 (die Stimme des Propheten).
71   Herod: 'So hört: Ich verbiete ihm, die Toten zu erwecken! Es müsste schrecklich sein, wenn die Toten wiederkämen!' (Strauss, *Salome*, Rehearsal Figure 214.) ['So be it: I forbid him to raise the dead. It would be terrible if the dead came back!' (adapted from Wilde, 'Salomé', p. 565)].

know whether these passages were also musically omitted, or whether words only were removed from the ongoing musical flow, which I think more likely.[72]

Most curious is that this unnamed Prophet was not allowed certain body parts – for instance, a body (Leib) or a mouth (Mund), not to mention his head – and as a result these words were also suppressed in the censored libretto. Mention of his eyes, however, did not provoke any changes. The situation with his hair was more varied, as it was occasionally acceptable for the Prophet to have hair, but in other instances the Prophet's hair was erased from the libretto, and certainly it was not to be touched by Salome. In the original libretto Salome expresses her desire to touch (berühren) Jochanaan's hair whereas in the bowdlerized libretto she wishes to look at (beschauen) the Prophet's hair. Nevertheless, Salome's famous exclamation 'Dein Haar ist grässlich!' ['Thy hair is horrible!] was preserved.

Table 4.2   'Veiling' the Prophet's body parts

The original libretto	The bowdlerized libretto
Gewiss ist er keusch wie der Mond. [I am sure he is chaste as the moon.]	Gewiss ist er schlank wie ein Tann. [I am sure he is slim as a fir tree.]
Sein Fleisch muss sehr kühl sein … [His flesh must be very cold …]	Ja, er muss sehr kühl sein … [Yes, he must be very cold …]
Dein Leib ist grauenvoll. [Thy body is hideous.]	Weh! Du bist grauenvoll. [Alas! Thou art hideous.]
Dein Leib ist weiss wie der Schnee auf den Bergen [*sic*] Judäas. [Thy body is white like the snows that lie on the mountains of Judaea.]	Denn Du bist weiss wie der Schnee auf den Bergen [*sic*] des Nordens. [Because thou art white like the snows that lie on the Nordic mountains.]
Dein Haar ist wie Weintrauben … [Thy hair is like clusters of grapes …]	Du bist schwarz wie Weintrauben … [Thou art black like clusters of grapes …]
Lass mich es berühren, dein Haar! [Let me touch thy hair.]	Lass mich es beschauen, dein Haar! [Let me look at thy hair.]
Laß mich ihn berühren, deinen Leib! [Let me touch thy body.]	Lass mich Dich beschauen, O Prophet! [Let me look at thee, O Prophet.]
Dein Mund ist wie ein Scharlachband … [Thy mouth is like a band of scarlet …]	Du bist wie ein Scharlachband … [Thou art like a band of scarlet …]
Nichts in der Welt ist so rot wie dein Mund. [There is nothing in the world so red as thy mouth.]	Nichts in der Welt ist so rot wie Du es bist. [There is nothing in the world so red as thou art.]
Den Kopf des Jochanaan. [The head of Jochanaan.]	Das Blut der Propheten dort. [The blood of that Prophet.]

---

[72]   *The Bristol Times*, 9 December 1910, reports that the music of Strauss's *Salome* score remained intact.

In the original libretto Salome asks several times for the head of Jochanaan. Curiously, Kalisch replaced the problematic head with blood, making Salome nauseously blood-thirsty, as she keeps on requesting the Prophet's blood. In the original libretto she begs Herod after her dance: 'Gib mir den Kopf des Jochanaan!' ['Give me the head of Jochanaan!']. In the bowdlerized libretto this becomes 'Gib mir das Blut des Propheten dort!' ['Give me the blood of that Prophet!']. Ackté considered this an outrage, as she wrote to her husband:

> Instead of kissing John's lips I had to drink his blood. Is this any purer? What a bunch of hypocrites these English are. In their position I would be ashamed.[73]

> [Sen sijaan että nyt Johanneksen huulia suutelen, sain juoda hänen vertansa. Onko se puhtaampaa! Mikä hypocritijoukko tämä englantilainen [.] Heidän sijassaan häpeisin.]

The censor's difficulty with the Prophet's body parts allows for another reading of the infamous kiss to Lawrence Kramer's psychoanalytical interpretation where he concludes that the kiss has two meanings. On the one hand, Kramer sees the kiss as representing a submissive act, 'a symbolic act of fellatio', but on the other hand, as celebrating Salome's 'triumphant incorporation of the male power of speech'.[74] However, in the context of the systematic censorship in London, Saint John, as a Scriptural figure and precursor of the Messiah, could not become divided into bodily parts that in turn could become fetishized and the objects of Salome's desire. Furthermore, the idea of Salome desiring physical contact with the Prophet, for instance by touching his hair or body, was unbearable, and such passages became heavily modified in the libretto. Kissing the decapitated head would have meant a double transgression; first of all the Prophet would have been divisible to his bodily parts, epitomized by the decapitated head, which at all costs was to remain unseen and unmentioned in the London performances. Secondly, Salome's kissing of the lips of the decapitated head would have signalled a nauseous intimate encounter between the two protagonists, the pure and the impure, the dead and the living. Thus Salome's desire to kiss the prophet was so abhorrent that it was not only impossible to show it on stage, it was also entirely erased from the libretto.

Executing the Revisions

On 24 November the libretto was in the hands of Aino Ackté, and it is probable that the other performers also received their texts around the same time. Besides

---

[73]   Aino Ackté's letter to Heikki Renvall, London, 9 December 1910, NA HR 4.

[74]   Lawrence Kramer, 'Culture and musical hermeneutics: the Salome complex', *Cambridge Opera Journal*, 2/3 (1990): pp. 269–94, p. 280.

Ackté, the censored libretto required extra work from the performer of Jochanaan, Clarence Whitehill, whose original lines containing Scriptural prophesies and references were heavily rewritten. The changes for the other performers, with the exception of the Five Jews [renamed The Five Learned Men], were less substantial as they contained less Scriptural references. Ackté was dismayed on seeing the alterations and wrote to her husband:

> But you should see the Salome text as it is now. It is so utterly stupid that it makes you want to cry. One would not expect intelligent people these days to cook up something like that. It's shameful for the English. One can't speak about God but Gods. Jochanaan who is some prophet, cannot say Gott but Götter! Words like Tyrus, Moab, Palästina are Arkadien, Hellens; the Jews are "gelehrte". I can't say to the prophet Dein Mund ist roth but Du bist roth! I can't say "dein Haar ist schwartz wie Weintrauben" but "Du bist schwartz wie Weintrauben['] etc. I could tell you of hundreds of words which are more and more idiotic.[75]

> [Mutta näkisit Salometextin sellaisena kuin se nyt on. Se on niin perin enfaldigt, että sitä voi itkeä. Ei luulisi viisaitten ihmisten meidän päivinämme voivan sellaista keittää. Se on häpeä englannin kansallisuudelle. Siinä ei saa puhua Jumalasta, vaan Jumalista. Jochanaan, joka on joku profeetta, ei saa sanoa Gott, vaan Götter! Sanat kuten Tyrus, Moab Palästina ovat Arkadien, Hellenit; juutalaiset ovat "gelehrte" Minä en saa sanoa: "profetalle" dein Mund ist roth; vaan Du bist roth!! minä en saa sanoa "dein Haar ist schwartz wie Weintrauben" vaan "Du bist schwartz wie Weintrauben['] etc. Satoja sanoja voisin kertoa toinen toista idioottisempi.]

It must be remembered that it was not only new words that Ackté and Whitehill had to memorize, for extra work was required to adapt the new text to the melodic line and the singing body. This was something they had not expected, and were not paid any extra for. Understandably, the singers protested to Beecham about the textual alterations, but to no avail. Ackté obviously caused more trouble than the others for the opera administration, as attested by the following letter sent from The Thomas Beecham Opera Company to Aino Ackté:

Covent Garden, 30th. November 1910

Dear Madam Ackte [*sic*],
Will you please carefully bear in mind the fact of the alterations in your part of "Salome" must be sung. The Lord Chamberlain's representative will be present at the Dress Rehearsal and if he hears the old version he has declared

---

[75]   Aino Ackté's letter to Heikki Renvall, London, 22 November 1910, NA HR 4.

his intention of putting a stop to the performance. We trust you will not sing anything that will put Mr. Beecham in such an awkward situation.

Yours sincerely, Albert Archdeacon[76]

Censorship and the Prima Donna

The representative of the Lord Chamberlain, Douglas Dawson, as well as the author of the bowdlerized libretto Alfred Kalisch came to see rehearsals, Kalisch perhaps more out of interest than Dawson, whose duty was to control how the modifications were observed. These occasions offered Ackté a chance to make direct contact with the Lord Chamberlain's officials. She used this opportunity to her advantage to remould her role, both the text to be sung and her stage performance.

Ackté had been particularly displeased with a certain passage in the opera and asked for a change in the libretto directly from Kalisch, as evidenced by Kalisch's letter to Ackté after one of the early rehearsals, probably on 1 or 2 December 1910:[77]

> Dear Madam, I have been thinking about what you were so kind as to tell me at the rehearsal about the change you desire for Salome's words ["]Wer ist das, des Menschen Sohn?"[78] – And I think I have found an idea – the words which I am sending you on the enclosed sheet "O Prophet, verstoss' mich nicht: Lass mich, mit dir vereint, dir folgen bis zum Tod[!]" [O Prophet, do not hurt me! Let me be united with thee, to follow thee until death!] – which will allow you to employ the caressing loving accent which you described to me – and at the same time the grandmothers could believe (if it gives them pleasure) that this is for a good cause – and the morals of England will be saved! In the hope that you will accept my idea, I am your very devoted A. Kalisch[.][79]

---

[76]   Albert Archdeacon's letter (The Thomas Beecham Opera Company) to Aino Ackté, 30 November 1910, NL AAJ, Coll. 4.16.

[77]   Aino Ackté's letter to Heikki Renvall, London, 3 December 1910, NA HR 4.

[78]   The original text reads as: 'Wer ist das, des Menschen Sohn? Ist er so schön wie du, Jochanaan.' ['Who is he, the Son of Man? Is he as beautiful as thou art, Jochanaan?'] In line with the Lord Chamberlain's policy on Scriptural references, this sentence was modified to avoid the obvious sensual allusion both to Jesus and to Saint John. Kalisch's first version, unsatisfactory to Ackté had been: 'Was tat ich, dass Du mich sendest in die Wüste, Prophet!' ['What did I do, that thou sendest me to the desert, Prophet!']; see BL LCP 1910/31 (Salome) T, p. 11.

[79]   Alfred Kalisch's letter to Aino Ackté, 4 December 1910, NL AAJ, Coll. 4.10. This letter has been listed erroneously in the catalogue under the name A. Kolisch. Translation by Clair Rowden.

[Chère Madame, J'ai pensé à ce que vous avez bien voulu me dire à la répétition à propos du changement que vous désirez dans les mots de Salome. ["]Wer ist das, der Menschen Sohn?" – Et je crois avoir trouvé une idée – des mots que je vous envoie sur la feuille ci-jointe "O Prophet, verstoss' mich nicht: Lass mich, mit dir vereint, dir folgen bis zum Tod[!]" – vous permettant, j'espère d'employer l'accent de câlinerie amoureuse que vous m'avez décrit – et en même temps les grand-mères pourront croire (si ça leur fait plaisir) que c'est pour le bon motif – et la morale de l'Angleterre sera sauvée! Dans l'espérance que vous approuverez mon idée, je suis votre très dévoué A. Kalisch[.]]

From the temporal distance of over a hundred years, one may surmise that Kalisch shared Ackté's rather ironic view of libretto modifications. Through the short musical excerpt attached to this letter, the lines which Kalisch modified to meet the standards of both the Lord Chamberlain and the prima donna may be accurately located. Moreover, he was tampering with a text which, as stipulated in the terms of the licence, should only have been performed as originally licensed (see Figure 4.1). Kalisch's second version avoids any Biblical connotations but it retains Salome's desire for intimate contact with the Prophet, which, as Kalisch trusts, may be understood to be motivated not by erotic but by religious fervour, and hence acceptable even to the 'grandmothers' of the Covent Garden audience.

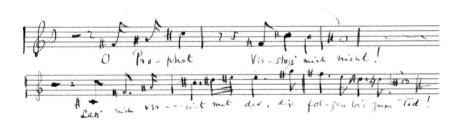

Figure 4.1   Short musical excerpt indicating a change in Kalisch's bowdlerized *Salome* libretto which Ackté had requested in rehearsal, drawn from Alfred Kalisch's letter to Aino Ackté, 4 December 1910

Source: Aino Ackté–Jalander Archive Coll. 4.10, National Library of Finland.

The Capital Problem Returns

According to Douglas Dawson's guidelines, passed also to the Advisory Board on 23 November 1910, no decapitated head was to be present on stage, neither on a silver charger (as in the original libretto), nor anywhere else. However, presenting John the Baptist's head had been possible for Maud Allan in 1908 who gave some 250 performances of *The Vision of Salome* at the Palace Theatre of Varieties in Cambridge Circus. Barefooted, Allan had caressed the decapitated head and kissed its lips. Not a stage play but a music-hall performance, Allan's *The Vision of Salome* escaped the censor's grip.[80] But the Covent Garden performances were monitored closely by the Lord Chamberlain's office which would allow no head. This was made clear to Ackté through her trusted friend Papa Hartl before the dress rehearsal:

> Can you imagine that yesterday they sent Hartl to seriously ask me if I could sing Salome without the charger. They don't know how to make a sensation and they don't know that for Salome I don't need anything like this to make it 'interesting'. They probably wanted a scandal so that after this refusal, the whole of London would run to see me. I laughed at Hartl to his face. Isn't this country splendid – nothing but hypocrisy. But don't make this public as it could cause me great harm.[81]

> [Ajattele että eilen lähettivät Hartl'in på fullt alvar kysymään enkö voisi laulaa Salomea ilman maillota Eivät tiedä kuinka tehdä sensationia, eivät tietysti tiedä että Salomessa en tarvitse tuollaista 'intreserataksein' [.] Luultav. tahtoivat skandalin, niin että koko Lontoo kiellon jälkeen juoksisi minua katsomaan. Nauroin Hartl'ia suoraan naamaan. Eikö tämä maa ole mainio – ei mitään muuta kuin hypocritiaa. Älä tätä nyt vaan publiceraa, siitä voisin saada suurta harmia.]

But what she probably was not told was that instead of the head or the charger, she would receive a bloody sword as a reward for her dance, as stipulated in the censor's guidelines for *Salome*.[82] This highly phallic object stained with blood may have looked acceptable from the Lord Chamberlain's perspective but it proved problematic for Ackté, as the red paint would stain her unique Worth-tailored Salome dress (see Plate 3). This incident caused minor turmoil in rehearsal which Ackté described to her husband:

> My own, my love, I write like this rather than that you receive no letter at all. The rehearsals kill me. I have tried to sing with half a voice but it displaces the voice. Yesterday I did not want to attend but lie down instead but I was intimidated that Beecham would never forgive me. Today we had the "dress["]. 1½ h before, I received a message that I should come in costume – which I refused, as did the other artists. Just before the start, I received word that I should sing and act as in the performance, as otherwise Beecham would stop the rehearsal. I answered that I am not paid for rehearsals, so B. can stop if he so wishes. In any case I

---

[80]   Cherniavsky, *The Salome Dancer*, pp. 160–89; Lucas, *Thomas Beecham*, pp. 54–5. A year earlier, a report of the Joint Select Committee had suggested imposing censorship also for music halls; see Nicholson, *The Censorship of British Drama*, vol. 1, pp. 71–2.

[81]   Aino Ackté's letter to Heikki Renvall, London, 30 November 1910, NA HR 4.

[82]   Douglas Dawson's letter to members of the Advisory Board, London, 23 November 1910, BL LCP CORR –Salome – 1910/815 T.

tried to act and sing so that the audience – at least 200 journalists and others could get the idea. The others gave even less, but nonetheless the rehearsal was good. I was handed a bloody sword from the cistern instead of the head. I got red paint all over my hands and asked for a clean sword as I couldn't possibly hold something like that. Suddenly the representative of the censor [Douglas Dawson] sent a message that I may have a silver charger in my hands <u>without</u> the head. I was saved. I acted as if the head had been on the plate. Afterwards I received from that count (representative of the censor) many compliments – as well as from many other quarters even though I had given only a half [of what I would give in the performance] and without my costume. We'll see about tomorrow. Towards the end of the rehearsal I saw only stars before my eyes. Now I am in bed and have taken migräin [Ackté's nomination for the painkiller for a headache]. I am so tired because of everything, interviews etc. and I can't eat anything because the food is utterly bad. I have lost weight so that there is nothing of me except for bones and nerves.[83]

[Minun omani, minun rakkaani – kirjoitan näin mieluummin kuin että jäisit taas ilman kirjeitä. Harjoitukset minua tappavat. Olen koittanut laulaa puolella äänellä, mutta se deplaceraa ääntä [ransk.; muuttaa äänen sijoitusta]. Eilen en tahtonyt mennä, vaan maata, mutta peloitettiin että Beecham ei koskaan antaisi anteeksi. Tänään oli „kenraali["]. 1½ t. ennen sain sanan että tulisin kostymissä – kieltäydyin, niin muutkint artistit. Juuri ennen alkua sain sanan että laulaisin ja näyttelisin kuten representationissa, muuten Beechman katkaisisi harjoituksen. Vastasin, että en ole maksettu harjoituksia varten ja että B. katkaiskoon jos tahtoo. Koitin sitten kuitenkin näytellä ja laulaa niin paljon että yleisö – ainakin 200 journal. y.m. saisivat idean. Muut eivät sitten niinkään paljon antaneet, mutta harj. oli siltä hyvä. Annettiin kaivosta verinen miekka pään sijasta. Sain punaista sminkkiä kädet täyteen ja pyysin saada puhtaan miekan, sillä en voinut pitää tuollaista käsivarsissani. Yhtäkkiä tuli sensorin representantilta sanan että saan pitää hopealautasen <u>ilman</u> päätä käsissäni. Olin pelastettu. Näyttelin aivan kuin jos pää olisi lautasella ollut. Sain sitten tuolta kreiviltä paljon komplimangia – niin muutenkin joka taholta, vaikka olin tehnyt vaan puolet ja ilman kostymia. Saa nyt nähdä huomenna. Harj. lopussa en nähnyt kuin tähtiä silmien edessä. Nyt olen vuoteessani ja olen migräinin ottanut. Olen niin vsäynyt kaikkien hommien takia interw. y.m. ja syödä en voi yhtään kuin ruoka on niin perin huono. Olen laihtunut niin ettei ole minussa kuin luita ja hermoja.]

The incident with the bloody sword was reported also by the press present at the eventful dress rehearsal, who had a field day. Uncharacteristically, Beecham conducted his orchestra in his shirt sleeves; Ackté appeared in a short, black walking skirt and white blouse, Herod (Ernst Kraus) in a lounge suit, and Herodias (Ottilie Metzger) in black silk dress with a large 'Dorothy' bag

---

[83]   Aino Ackté to her husband Heikki Renvall, 7 December 1910, NA HR 4.

on her arm, which had created considerable dramatic incongruence. Moreover, Beecham had interrupted the rehearsal when Clarence Whitehill had missed his first cue. 'Where's the Prophet?', Beecham was reported to have roared, and after another similar disruption the stage manager [Louis Verande][84] finally succeeded in placing the Prophet in the cistern.[85] Another disturbance took place when Ackté was indeed handed a bloody sword as a reward for Salome's dance. '"I cannot do with it," she said in broken English. ... Mme Ackté then explained, quite pathetically, "I must be clean".'[86] Ackté continued: 'I cannot act unless my hands are clean!'.[87] Her anguish was seconded by Beecham's shout 'Clean the sword!', and in the meantime Ackté wiped her hands on the costume of the nearest soldier.[88] They were joined by the stage manager 'with many gesticulations and a troubled countenance: "A clean sword," he said, "I cannot do it! It is too great a proposition." "You must!" cried Acté [*sic*], making a grimace over her fingers. "I will not act stained like this!". "Alas!" murmured the stage manager and fled to the wings to do the great lady's bidding.'[89] He came back after a while, stopping the rehearsal one more time, bearing the solution to the problem: '"I have just received a message that we may use the charger instead of the sword; but not the Head!" "Oh, joy!" cried Acté [*sic*], clasping her hands over her heart.'[90]

This quasi-operatic incident, recounted in slightly different versions in the newspapers mentioned above, places Ackté in the centre of both the actual Covent Garden stage as well as the public stage of the newspapers. Because of her diva protest, Douglas Dawson, embodying the Lord Chamberlain's authority, was ready to give up his own idea of the bloody sword and seek a compromise that let Ackté off the hook. Moreover, in her autobiography, Ackté recounts how *her*

---

[84]   Jefferson, *The Operas of Richard Strauss*, p. 47.

[85]   'Salome to-night. The event of the opera season. Rehearsal comedies', *The Sketch*, 8 December 1910; 'Dress rehearsal of "Salome"', *The Morning Leader*, 8 December 1910; '"Salome" at Covent Garden. The grand rehearsal. Mme. Ackté & the blood-stained sword', *The Daily News*, 8 December 1910; '"Salome." Foreglimpse at what the audience will see to-night', *The Star*, 8 December 1910; '"Salome" rehearsal. The light side of opera. Incidents at Covent Garden', *Pall Mall Gazette*, 8 December 1910.

[86]   '"Salome" at Covent Garden', *The Daily News*, 8 December 1910.

[87]   'Dress rehearsal of "Salome"', *The Morning Leader*, 8 December 1910.

[88]   Ibid. See also Lucas, *Thomas Beecham*, p. 68.

[89]   'Dress rehearsal of "Salome"', *The Morning Leader*, 8 December 1910.

[90]   Ibid. According to Steve Nicholson, Douglas Dawson received a note from Ackté after a stage rehearsal pleading 'Sir, I entreat you, give me the head.' ['Monsieur, je vous prie, donnez-moi la tête.'] See Nicholson, *The Censorship of British Drama*, vol. 1, p. 74. He references the Lord Chamberlain's collection of letters, but I have found no trace of this letter, nor could I corroborate the incident on the basis of Ackté's own correspondence where she graphically describes the course of events. This, however, does not exclude that such a note might have been sent by Ackté.

Figure 4.2   Engraving by F. Matania of the Covent Garden production with
Aino Ackté as Salome, holding the charger aloft, *The Sphere*,
17 December 1910

Source: Aino Ackté–Jalander Archive Coll. 4.49, National Library of Finland. Ackté chose
this picture for her autobiography, *Taiteeni taipaleelta* (1935).

suggestion – the charger without the head – had been accepted.[91] Nevertheless,
Ackté still considered not having the head odd, as she wrote in a letter to her
husband after the premiere:

> Of course the illusion had to be the greatest as I had to sing to an empty charger.
> Luckily it did not become too ridiculous because that would easily have spoiled
> the whole effect.[92]

> [Tietysti täytyi illusioni olla suurin kuin sain laulaa tyhjälle lautaselle. Onneksi ei
> se käynyt liian ridiculiksi, vaikka helpolla tuo olisi voinut koko affektin pilata.]

For successive performances the charger was not to remain empty but received
a coating of red paint to suggest the Prophet's blood.[93] It is probable that the

---

[91]   Aino Ackté, *Taiteeni taipaleelta* (Helsinki, 1935), p. 180.

[92]   Aino Ackté's letter to Heikki Renvall, London, 9 December 1910, NA HR 4.

[93]   *Reynold's Weekly Newspaper*, 11 December 1910; 'The head problem in Salome.
Censor sanctions a new arrangement', *The Morning Leader*, 30 December 1910; *Lancashire
Evening Post*, 31 December 1910.

paint was not added on Ackté's initiative as there is no mention of this in her correspondence or interviews. And yet it seems as if an empty charger was also unbearable, as suggested in one review:

> The substitution of an empty silver salver for the severed head makes the horror more imaginative than actual [...] Evidently the authorities concerned have not thought out the dramatic purport of the empty vessel.[94]

As Lawrence Kramer concludes:

> Confronted with that emptiness, the observer may choose whether or not to fill it. *No one is compelled to imagine John the Baptist's head on that plate.* For those who leave the plate empty, the Salome complex begins to disintegrate.[95]

Saving Face, if Not the Head

If Ackté had proved somewhat difficult in the dress rehearsal and had challenged the censor, she caused a major catastrophe at the premiere, at least from the point of view of the Lord Chamberlain. This is how Beecham recounts the events:

> For about half an hour all went just as had been planned, everyone singing their innocent phrases accurately, if somewhat frigidly. But gradually I sensed by that telepathy which exists between the conductor of the orchestra and the artists on the stage, a growing restlessness and the excitement of which the first exhibition was a slip on the part of Salome, who forgot two or three sentences of the bowdlerized version and lapsed into the viciousness of the lawful text. The infection spread among the other performers, and by the time the second half of the work was well under way they were all living in [*sic*] and shamelessly restoring it to its integrity, as if no such things existed as British respectability and its legal custodians.[96]

Beecham had been particularly worried about some orchestral pianissimi in Salome's monologue at the end of the opera which would reveal the original libretto. However, instead of a public reproach from the Lord Chamberlain's office following the performance, they came to thank Beecham and his colleagues for the

---

[94]   C.K., 'Production of "Salome"', *The Morning Leader*, 8 December 1910.

[95]   Kramer, 'Culture and musical hermeneutics', p. 294; emphases in the original. In this article, Kramer reveals a set of cultural anxieties of the body, desire, dance, voice and the gaze, as embodied by Salome.

[96]   Beecham, *A Mingled Chime*, p. 150.

utterly satisfying way in which they had gratified the censors' wishes. Beecham remained baffled:

> To this day I do not know whether we owed this happy finishing touch to the imperfect diction of the singers, an ignorance of the language on the part of my co-editors of the text, or their diplomatic decision to put the best possible face on a dénouement that was beyond either their or my power to foresee and control.[97]

But the Comptroller of the Lord Chamberlain, Douglas Dawson, who indeed knew German and had made some alterations to the German text himself, was truly pleased, even writing a congratulatory letter to Ackté the day after the premiere:

> Dear Madam,
> let me offer you, on Lady Dawson's behalf as well as my own, our warmest congratulations for the great success of yesterday evening. I cannot recall ever having seen such enthusiasm at Covent Garden, and I wish to tell you also how I heard only the most flattering accolades on leaving the Foyer, above all on the manner in which you rendered the role of Salome.
> With respectfully devoted regards,
> Douglas Dawson[98]

> [Chere [*sic*] Madame,
> Permettez-moi de vous offrir, de la part de Lady Dawson et de moi-même, nos meilleurs félicitations sur le grand succès d'hier soir. Je ne me rapelle jamais [*sic*: d'avoir] vu pareil enthousiasme à Covent Garden, et je tiens aussi à vous dire qu'en sortant du Foyer je n'ai entendu que des éloges les plus flatteuses, surtout sur la manière dont vous avez rendu le rôle de Salome.
> Agréez, Madame, je vous prie, l'assurance de mes sentiments respectueusement dévoués.
> Douglas Dawson]

Nothing in this letter suggests exasperation at Ackté's performance of the original libretto or includes recommendations requiring changes to the (un)bowdlerized text. Indeed, perhaps the general enthusiasm in the auditorium had been strong enough to prevent any further action from the Lord Chamberlain's office.

But why did Ackté use the original, uncensored version of the text? Did she forget? Or did she rebel? Judging from the letter to her husband on 24 November, the reason was a simple misunderstanding: 'Luckily the director [Beecham] said to

---

[97]   Ibid., p. 151.

[98]   Douglas Dawson's letter to Aino Ackté, 9 December 1910, NL AAJ, Coll. 4.8.

me that at the premiere I could sing it as it was in the original [German libretto].'[99] Obviously Ackté had assumed that she would only need to use the altered text in the dress rehearsal with the censors present. However, in her autobiography, written and published some 25 years after the first run of *Salome* performances in Covent Garden, she gives a slightly different explanation. Annoyed by the ridiculous textual changes, Ackté supposedly decided to stick to the bowdlerized libretto for rehearsals and the premiere, but in the successive performances, to slip back to the original text.[100] Whatever the case, Ackté hot-headedly resisted the censor's requirements and contributed to the undoing of the censor, whose ridiculousness was claimed also in public:

> Probably, too, this production of "Salome" will be historical as having ultimately and finally killed the Censor by ridicule. The alterations in the text are merely ridiculous, and the final one, which makes Salome declare that she will follow the prophet supremely so. As if alterations of words could change the action and the drift of the music![101]

Furthermore, Ackté's 'Dance of the Seven Veils' did nothing to suggest religious passion; it was purely erotic and seductive, an 'embodiment of seductive suppleness'.[102] In addition, many newspapers pointed out how the censorship had failed; the Prophet resembled a conventional depiction of Saint John,[103] and Salome's feelings towards the Prophet were not understood as religious but erotic:

> Every gesture, every movement, every inflection of her voice told the tale that needed no words. What did it matter what phrases she sang at the tall, dark stern figure before her; it was a language every Englishman in the place could understand. That she was infatuated beyond reason by him was unmistakeable. … For instance in the duologue between the Prophet and Salome, Mme. Ackté almost saved the situation by her wonderful resourcefulness.[104]

Ackté's sensuous performance appealed also to the Prophet himself, Clarence Whitehill who, in his letter congratulating Ackté for her colossal victory, made a case for Ackté's charm:

> Dear friend, a thousand bravos! You have had one of the greatest successes of the century and I hope that you are happy. All the newspapers – and I have read

---

99 'Onneksi sanoi tirehtöri minulle että premiärissä laulaisin kuten originalissa!' Aino Ackté's letter to Heikki Renvall, 24 November 1910, NA HR 4.

100 Ackté, *Taiteeni taipaleelta*, p. 180.

101 *The Daily News*, 13 December 1910.

102 *Daily Mail*, 9 December 1910; see also *The Irish Times*, 9 December 1910.

103 *Liverpool Daily Post*, 9 December 1910.

104 *Evening Standard*, 9 December 1910.

1   Gustave Moreau, *Salome Dancing before Herod*, 1874–76.
Oil on canvas, 56 1/2 × 41 1/16 in (143.5 × 104.3 cm).

2   Scenery design by Maxime Dethomas for *La Tragédie de Salomé*

The Latest Scientific Wonder: Photography in Colours.

Salome.

FROM AN UNTOUCHED COLOUR-PHOTOGRAPH: MME. AÏNO ACKTÉ AS SALOME,
IN RICHARD STRAUSS'S OPERA "SALOME," AT COVENT GARDEN.

We would emphasise the fact that this reproduction is made from a direct colour-photograph: that is to say, not from an ordinary black-and-white photograph coloured by hand. For this reason as well as for its actual merits it is of exceptional interest.

Dovertype specially taken for "The Sketch" by the Dover Street Studios.

3   The Dover Street Studios had exclusive rights for Ackté's Salome photographs. This only remaining colour photograph allows observation not only of the colours but also the textures of the cloth. Ackté's costume was tailored by the Parisian Worth, according to her own model. Supplement to *The Sketch*, December 1910.

4   Peter Konwitschny's production of *Salome*
at De Nederlandse Opera, Amsterdam, 2009

5   Robert Tear as Herod surrounded by the Five Jews, from
the Canadian Opera Company's production of *Salome*, 2002

6   Veruschka as Myrrhina in Carmelo Bene's *Salomè* (Italy, 1972)

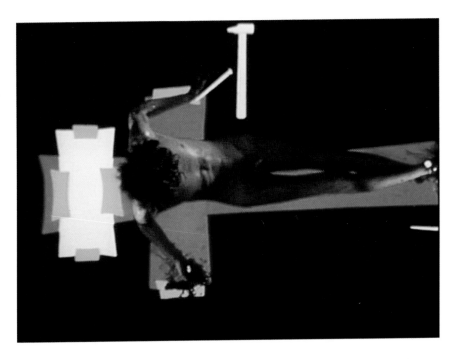

7   Franco Leo as Jesus Christ in Carmelo Bene's *Salomè* (Italy, 1972)

8   Donyale Luna as Salomè in Carmelo Bene's *Salomè* (Italy, 1972)

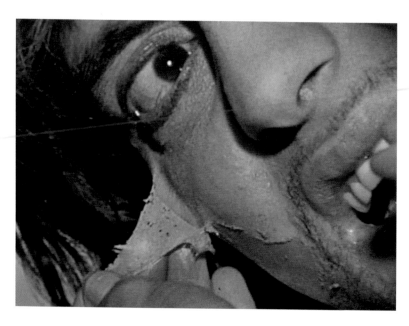

9   Carmelo Bene as Herod in *Salomè* (Italy, 1972)

RICHARD STRAUSS'S "SALOME" AT COVENT GARDEN
THE FASCINATION OF JOHN THE BAPTIST FOR SALOME

THE GRAPHIC, DECEMBER 17, 1910

Salome's desire for John the Baptist, who appears in the Covent Garden version of Dr. Strauss's great opera as " A Prophet," and his repudiation of her, are the two chief motives in the opera. In this picture we see her (as played by Mme. Aino Ackté) trying to fascinate the Prophet, although the body of her lover Narraboth, who has helped her to come to close quarters with the Prophet, is lying on the spot where he fell by his own hand before her very eyes.

DRAWN BY GILBERT HOLIDAY

Figure 4.3   Engraving by Gilbert Holiday of the Covent Garden production
with Aino Ackté as Salome and Clarence Whitehall as the Prophet,
The Graphic, 17 December 1910

Source: Aino Ackté–Jalander Archive Coll. 4.49, National Library of Finland.

them all – are full of you. I have only one regret, that I cannot see you from the auditorium.

You were so seductive the other night that I hardly could resist you.

Who knows – if another time (perhaps even tonight) I would do that.

A thousand regards, Clarence Whitehill[105]

[Chère Amie, Mille Bravo!

Vous avez un des plus grands succès, du siècle et j'espère qu'il vous contente.

Tous les journaux – et je les ai lu tous – sont pleins de vous. Je n'ai qu'un seul regret, c'est que [je] ne peux pas vous voir de la salle.

Vous étiez si séduisante l'autre soir que j'ai pu à peine vous résister.

Qui sait – si une autre fois (ce soir même) j'en aurai la faire [*sic*].

Milles amitiés, Clarence Whitehill]

Towards the End

Ackté performed Salome 9 times. For one performance (on 12 December), the Swedish singer Signe Rappe (1879–1974) had a chance to go on as Ackté was under contract to give a concert in Edinburgh, but Rappe's success remained modest compared with Ackté's, and no further performances were allotted to her. After four performances, Beecham substituted new performers for Herod (Ernst Kraus was replaced by Franz Costa) and Herodias (Ottilie Metzger was replaced by Elly Petzl-Demmer), but retained Ackté, Clarence Whitehill and Maurice D'Oisly (Narraboth).[106]

Towards the end of the run, the charger filled with blood began to bother Ackté. Of course the entire dramatic set-up for her final monologue was strange and unsatisfactory, being deprived of the Prophet's head. In her Continental performances, Ackté was used to addressing her words to the decapitated head, as may be read in her personal score of *Salome* which comprises her autograph performance instructions. On European stages, Ackté used the charger for lifting up the head as the sign of victory, and later, when her monologue had progressed further, she would lift up the head by its hair, holding it closer to her so that she could speak to its face: 'Ich lebe noch, aber du bist tot ...' ['I still live but thou, thou art dead ...'] And eventually she would kiss the head's lips. Strauss approved of Ackté's choreography; he only suggested that Ackté should put Jochanaan's head down immediately after receiving it, and not lift it into the air. But Ackté had

---

[105]   Clarence Whitehill's letter to Aino Ackté, London, 10 December 1910, NL AAJ, Coll. 4.15.

[106]   Jefferson, *The Operas of Richard Strauss*, p. 47. Access to the other performers' papers and scores would offer broader scope for the study of the *Salome* performances in Covent Garden 1910; however, this was not feasible for this chapter.

her own opinion and she held the head in her hands as long as her scenic instinct suggested.[107] Nothing of this however, could be seen at Covent Garden as, in the final monologue, Salome poured her heart out to a charger, filled not with a head but with a red liquid supposed to be the Prophet's blood. It is probable, therefore, that it still imposed restrictions on Ackté's movements as there was once again a risk of the fabric of her dress becoming stained. Ackté thus wanted the real liquid to be replaced by a cloth. But this modification again had to be requested from the Lord Chamberlain's Office:

> Madame Ackte [*sic*] has asked me to write to you to know if you will grant her permission to use the tray in "Salome" – which is supposed to contain the head of the Prophet – covered with a cloth. She deplores the inartistic and rather repulsive state of things, namely singing into this tray filled with blood, and suggests that if the tray is covered with a cloth, people may imagine what they like, but they cannot see anything. Therefore we would still be acting within the license [*sic*] so kindly granted by the Lord Chamberlain. Madame Ackte [*sic*], as an artist feels very much ridicule which is being cast upon this scene of the play, and is most anxious that if it is possible a change may be made for next Monday's performance.[108]

After swift negotiation in the run up to Christmas this was granted, as reported by Douglas Dawson to Archdeacon: 'I have shown the Lord Chamberlain your letter of today. Lord Spencer says "yes", the tray can be covered with a cloth, *only care must be taken not to build up a great heap in it which would look suggestive.*'[109] This improvement was also reported in the press.[110] The enchanted, gallant and devoted Dawson also wrote a kind letter to Aino Ackté on 24 December:

---

[107]   Ackté, *Taiteeni taipaleelta*, p. 153. It is probable that Strauss indeed objected to the head of Jochanaan being lifted and swung in the air, because in doing so Salome would not arouse compassion, but only disgust and horror. See Kramer, *Opera and Modern Culture*, p. 164, where he quotes Erich Leinsdorf, *The Composer's Advocate: A Radical Orthodoxy for Musicians* (New Haven, CT, 1981), p. 57n. According to Kramer, Strauss indeed believed this was no way 'to treat a man's head: a phallus deserves more respect!'. As mentioned earlier, in her Continental performances Ackté showed very little respect for the 'phallus'.

[108]   Albert Archdeacon's letter to the Lord Chamberlain, 22 December 1910, BL LCP CORR – Salome – 1910/ 815 T.

[109]   Douglas Dawson's letter to The Thomas Beecham Opera Company/Albert Archdeacon, 23 December 1910, BL LCP CORR – Salome – 1910/ 815 T; my emphasis.

[110]   *The Morning Leader*, 30 December 1910; *Lancashire Evening Post*, 31 December 1910.

Medmenham Abbey, Marlow.

Dear Madam,
your letter yesterday caught me at the station as I was leaving for a short Christmas break.
I had already responded to Mr. Archdeacon's message which I received yesterday, granting him, on behalf of the Lord Chamberlain, the permission he sought. I hope that with this, we have found the necessary solution, and that you will have on Monday as great a success as before.
With all my friendship and my best wishes for the Christmas, Madam, my respectfully devoted regards.
Douglas Dawson[111]

[Medmenham Abbey, Marlow.

Chere [*sic*] Madame,
Votre lettre d'hier m'a trouvé à la gare, partant pour un petit congé de Noël.
J'avais déja repondu [*sic*] à un mot que j'avais reçu de M. Archdeacon hier, en lui accordant, de la part du Lord Chamberlain, la permission qu'il chercherait.
J'espère, que avec ça [*sic*], nous aurons trouvé la solution nécessaire, et que vous aurez en lundi un plus grand succès même qu'autrefois.
Avec toutes mes sympathies, et mes meilleurs souhaits pour Noël, je vous prie de croire, chere [*sic*] Madame, à mes sentiments respectueusement dévoués.
Douglas Dawson]

Conclusions

The material presented above allows a close look at the behind-the-scenes activities surrounding *Salome* in London in 1910. This detailed reading reveals new kinds of interconnections between people and institutions, as well as public and private motivations. It becomes evident that the Lord Chamberlain's office was not an entirely independent organization in decision making, but tied to politics and public opinion, and even personal tastes. As a result, that which may have been considered a constant unit – the Lord Chamberlain's office – appears to be in constant flux. At the time of licensing *Salome*, the Examiner A.G. Redford was losing influence as his superiors were growing displeased with his work and they were looking for a means to action his dismissal. Soon after the *Salome* performances were over in 1911, Charles Brookfield was nominated co-examiner to Redford. This step divided not only the workload but also the Examiner's salary, and after a month, Redford chose to resign, only to find a position in 1912 with

---

[111]   Douglas Dawson's letter to Aino Ackté, 24 December 1910, NL AAJ, Coll. 4.8.

the British Board of Film Censors where he remained until his death in 1916.[112] This internal turmoil at the Lord Chamberlain's office explains why Redford was kept out of the 1910 licensing process of *Salome*, despite having been involved in 1909 when Beecham made his first application for a licence. Therefore, instead of the Examiner, the active role within the Lord Chamberlain's office was played by Douglas Dawson, whose personal feelings towards Ackté certainly helped to reach many compromises. Perhaps negotiations with G.A. Redford would not have led to such solutions.

The greatest external challenges for the Lord Chamberlain came from three sides: from the Prime Minister of England, Aino Ackté and from public pressure expressed through the newspapers. It was the Prime Minister's involvement that electrified Lord Spencer to initiate the licensing process of *Salome*, and to do so within the terms close to the Lord Chamberlain's general procedure. Moreover, the Prime Minister's and his wife's personal friendship with Maud Allan was an advantage in Beecham's case.

The newspaper critics openly stated the failure of the censor's intentions as they, as well as the wider audience, knew exactly what the drama was about: The Prophet was easily recognized as Jochanaan, who even visually resembled the traditional image of John the Baptist. And Salome's fervent desire was not construed as religious passion, as intended in the bowdlerized libretto, but was seen as openly erotic. According to Ernest Newman:

> *Our* John the Baptist was really John the Baptist, not "A Prophet" named Mattaniah; *our* scene was really laid in Jerusalem, not in Greece; and *our* Salome really said to the Baptist just what Wilde and Strauss make her say, not what the girl would have said had the Censor [G.A. Redford] had the bringing up of her.[113]

All in all, the Lord Chamberlain's censorship activities became a laborious political performance with little effect on the eventual outcome of the operatic performance – with the exception of the missing head. Ultimately, in the course of her performances, the diva restored her original lines, returning to the unlicensed text, and swept the other performers along with her, thus unveiling the Lord Chamberlain's meticulously bowdlerized text and its hypocrisy.

It is, of course, general knowledge that *Salome* was performed in London in 1910 and ran into difficulties due to censorship. By taking a microhistorical approach to the facts, however, one can explore what Jacques Revel[114] and

---

[112]   Nicholson, *The Censorship of British Drama*, vol. I, p. 72; Johnston, *The Lord Chamberlain's Blue Pencil*, p. 54; Shellard and Nicholson with Handley, *The Lord Chamberlain Regrets ...*, pp. 64–5.

[113]   Newman, 'Strauss's "Salome"', *The Nation*, 17 December 1910; emphases in the original.

[114]   Revel, 'Micro-analyse', pp. 61–5.

Giovanni Levi[115] regard as one of microhistory's central characteristics: variation in scale or the interplay of scales. The method of performing a scale change – zooming – allows us to perceive the personal, professional, institutional and even political networks involved in making the *Salome* performances possible. As Paul Ricoeur puts it:

> [t]he key idea attached to the idea of a variation in scale is that, when we change scale, what becomes visible are not the same interconnections but rather connections that remained unperceived at the macrohistorical scale.[116]

In this chapter, the manoeuvring between scales reveals agencies and their interconnections that previously have received very little or no attention at all, such as the roles of Alfred Kalisch or Douglas Dawson who contributed to the supposed purifying of the *Salome* libretto of Scriptural references and moral anxieties that were deemed unbearable for the 1910 British public.

Furthermore, this approach allows Aino Ackté to emerge not only as a skilful executor of Richard Strauss's ingenious score but also as an outspoken subject of her own art, *her* Salome, whose artistic choices challenged and transgressed the Lord Chamberlain's institutional norms. The only thing she could not have was the decapitated head of the prophet which, in this analysis, emerges as the greatest taboo that continued to characterize the '*Salome* problem' from the first initiatives to have the opera licensed, to the last week of its London performances.

---

[115]   Giovanni Levi, 'On microhistory', in Peter Burke (ed.), *New Perspectives on Historical Writing* (Pennsylvania, PA, 2008), pp. 99–102.

[116]   Paul Ricoeur, *Memory, History, Forgetting*, trans. Kathleen Blamey and David Pellauer (Chicago, IL, 2006), p. 210.

Chapter 5
Seven Veils, Seven Rooms, Four Walls and Countless Contexts

Hedda Høgåsen-Hallesby

'Salomé dances the dance of the seven veils', Wilde states laconically in his stage directions, as if ignoring over a thousand years of elaborations of this dance, in texts, on stage and in paintings, from Botticelli to Moreau, from late-medieval mysteries to Heine and Flaubert, and from Alessandro Stradella's 1675 oratorio *San Giovanni Battista* to Massenet's opera *Hérodiade* (1881). Due to the way it names an otherwise nameless yet known event with Biblical origins, Wilde's terse statement is nevertheless important in the history of Salome renderings. His naming of the dance provided a suggestive mist that has surrounded interpretations and re-tellings of the young princess's performance both before and after the emergence of the scandalous Irishman's drama.[1]

One example of this name's constitutive effect is found in Richard Strauss's operatic version. Strauss constructed the dance as an enormous crescendo built up in seven sections (ABACA, plus introduction and coda), and spiced it up with Oriental-sounding musical tropes. Where Wilde left an open space in his text, framed by the context-bound associations of the name, Strauss captured the dance within a score, as well as in a fixed time frame. The way one leitmotif is interwoven with the next creates a dense musical structure which has proved almost impossible to cut. Yet, like Wilde, Strauss left an open space that has to be filled on stage, where the process of 'filling-in' must happen through interpretational and associative pursuits bound by the fixed frames of opera: words and music.

This process is ongoing. In 2008, the unruly young princess appeared at The Royal Opera House in London in a production by David McVicar. The whole story was set in a kitchen-cum-cellarage except for one part: the dance. As the famous ostinato was played, the large-scale set was dismantled, presenting the audience with a new, empty room containing nothing but a chair, a rag doll, Salome and Herod who then proceeded to dance through several different rooms. In 2009, it was Amsterdam's turn to be presented with the old myth in a new production by Peter Konwitschny (see Plate 4). This time, the story was placed in a sealed bunker,

---

[1] On this 'retroactive instrumentality' of Wilde's *Salomé*, see Megan Becker-Leckrone, 'Salome©: The Fetishization of a Textual Corpus', *New Literary History,* 26/2 (1995): pp. 239–60, p. 254.

with the dance functioning as a turning point that changed both the conception of the physical room on stage and the characters' confined situation.

As rooms and spaces have been effectively utilized in recent productions of *Salome* to better understand the somewhat strange story and motives of the young princess, I will argue in this essay not only for the usefulness of such concepts in understanding the phenomenon of opera production generally, but also as a means to capture a 'limited openness' appearing in Salome's dance. On the one hand, the open space left by the musical interlude demands visual expressions and interpretations of the 'opera text'. On the other hand, this pursuit of 'performance texts' is simultaneously limited by the opera text itself, as well as by practical factors.[2] This dependent and continuous process of 'filling-in' has left the dance in a paradoxical position where insights into the phenomenon of canonization may be provided.[3]

I start by examining how different kinds of spaces are produced in opera, and the consequences these spatial existences might create in Salome's dance in particular, then continue by looking at the inherent tension the dance vehicles. After explaining one way in which this tension can be understood, I describe how it is resolved in productions spanning from 1949 to 2009. These productions lead me to my conclusion where I discuss how different kinds of margins, borders and limits have fostered the radical openness and innovations in the production history of Salome's dance, as well as the history of opera production in general.

Production of Operatic Spaces

Despite its existence as a temporal art form, opera has several ties to the concepts of rooms and space, which might refer to several phenomena: an audience's experience is determined by the physical rooms in which the opera is set; spaces and places are established and represented within the operatic event; notions of

---

[2]　For heuristic reasons, I have chosen to adopt David Levin's terms 'opera text' as referring to the score, the libretto and the stage directions, and 'performance text' as the performance and the event. David J. Levin, *Unsettling Opera: Staging Mozart, Verdi, Wagner, and Zemlinsky* (Chicago, IL, 2007), p. 11.

[3]　On opera and canonization, see James Hepokoski, 'Operatic Stagings: Positions and Paradoxes. A Reply to David Levin', in Fabrizio Della Seta, Roberta Montemorra Marvin and Marco Marica (eds), *Verdi 2001: Atti del Convegno Internazionale, Parma, New York, New Haven, 24 gennaio–1 febbraio 2001* (Firenze, 2003), pp. 477–83. Although Richard Strauss's *Salome* could be considered a 'youngster' in the formal canon of Western opera, it is nevertheless included in the group of works that are frequently produced. There does not seem to exist an official and updated list of 'most performed operas', although a limited version can be found in David T. Evans, *Phantasmagoria: A Sociology of Opera* (Aldershot and Vermont, 1999). However, a quick online search shows several unofficial lists from North American and European opera houses where *Salome* is among the 20 most-performed operas, between 1980 and the present day.

spaces, rooms and unities also operate in understandings of opera as the ultimate expression of wholeness. Moreover, these different productions of spaces are related in a triadic relationship. Sociologist and philosopher Henri Lefebvre's mapping of spatial categories in *The Production of Space* (1974) differentiates these levels, while also emphasizing their interdependency.[4] Lefebvre separates between: 1. Material spatial practices; 2. Representations of space; 3. Spaces of representation/representational spaces. Where the first refers to physical and material conditions, the second concerns significations, codes and symbolic representations that allow physical spaces to be understood in a certain way. The third level refers to mental constructions, such as imaginary landscapes or science fiction ontologies.[5] My essay concerns all three as they operate in *Salome* and in operatic production. The first represents the physical room, and how the construction of the auditorium inflects the listener's experience directly. The second level refers to the representations of rooms on stage, as clearly demonstrated in productions by McVicar and Konwitschny. These two productions also exemplify how such spaces include not only representations of physical rooms, but also of psychological or mental spaces.[6]

With regard to the third level, spaces of representation occur in at least four different ways in opera:

- In the open spaces left for visual elaborations and interpretations in the libretto and score. These are enclosed with intertextual references and associations surrounding text and music, such as Wilde's naming of the dance, but also by established musical tropes as well as the time frame set up by the music.

---

[4]   Henri Lefebvre, *The Production of Space*, trans. Donald Nicholson-Smith (Oxford, 1991). Critical space theory has achieved a considerable position in recent decades and contributions have come from several academic disciplines. Lefebvre's texts have served as an important basis for critical elaborations by David Harvey, *The Condition of Postmodernity: An Enquiry into the Origins of Cultural Change* (Oxford, 1989), and Edward W. Soja, 'Thirdspace: Expanding the Scope of the Geographical Imagination', in Philip Sarre, John Allen and Doreen Massey (eds), *Human Geography Today* (Cambridge, 1999), pp. 260–77. Foucault and Bakhtin are also names that figure frequently in these texts, offering other spatial notions, such as 'heterotopia' and 'the chronotope'. See Michel Foucault, 'Of Other Spaces', trans. Jay Miskowiec, *Diacritics: A Review of Contemporary Criticism*, 16/1 (1986): pp. 22–7; Mikhail Bakhtin, 'Forms of Time and Chronotope in the Novel', in Michael Holquist (ed.), *The Dialogic Imagination*, trans. Caryl Emerson and Michael Holquist (Austin, TX, 1981), pp. 84–258.

[5]   See also Harvey's explanation and elaboration of Lefebvre's three dimensions in Harvey, *The Condition of Postmodernity*.

[6]   As Harvey describes, at the second level we can find personal spaces and mental maps of occupied space, in addition to symbolic representation of spaces. Ibid., p. 221.

- In established understandings of organic unity and wholeness as upheld by several theorists of opera, and confirmed by Wagner's notion of the *Gesamtkunstwerk*.
- The spaces constituted by the 'in-betweenness' of opera:[7] its straddling of text (both score and libretto) and performance, representations and living bodies, expectations and practical solutions.
- The operatic construction of 'other rooms', a kind of heterotopic 'third space' where the impossible might possibly happen, rooms where the 'suspension of disbelief' dwells supported by the metaphysical worlds set up by the music.[8] This 'other space' of opera simultaneously maintains and challenges established representational structures, yet they are also dependent on physical rooms (they are not utopias!).

Lefebvre's aim was to show how it is useless to separate between metaphorical and physical spaces: the metaphorical space is always infected by the experienced, and the physical cannot be grasped outside processes of representation.[9] In a similar vein, I believe the production history of Salome's dance can reveal how different kinds of rooms or spaces work together in opera, creating a multidimensional room between the physical, the representational and the imagined. With this in mind, let Salome lead us to discover how such rooms are opened up, filled and dismantled.

Salome's Dance, Visuality and Unified Spaces

So sparsely described and surprisingly deprived of sensory details, yet promising both embodiment and an intense effect of visual performance, Salome's dance has become an undefined icon of movement and imagery that definitely calls for elaboration.[10] Salome's nomadic route through literature, art, stage and music

---

[7] On the notion of 'third space' as an 'in-between space', see Homi K. Bhabha, *The Location of Culture*, (London and New York, 1994), p. 141.

[8] On 'heterotopia' as a kind of 'third space' and space of otherness, transition, revelation and ambivalence, yet with direct connections to physical spaces, see Foucault, 'Of Other Spaces'. Heterotopias are hybrid places. The way Bhabha relates the notion of 'third space' directly to hybridity is interesting as far as the hybrid form of opera is concerned: 'hybridity to me is the third space which enables other positions to emerge. This third space displaces the histories that constitute it and sets up new structures of authority'. Jonathan Rutherford, 'The Third Space: Interview with Homi Bhabha', in Jonathan Rutherford (ed.), *Identity, Community, Culture, Difference* (London, 1990), pp. 207–21, p. 140.

[9] Lefebvre, *The Production of Space*, p. 16.

[10] On the indescribability of this dance, as discussed by Françoise Meltzer and Stéphane Mallarmé, see Marjorie B. Garber, *Vested Interests: Cross-Dressing and Cultural Anxiety*, (New York, 1991), p. 341. See also Zagona, who points to how representations of the dancing Salome after 1000 AD appeared frequently on 'walls, stained-glass windows, and in the illuminated pages of sacred manuscripts and on tympanums of medieval

transfers her into a mythic, canonizing structure, while simultaneously revealing the open ends of such processes and how its origins are fragmented, polyphonic and polymorphous, with no firm basis or starting point.[11] If there should be some kind of core behind the many and perambulating representations of this mythic, nearly encyclopaedic character and her actions, it must be something essentially ambivalent: something visual without description, a 'blank visuality' or an empty, yet overfilled space asking to be interpreted, embodied and revitalized again.[12]

However, there are at least two consistent elements in the corpus of re-tellings describing the death of John the Baptist and the dancing princess. One is active, alive and in motion, namely the dance; the other, the decapitated head, is passive, dead and still. Both are mute and associated with physical bodies.[13] As these are two *visual* components, the head and the dance contribute in making the phenomenon of spectacles, and the act of looking into, a structuring principle of the narrative.[14] Transferred to a physical stage and to opera, this process is supported by the phenomenology of performing arts, an attentive audience, as well as acting bodies. Thus, the textual leitmotifs of Wilde's drama reflect processes within the medium in which it is adapted.[15] Salome's dance in front of Herod reveals how the object of the gaze is parasitic on an external eye: the eyes of those who have perceived, enjoyed, condemned and/or interpreted. A recipient is needed, someone looking at the dancing body, someone who is willing to pay for it (be it just a ticket, their time, or rather the life of a (holy) man), an observer who becomes absorbed in the structure of the repeated story of the dancing girl.

---

churches'. Helen Grace Zagona, *The Legend of Salome and the Principle of Art for Art's Sake* (Genève, 1960), p. 21.

[11] The name of the girl does not appear in the Gospels, but comes from Josephus's *Antiquities of the Jews*, dating from approximately 94 AD. Yet Josephus neither mentions the head nor the dance.

[12] Conrad describes the many Salome representations as exhibits in a museum, an institution that 'equalizes all periods of time and juxtaposes the furthest reaches of space. Salome in particular unfurls into an array of images, hung in a gallery which is a shadowy mental theater where each spectator can find the fantasy which suits him.' Peter Conrad, *Romantic Opera and Literary Form* (Berkeley, CA, 1977), p. 167.

[13] The dancing body and the bleeding head are also what have become responsible for the attention, disgust, shock and curiosity this story has evoked throughout times. Moreover, both are related to Freudian fetishes: the eye and the mouth, associated with ambivalence and lack – a negotiated, yet dependent place of openness.

[14] The act of looking and the gaze as a structural element in Wilde's drama is briefly discussed in the introduction to this volume, and explored further in other chapters.

[15] Moreover, *Salomé* is also structured around an encounter with a particular voice. Thus the opera can be interpreted as commenting on several aspects of the operatic form. As the media theorist Friedrich Kittler states, '*Salome* sets up a perfect world of seeing and hearing.' Friedrich A. Kittler, 'Opera in the Light of Technology', in Beate Allert (ed.), *Languages of Visuality: Crossings between Science, Art, Politics and Literature* (Detroit, MI, 1996), p. 82.

The way Salome's narrative is reflected in the phenomenology of the form points to the fact that although opera is known primarily as a musical form, it has, as the Salome myth itself, several footholds in visual culture. Opera houses are often built as fairy-tale castles in different architectonic styles, bearing witness to opera's associations with enchantment, dreams, and seduction. And as physical rooms directly inflect experiences, several theorists and practitioners of opera have been concerned with the architecture of the opera house and the design of the auditorium. Indeed, Richard Wagner himself was on a quest for unity and control within the whole operatic process which led to detailed descriptions of how the singers should express their roles, and how their bodies should follow each musical gesture.[16] According to his assistant Heinrich Porges, Wagner's ultimate goal was an expression of unity between the dramaturgical logic, the music, and the visual expression – as 'an organic union' and 'a living, breathing organism'.[17] Another contributor to the conception of operatic unity in Wagner's operas, was the architect and stage designer Adolphe Appia. Appia understood operatic production as a series of rooms, both literally, as he replaced two-dimensional painted sets with three-dimensional spaces, and figuratively, as he believed in an ultimate artistic unity constituted by light, music, space and the human body. To Appia, this dramatic space was also constituted by the *time* of music, situating the body on stage in a fixed time frame. Ultimately, the unified space should, according to Appia, present a different atmosphere, a kind of outer-space, with 'a new life far richer than everyday reality'.[18] One of the many who was inspired by Appia was Max Reinhardt who experimented with material spaces in his theatre productions. What Reinhardt, Appia and the French symbolists, including Wilde, shared was the concept of the 'total theatre', where Wagner's notion of *Gesamtkunstwerk* served an important inspiration, implying an indivisible staged entity of sound, words, light, decor, music and dance.[19] Wagner's, Appia's and Reinhardt's endeavours reveal the importance of the physical room, and the way in which it was used in

---

[16]   See, for example, Wagner's 'Staging notes on *Der fliegende Holländer*', cited in Thomas Grey (ed.) *Richard Wagner: Der fliegende Holländer* (Cambridge, 2000), pp. 193–200, p. 197. On the constructions, design and productions of the *Festspielhaus* in Bayreuth, see Patrick Carnegy, *Wagner and the Art of the Theatre: The Operas in Stage Performance* (New Haven, CT, 2006).

[17]   Heinrich Porges, *Wagner Rehearsing the 'Ring': An Eye-Witness Account of the Stage Rehearsals of the First Bayreuth Festival* (Cambridge and New York, 1983), pp. 3–4.

[18]   Adolphe Appia, *Music and the Art of the Theatre*, trans. Robert W. Corrigan and Mary Douglas Dirks, foreword by Lee Simonson, ed. Barnard Hewitt (Coral Gables, FL, 1962), pp. 18, 34.

[19]   See William Tydeman and Steven Price, *Wilde: Salome*, Plays in Production (Cambridge and New York, 1996). Wilde's position as an advocate for total theatre is confirmed in his essay 'The Truth of Masks', where he talks about the stage as 'the meeting-place of all the arts', where one single mind should direct the whole production and where the essence of the artistic effect should be unity. Oscar Wilde, 'The Truth of Masks', in *Complete Works of Oscar Wilde* (London and Glasgow, 1948, reprinted 1977), pp. 1060–78.

the operatic representation of spaces to create an organic unity where the borders between the different artistic expressions had to be dissolved, making the fairy-tale castles contain other and alternative worlds: the 'third space' or heterotopia of opera.

Yet, this might be a world on shaky ground. In spite of Wagner's – many would say successful – attempts to create wholeness and unity in the total operatic experience, it is nevertheless striking how his musical dramas are filled with scenes almost impossible to stage convincingly, comprising funeral pyres, rainbow bridges and dragons. The materiality, practicality and visuality of performance in these scenes collides with the metaphysical, imaginable world supported by the music. Carolyn Abbate describes such a collision as a 'quintessential operatic phenomenon'.[20] Yet, even if this may be typically operatic, it represents a challenge to the quest for wholeness in the experience that might point back at the (lack of) desired unified space. A similar collision also concerned the French symbolists: as their ideas turned from the printed page to the stage, the delicate sensations and alternative spheres of existence collided with the tangibility and realism of a physical theatre.[21] However, Wilde never got the chance to see his vision of *Salomé* realized, as he was serving his sentence for acts of 'gross indecency' when the drama was premiered in Paris in 1896.[22] He did, however, state that apart from his illustrator Aubrey Beardsley, there was no one beside himself who really could see 'that invisible dance'.[23] To Wilde it remained a dream or a utopia.

One who *did* see several versions of the dance was Richard Strauss, who in turn became responsible for the version in which it has become best known, as he turned Wilde's drama and illusions into opera, thus demanding the dance to be carried out and embodied as a material spatial practice. Yet the fact that over 15 years after *Salome* was first performed, Strauss wrote a detailed stage direction for the dance, points not only to Strauss's willingness to be involved in the opera as a unity that includes choreography and stage design, but also towards an inherent difficulty related to the dance's position as a visual icon, and how that visuality might threaten the desired operatic unity.[24] In what follows, I will elaborate on how the dance represents both the production of, as well as the tension between, different kinds of spaces in opera: the experienced, the perceived and the imagined.

---

[20]   Carolyn Abbate, *In Search of Opera*, Princeton Studies in Opera (Princeton, NJ, 2001), p. vii.

[21]   Tydeman and Price, *Wilde: Salome*, p. 4.

[22]   On Wilde's dreams of Salome performances, see Tydeman and Price, *Wilde: Salome*, pp. 15–24.

[23]   Oscar Wilde, *The Letters of Oscar Wilde*, Rupert Hart-Davis (ed.) (London, 1962), p. 348.

[24]   Reprinted as an appendix in Derrick Puffet (ed.), *Richard Strauss: Salome*, Cambridge Opera Handbooks (Cambridge, 1989).

The 'Clean Slate'

In spite of its 'blank visuality', Salome's dance does not appear as a 'clean slate'. On the contrary, the expectation of Salome's dance, on and off stage, runs high. This intertextual framework of expectations is firstly constituted by the narrative structure, secondly, by previous renderings and the dance's mythic status.[25] In the opera, it is given nine precious minutes of the total 90, it has an audience both on and off the stage, and it is rewarded with *everything* in the world, even before any move is made. Thus, 'The Dance of the Seven Veils' represents the pinnacle of all dances, similar to the Orpheus myth for song.[26]

Like her appearances in different art forms, Salome – the opera, the character and her dance – has served as an open symbol or space of representation on which to write meaning, agendas and interpretations. This trend is equally true in musicological study, where the notion of unity or disruption of unity plays a crucial role.[27] Strauss's score demonstrates a remarkable level of unity, following along the lines of Wagner's leitmotif-driven dramas, where almost every note can be traced back to a set of motives, and where the short prelude becomes an entry into a seemingly closed world. Such an impression is supported by the consistent symbolism of Wilde's text,[28] as well as the simple fact that there is just one act that takes place within one room,[29] placing the story within confined spaces, physically, representationally and imaginatively. Through unity of action, place and time, and being sewn together by nearly seamless music, *Salome* is close to a perfect tragedy

---

[25]   According to Kristeva's understanding of 'intertextuality', a text is a permutation of texts, a '*space* of a given text' where several utterances that are also taken from other texts intersect one another. Julia Kristeva, *Desire in Language: A Semiotic Approach to Literature and Art*, Leon S. Roudiez (ed.) (New York, 1980), p. 38, my emphasis.

[26]   This has made the legend of the dancing Salome into one of the best narratives for dance. This was confirmed by the way dancers, especially around the turn of the twentieth century, used this narrative to create and perform, a trend that has been called 'Salomania'. See Clair Rowden's chapter in this volume.

[27]   The following articles were briefly discussed in the introduction to this volume: Lawrence Kramer, 'Culture and Musical Hermeneutics: the Salome Complex', *Cambridge Opera Journal*, 2/3 (1990): pp. 269–94; Susan McClary, *Feminine Endings: Music, Gender, and Sexuality* (Minneapolis, MN, 1991); Carolyn Abbate, 'Opera: or, the Envoicing of Women', in Ruth A. Solie (ed.), *Musicology and Difference* (Berkeley, CA, 1992), pp. 225–58; Linda Hutcheon and Michael Hutcheon, *Bodily Charm: Living Opera* (Lincoln and London, 2000).

[28]   Wilde himself described *Salomé* as containing 'refrains whose recurring *motifs* make *Salome* so like a piece of music and bind it together as a ballad'. Oscar Wilde, 'De Profundis', in *Complete Works*, pp. 873–957, p. 922.

[29]   Wilde's stage directions, describing the opening of the cistern on the left, a staircase to the right, a moon above and a dungeon beneath set up a visual frame and a confined space in which the action takes place. These are reproduced in Tydeman and Price, *Wilde: Salome*, p. 47.

that could absorb the audience and lead them towards a catharsis evoked by pity, fear and a deranged young woman who must be obliterated.

As this unity is dependent on the endeavours of a physical body on stage, either through song or movement, it contains an operatic tension that often leaves the audience of Salome's dance more embarrassed than seduced. When this is the case, explanatory factors relate to the different kinds of spaces I have outlined, as the heterotopia of a dance has to be replaced by a particular embodiment of a singer on stage and her material spatial practice. The opera singer is deprived of her most important medium and is forced to dance (convincingly) to fill a wordless and song-less zone of dramatic and visual space carved out by Strauss's music. Where a highly specialized and trained singer may well fulfil the role as the singing Orpheus, she might fall short when she is forced to be quiet, and to convince and seduce through visual means alone. While the body on stage is situated within an uncomfortable physical and temporal space, it also appears as a situation in itself, situating the staged body: the fact that the singer, both as agent and as medium, is left with a handicap, also affects the representation of the character. What emerges is a tension between narrative representational spaces, portraying Salome as a convincing dancer, and the material spatial practices, where the body is forced to abandon vocal utterances for visual expression – a tension that represents a threat to the audience's impression of unity in the musical drama, as the perceived, the experienced and the imagined do not fit together.[30]

Situated Bodies and the Potentiality of Music

To better understand this complex situation, perspectives from another feminist icon – Simone de Beauvoir and her phenomenological understanding of 'situation' – might be useful.[31] According to Beauvoir, a body is situated by myths, representations and physical restrictions. As it serves as an instrument for change and transcendence (while also being a limiting factor), the physical body can be understood as a situation itself, functioning – as Beauvoir describes – as 'our grasp on the world and an outline for our projects'.[32] This relationship between the physical body's possibilities and restrictions on the one hand, and representational structures on the other (taking

---

[30]   As the music carves out rooms of time that have to be filled with visual content, this tension might especially occur in dances and interludes, where words and voices are lost on the way towards a sonic image or a symphonic poem. Musical interludes have often posed dramaturgical and directorial challenges, but also interpretative possibilities. See the writings of opera producer Boris Goldovsky, *Bringing Opera to Life: Operatic Acting and Stage Direction* (New York, 1968), p. 339.

[31]   As described in *Pyrrhus et Cinéas* (1944), *Pour une morale de l'ambiguité* (1947) and *Le Deuxième Sexe* (1949).

[32]   Simone de Beauvoir, *The Second Sex*, trans. Constance Borde and Sheila Malovany-Chevallier, introduction by Judith Thruman (New York, 2010), p. 49.

place in the life of every human being) creates a 'limited openness' reminiscent of the relation between the singer and a character, which has to be created anew in every production. As the character situates the singer, the body of the singer situates the character and creates an oscillation between 'having a body' and 'being a body', between the semiotic and the phenomenal body, which is simultaneously restricted and limited, open and undefined.[33]

In Salome's dance, the practical restrictions together with the framing of the fixed opera text on the one hand, and the openness represented by the need to refill and embody anew on the other, are what constitute the situation in which the body on stage and the staged body are placed. By exemplifying such a dependency, but also the tension that might be the result, the dance thus demonstrates the ongoing oscillation between physical body and representation. This tension can potentially lead the audience for a moment to leave the absorption or the 'suspension of disbelief' – the metaphysical, imaginable 'third room' – and see the bodies on stage as just that: as material spatial practices or bodies in uncomfortable situations, caught in the materiality and practicality of opera.

This does not mean that the dance has always been a tiresome affair. However, the production history of *Salome* bears witness to multiple attempts to escape the 'horror of the vacuum' and avoid the potential embarrassment through numerous directorial inventions to lead the attention away from the dancing opera singer. If not intending to replace the singer with a ballerina, directors and producers tend to cling to contexts that have surrounded the opera and fill the room with intertextual references that easily 'stick' to the music, filling the open space of representation.

A premise of opera is the understanding of music as something far from being pure or autonomous, but rather deeply influenced and inflected; it will attach itself to nearly any character, text or plot.[34] In his essay 'Rasch', Roland Barthes describes Schumann's music phenomenologically, calling music 'a field of signifying and not a system of signs'.[35] Music functions as a 'signifier' without a clear 'signified'; thus it points back at the phenomenon of interpretation and the process of meaning-making itself.[36] Nicolas Cook describes a similar characteristic of music generally, when he discusses the *potentiality* of music.[37] The music does not have meaning, he claims, for meaning is something the music *does* within the contexts in which it appears. Music can for instance convey meaning to images, but images can also

---

[33] 'Being a body' through 'having a body', the importance of the phenomenal body in the constitution of a semiotic body, is described by Erika Fischer-Lichte, *The Transformative Power of Performance: A New Aesthetics* (London, 2008), p. 82.

[34] Roger Parker, *Remaking the Song: Operatic Visions and Revisions from Handel to Berio*, Ernest Bloch Lectures (Berkeley, CA, 2006), p. 11.

[35] Roland Barthes, *The Responsibility of Forms: Critical Essays on Music, Art and Representation*, trans. Richard Howard (Oxford, 1986), p. 308.

[36] Lawrence Kramer has also recently described this phenomenon in *Interpreting Music* (Berkeley, CA, 2010), p. 19.

[37] Nicholas Cook, *Analysing Musical Multimedia* (Oxford, 1998), p. 23.

give meaning to the music, the process works both ways. As music is constantly situated and situating, it is 'never alone'. What it is inflected *by*, however, is not determined, but rather open for debate. When the music is deprived of words, as in dances and interludes, this negotiation becomes even more open. What emerges is an open representational space, whose enormous potentiality results in imaginary 'third spaces' beyond physical rooms and limited representations.

According to Peter Conrad, Salome becomes more like an image or painting when she dances.[38] This might be interpreted as some kind of limiting objectification, freezing her into an image that contributes to a stiff representation across timespans and places. However, it might also imply that the character is released from some of the representational framework constituted by the libretto and thus more open to a dialogue between the potentiality of the music and the total visual set-up on stage. Yet, as we will see later, the libretto can also be used as an interpretational basis to access archives of hidden images and suppressed stories. Moreover, the limitations set up by opera texts might be the key to fostering the radical openness and visual inventions of performance texts.

The 'Filled Slate'

What is the potential in Strauss's music for Salome's dance? While the music carves spaces of blank visuality, these rooms are also overfilled with potential meaning, stemming from the structure and musical tropes of the dance music, as well as hundreds of years of retellings of the Salome myth that have established links to historico-cultural contexts and constituted an archive of interconnections between the extra-operatic and intra-operatic.

One reference often used in the filling of this open space is the dance as an expression of European Orientalism, placing it in a line of Orientalist operas from the late-nineteenth century. As this affinity is present in structures within the opera text, especially in the score, it might be latent in every production. A solo oboe playing an embellished line that stresses the raised fourth degree is followed by a sliding chromaticism appearing over a rhythmic ostinato. Glittering timbres infuse Strauss's otherwise colourful palette of instrumentation. The use of Orientalist musical elements was explained by Strauss himself: 'operas based on oriental and

---

[38] '... she ceases to be a character and becomes an *image*, and opera turns simultaneously into a symphonic poem, into a ballet, and into a *painting*.' Conrad, *Romantic Opera and Literary Form*, p. 155, my emphases. Conrad further compares the many Salome representations with exhibits in a museum, an institution that 'equalizes all periods of time and juxtaposes the furthest reaches of space. Salome in particular unfurls into an array of images, hung in a gallery which is a shadowy mental theater where each spectator can find the fantasy which suits him' (p. 167).

Jewish subjects lacked true oriental colour and scorching sun'.[39] The composer's statement bears witness to how representations of geographical spaces and peoples in music are intimately related to imaginary 'other spaces', containing notions of something true, real and sensuously perceptible.

As Orientalist expressions have been closely connected to visual culture through exhibition, consumption and control, it is likely that the part of opera where the visual elements are most accentuated is also the part where the exotic is especially highlighted.[40] In Strauss's opera, the most Oriental-sounding music is associated with a moving body that is deprived of language and voice, as opposed to the rational thought traditionally associated in the West with the disincarnate 'masculine' mind. This opposition is underpinned in *Salome* by setting up Jochanaan's offstage male voice and bodiless head as a contrast to the silent and dancing female body. We could go even further and presume that if aural expressions represent the norm of opera, the visual form of ballet becomes the Other: a foreign medium pointing towards the strange and abnormal.[41] Established Oriental stereotypes' dependence on visuality are thus confirmed through the combination of the position of the dance as visual icon on the one hand, and the sound of oboe, tambourines, castanets and exotic scales on the other, establishing a 'musical gaze' on exotic parts of the world.

If this reference connecting intra-operatic and extra-operatic perspectives is latent in every performance of this dance, Götz Friedrich's film production from 1974 in particular plays this specific card. Here Salome, embodied by Theresa Stratas, is portrayed as an over-emotional, Oriental princess in a garish and tacky setting, surrounded by black slaves ecstatically playing jungle drums. This version becomes a caricature of Western Orientalism, a tableau similar to Jean-Léon Gérôme's detailed and colourful representations of the Arab world, where the naked, young boy's performance in *The Snake Charmer* (1870) is accompanied not just by a recorder-like instrument, but also by the eyes of a group of mercenaries, willing to pay for the entertainment. Because of the many veils covering Stratas's body and the ballet dancers encircling her (dancing a version of a south-east Asian oil-lamp dance), the opera singer does not have to move that much at all. Indeed, the body performing for the filmed spectators is not captured as the focal spot of the spectators' gaze, only by the lens of the camera. Friedrich's lenses focus just as much on the spectators as the spectacle, making the greedy eyes of the grape-eating Herod (framed by topless slaves) into an alternative object of the audience's observation. In this way, the dance certainly portrays the Oriental Salome as the

---

[39]   Richard Strauss, *Recollections and Reflections*, ed. Willi Schuh, trans. L.J. Lawrence (London, 1953), p. 150.

[40]   On Orientalism and visual culture, see Timothy Mitchell, 'Orientalism and the Exhibitionary Order', in Nicholas Mizoeff (ed.), *The Visual Culture Reader* (London, 1998), pp. 495–505; Edward W. Said, *Orientalism* (New York, 1978), pp. 118, 247.

[41]   See Daniel Albright, 'Golden Calves: The Role of Dance in Opera', *The Opera Quarterly*, 22/1 (2006): pp. 22–37.

object of the observing gaze, but it also portrays and reveals these representations' dependence on an external eye.

The combination of visual expressions and conceptions of the abnormal reappears in another contextual reference that has surrounded the Salome myth, especially from the late-nineteenth century onwards, strengthened by Wilde's connection of Salome and the moon through images of a mad, naked and desperate woman looking for lovers. The tragedy takes place the night of the full moon, the Baptist fears the night on which the moon becomes blood-red, and in turn-of-the-century writings that linked female hysteria and the lunar cycle, convulsive seizures were thought to take place during female menstruation.[42] The adolescent young girl of the Wildean/Straussian story has been interpreted as a hysterical patient from the very premiere of the opera. A journalist in *Deutsche Tageszeitung* described *Salome* as a 'symphonic poem with the translucent title Hysteria'.[43] Here *Salome*'s resemblance to a symphonic poem rather than an opera reappears. The symphonic poem does not have to follow a narrative or a literary text, but can musically illustrate a painting or landscape – a visual image. The title of this image, 'Hysteria,' could very well function as a subtitle to many of the more recent productions which have presented Salome as a wild and uninhibited person with convulsive movements, culminating in the dance, such as Petr Weigl's production at the Deutsche Oper (1990), with Catherine Malfitano. In this version, the tense coda of the dance (where the enormous crescendo stops on tremolo strings, and Salome's teasing motif is heard in flutes) is entirely devoted to portraying Salome's seemingly paroxysmal body kneeling on a raised, circled platform; her arms are outstretched and her body is covered by a transparent veil that she tears off. Surrounded by scrutinizing viewers, it recalls the events that were organized in the nineteenth century by the French neurologist Jean-Martin Charcot to display the spectacular characteristics of hysteria to an invited audience at the Salpêtrière hospital in Paris. The material spatial practice of this production can thus be seen as a representation of a particular historico–geographical space within the open-yet-situated representational spaces of the dance.

Salome's convulsions are not described in Wilde's text, however; neither do they appear in Strauss's sparse stage directions, nor in the score or in his later elaborations on how he thought the dance should be executed. Yet, these extra-textual references are nevertheless textually supported, not just by Wilde's symbolic imagery, but also by the increasing intensity of Strauss's dance music, ending in a nearly static standstill of tremolo strings, which have led interpreters (both scholars and producers) to emphasize its orgasmic qualities. These associations

---

[42]   See Janet L. Beizer, *Ventriloquized Bodies: Narratives of Hysteria in Nineteenth-Century France* (Ithaca, NY and London, 1994), p. 40.

[43]   Quoted in Anne L. Seshadri, 'The Taste of Love: Salome's Transfiguration', *Women and Music*, 10 (2006): pp. 24–44, p. 32.

confirm the connections to the diagnosis of hysteria,[44] which are furthermore sustained by other Salome portrayals both before and after the production of the drama and the opera. In this combination of production, historical contexts and reception history, increasing spasticity and wild behaviour have, similar to the Oriental clichés, become a repeated dramaturgical trope in productions of the dance, a way of visually 'filling-in' the open representational space.

Another example in similar vein appeared at the Royal Opera House in London in 1993. This production, directed by Sir Peter Hall, shows Maria Ewing as Salome who dances with more and more intensity and convulsions, and less and less clothes, before ending up completely naked under a full moon. At the climax of the dance, Ewing's gyrating, naked body is spotlit by the moonlight. When asked about the reasons for putting his ex-wife, Maria Ewing, completely naked on the opera stage (and in the less ephemeral video production), Hall's answer was: 'You cannot leave the "Dance" to the imagination'.[45] With this statement, Hall pointed right at the crux of Salome's dance: its position as something open and indescribable, a 'third space' left to imaginative elaborations and fantasies that in opera is forced to become embodied and visualized, to be moved from imagination to materiality.

In 1949, Peter Brook demonstrated another solution at the same opera house. Brook invited the surrealist artist Salvador Dali to design his production of *Salome*. Brook and Dali 'infected' the spatial material practices directly, and gave the singers handicaps and restrictions through enormous and extravagant costumes making it almost impossible to move, let alone dance. In his later writings, Brook asserted that these physical restrictions were intended: 'No singer is supposed to be a dancer', he stated, 'the more the dance could be carried by the orchestra and indicated by the singer, the less the embarrassment and the greater the illusion.' Brook thus preferred to emphasize the surrealism – the 'Other spaces' or heterotopias – as it emerged out of 'the strange, poetic and unrealistic' in the music and the libretto, which he believed should *not* be given a 'straight' visual counterpart, but which aimed to 'lift the audience into the strange Wilde–Strauss world'[46] (see Figure 5.1).

---

[44]   See, for instance, Lawrence Kramer, *Opera and Modern Culture: Wagner and Strauss* (Berkeley, CA, 2004), pp. 172–3. On the relation between hysteria and female orgasm, see Havelock Ellis, *Studies in the Psychology of Sex, Volume 1* (Rockville, 2008 [1900]), p. 160; Sander L. Gilman et al., *Hysteria Beyond Freud* (Berkeley, CA, 1993), p. 287.

[45]   Quoted in Puffet (ed.), *Richard Strauss: Salome*, p. 162.

[46]   Quotes from Peter Brook, *The Shifting Point: Theatre, Film, Opera 1946–1987* (New York, 1994), pp. 170–71.

Figure 5.1   Franz Lechleichner as Herod and Constance Shacklock as
              Herodias in the Covent Garden production of *Salome* (1949)
              produced by Peter Brook, designs by Salvador Dali
Source: Photo by Chris Ware/Keystone Features/Getty Images.

Alternative Rooms

There is definitely something strange about the abnormal rooms constructed within the fairy-tale castles of the opera houses. These 'outer-spaces' have their own gravity and concepts of reality and normality, or to paraphrase Appia, what happens there is something different from 'everyday reality'. Within these alternative rooms of opera the question of the normal and abnormal, the Other and the Same, is open for debate. *Salome* is a particularly illustrative example, as the three-bar prelude opens up a world where desire, fantasy, tonal infidelity and melodious excess are established as a norm. This fact inflects the operatic Salome's presumed position as an 'absolute Other'. Moreover, when the canonized and closed opera text encounters the premise of re-embodiment and the openness of visual recreation, the understanding of the character is doomed to be forever negotiated within the situating rooms and in-between spaces created between text and performance, past receptions and present productions.

In McVicar's production of 2008, the set design by Es Delvin moved location twice: both from the debauchery of the biblical Judaea, to the decadence of *fin-de-siècle* Europe, to the pre-War 1930s on the verge of a cultural and moral breakdown. The production shows the stage horizontally split in two. Herod's party takes place upstairs; his guests – dressed in deep-coloured silk, diamonds and pearls, sipping red wine from crystal glasses – are gathered around a beautifully decorated table. What takes place upstairs is reminiscent of a tableau; the *action*, however, takes place in the kitchen-cum-cellarage below, evoking something sterile, yet unhygienic and unsanitary. This room represents the flip side of the glossy image above, filled with dirt, violence, prostitution and malady. As the famous ostinato is heard, the large-scale set starts to move, as to initiate action, while the audience is introduced both to new material spaces and new representations of space.

Rather than seeing other characters on stage watching Salome, and thereby doubling the gaze on her and potentially objectifying her as Friedrich's version risks doing, the production takes the audience into closed rooms; yet what happens there is something we were not supposed to see. Through the use of the set and silent acting, but also by giving a visual correlative to parts of the music other than the Orientalist tropes or the frenzied crescendo, this version of the dance unveils something too. By highlighting the 32-bar Viennese waltz, which demands two dancers – both Salome and Herod – what is revealed is neither the princess's naked, hysteric or exotic body, nor the uncomfortable situation of the singer, but rather the story of a problematic and incestuous relationship. Together with Salome and Herod we move through seven different physical rooms and simultaneously through representations of their history together. Presumably inspired by the intertextual references of the story to Bluebeard's Castle's seven rooms, as well as Freudian theory linking abnormal behaviour to repressed childhood experiences, this production unveils what has happened in the locked chambers of Herod's castle. Like other productions, this one stages the dance through contexts inflecting the opera, but also on the intra-operatic frame constituted by Herod's line 'It may be that I have loved you too much'.[47]

Reviews of this production revealed the remarkably persistent conception of 'The Dance of the Seven Veils'. *The Observer* critic, Anthony Holden, wrote: 'The dance was the only scene in which the German soprano Nadja Michael's Salome

---

[47]   Oscar Wilde, 'Salomé', in *Complete Works*, pp. 552–75, p. 570.

also disappointed. But it is the only scene in which she is not required to sing.'[48] Although the review confirms the previously described in-built tension or problem of the dance, it seems that what really disappointed Holden was not Michael's performance, but rather the way in which the production deprived him of the chance to review the achievements of a performing female body situated in time, music and production on stage.[49] He overlooked how this Salome was located in other (material and represented) rooms, turning these nine minutes into a place not for seduction, but for comprehension. This was the result of possibilities offered by opera as visual and material-spatial expression, together with the open potential for visual elaborations, surrounded by a 'sticky' musical frame and clues in the libretto.

A final example also used architectonical, material rooms to tell another story within the open space of the dance. Where McVicar's *Salome* demonstrated how the concept of rooms and spaces, whether physical or representational, might imply that there is 'an outside' (or something not seen), Peter Konwitschny's 2009 production revealed how rooms can involve surveillance and/or claustrophobia. Instead of opening new rooms, this version was set in a locked and closed space. Here the Baptist was not the only one in prison; the story took place in a sealed bunker, with every character on stage from the very beginning, in a wild and highly decadent party, overflowing with sex, drugs and rock'n'roll. On reaching the waltz section of the dance, the main characters took up pencils and drew three strokes on the walls of the bunker, following the waltz metre of the music. When handles and keyholes appeared from their drawing, it became clear what their lines were intended to represent. As the music proceeded from the slow waltz to the more ecstatic crescendo, the characters started hammering on the doors they had drawn, desperately trying to get out of the room and situation. This visually portrayed confinement was supported by unifying musical and textual structures, as well as stage directions limiting everything that happened into one space. What emerged was a space *as* representation: a sealed unity of physical and representational space, supported by the reciprocal endeavours of the operatic expressions involved. Hence, the production demonstrated how the flip side of wholeness might be restriction or claustrophobia.

The Waltz

What is the matter with the accelerando 32-bar waltz setting off in C♯ minor in the middle of the dance? In several productions this is the point where the dramaturgy

---

48   Anthony Holden, 'Don't go and lose your head ...', *The Observer*, 24 February 2008, available at: http://www.guardian.co.uk/music/2008/feb/24/classicalmusicandopera. livereviews, accessed 10 February 2011.

49   My impression is primarily based on the reviewer's opening gambit, stating that 'Salome at the Royal Opera House is the least sexy she's been for years.' Ibid.

culminates or takes a new turn. Besides the productions just described, the waltz represents turning points in Hall's and Friedrich's versions as well: Ewing's convulsive body movements turn to slow motion, while Stratas loosens her hair and goes from a Turandotesque ice princess to become a hot-blooded harem-girl.

In mixing the romantic expressions of the Viennese waltz in the style of Strauss's namesake with the musical stereotypes of operatic nineteenth-century Orientalism, the dance can be seen to follow a tendency to portray the Oriental world through dance and light entertainment.[50] Robin Holloway harshly criticized the dance, labelling it 'bargain-basement Orientalism' that reaches its peak in the waltz, the place where Strauss's 'genius for bad taste' encounters the triumph of banality.[51] Yet as shown in the examples above, and due to the numerous possible interpretational spaces of the music, the waltz, when visualized in productions, can also be the opposite of kitschy Orientalism. With its clear rhythm, structural 'walls' and cultural-historical associations (i.e. its 'potentiality'), the waltz can function as a space for visual revelation outside the conceptual bonds of the text. Following a fermata in the densely written dance, it appears as a 'dance within the dance'. As a separated unit within the oceanic length of the piece, the waltz encourages a turn within the dramaturgy, an episode or section where a new relation between music and image can be established. The waltz is the point in McVicar's production where the dance actually becomes a dance – where the bodies on stage move in correspondence with the rhythm of the music. In a similar vein, in Konwitschny's version, the waltz is where the characters' situation is revealed through a visual action in accordance with the rhythmic pulse. These visual actualizations of a musical structure are realizations of the desired unity between music and image, creating a representational, imagined and occasionally experienced 'third space' of wholeness, deeply embedded in the dreams of the opera form.

Perhaps this waltz can reflect a potential function of the dance as a whole within the context of this opera: an open, but limited and bounded room constructed within the score and the libretto (the opera text), establishing a potential to be carried out in performance texts.[52] The dance becomes an intermezzo or a deferral of the action more than a climax, a space for reflection more than seduction, for retelling the story in a different way. This might also be an explanation why the most seductive music is saved for the 'perverted Liebestod' at the end of the opera, where Salome's imagination, and not her performing body, is the main agent of

---

[50]   Herbert Samuel Lindenberger, *Opera in History: From Monteverdi to Cage* (Stanford, CA, 1998), p. 186.

[51]   Robin Holloway, '*Salome*: art or kitsch?', in Puffett (ed.), *Richard Strauss: Salome*, pp. 145–60, p. 149.

[52]   The fact that the dance was written after the rest of the opera, even after the rest of the score was sent to the publisher, might be another explanation for its position as a fixed unit or an independent number, and thus a somewhat strange element within this opera otherwise written as an ongoing *Musikdrama*.

sexual arousal.[53] Let us not forget: Herod was seduced into promising Salome all she wanted not by her physical dance but by his own imagination and fantasies taking place in a heterotopic 'third space', where Salome's dance as myth has lingered, yet not without connections to the first and second spaces of materiality and representations.[54]

Conclusion: The 'Limited Openness' of Opera

Inspired by Lefebvre's spatial theories, I have argued for the usefulness of the concept of 'space' to capture the 'limited openness' of Salome's dance, but also to better comprehend the phenomenon of opera production generally. Understanding productions as rooms might refer to the multidimensionality constituted by the different forms of expressions. The way in which music creates spaces that must be filled is also implied. These are arguably more restricted in opera than in spoken theatre, as two of the walls – the music and the libretto – are consistent, one of them even determining the timing of the action.

Different kinds of walls set up in a production can certainly be limiting: to the singers, to the music, as well as to the story and overall expression. Yet, as the task of every production is to re-create within an already existing framework, these interpretations also represent a frightening openness, where the content can determine how the canonized myth or operatic work are experienced, perceived and imagined. The visual and recreational sides of opera, which might appear as a 'horror of the vacuum', or a threat to the unified experience, become, in such a perspective, the potential of operatic rooms. In a description which can be related directly to opera, Edward Soja defines Lefebvre's 'third space' as:

> a radical openness that enables us to see beyond what is presently known, to explore "other spaces" (see Foucault's *des espaces Autres* and "heteropologies") that are both similar to and significantly different from the real-and-imagined spaces we already recognize.[55]

Neither the regrettable fact that new operas are almost no longer produced (resulting in a closed canon of works), nor the fixed frames of opera texts have stopped an extreme and radical visual and contextual recreation within opera production. It is indeed this condition of opera that has turned it into a genre for interpretational radicalism via vast visual innovations, demonstrating the

---

[53]   Salome's monologue is described in this way by Michael Kennedy, *Richard Strauss* (Oxford, 1995), p. 134, and Richard Taruskin, *Music in the Early Twentieth Century*, The Oxford History of Western Music (Oxford and New York, 2009), p. 44.

[54]   His promise is made *before* she starts moving. Indeed, Narraboth states at the very beginning of the play, 'You would fancy she was dancing!' Wilde, 'Salomé', p. 552.

[55]   Soja, 'Thirdspace', p. 269.

production of potential *espaces Autres*. The paradoxical position occurs as both material spatial practices, and representational contexts have to be remodelled within the settled walls of libretto and music, which are seldom or never changed. The phenomenon of opera production can therefore exemplify the ways stronger limits and conservative conventions might provoke and demand more space and more openness in interpretations. Richard Taruskin points to this development in his provoking essay on opera production 'Setting Limits'.[56] While the textual basis, and especially the score, is considered binding and 'holy' – as a guarantee of fidelity to the author's authentic intentions and thus a way of validating the whole production – the visual performance grants unlimited licence: 'That is why we set limits. It is a perfect escape from freedom.'[57] Radical stagings of canonized operas, as represented by productions in the tradition of the *Regieoper* from the latter part of the twentieth century, are demonstrations of artistic productions voluntarily happening within a restricted freedom, the set-yet-open representational spaces of opera. Although I agree with Taruskin's observation that music in these productions is given a sacred, untouchable position, I reject his negative view, preferring its possibilities to open up feminist-inspired interpretations, as well as an understanding of canonization as a recreating, dependent practice.

As I see it, the restricted freedom, the 'closed openness' and dependent re-telling that characterize both this dance in particular, and new opera productions in general, might be *Salome*'s most important contribution to feminist opera scholarship, pointing to the paradoxical and double position that is the result of the encounter between bodies on stage and staged bodies, between past renderings and present performances, between spectator and spectacle, between music, text and visuality. These numerous 'in-between' positions (reminiscent of Beauvoir's phenomenological–representational use of 'situation') create different kinds of spatiality connecting the physical and representational, but also the spaces of negotiation emerging in the middle. This is where Salome, the character and the opera, is claustrophobically overflowing and empty at the same time.[58]

The numerous interpretations of *Salome* – on stage and in text – are the result of opera as a canonizing genre. The term 'canon' is associated with a closed set of texts that are considered to be authoritative, establishing a norm or a particular

---

[56]   Richard Taruskin, 'Setting Limits', in *The Danger of Music and Other Anti-Utopian Essays* (Berkeley, CA, 2009), pp. 447–65.

[57]   Ibid., p. 460.

[58]   As Joan W. Scott describes: 'We can write the history of that [political] process only if we recognize that "man" and "woman" are at once empty and overflowing categories. Empty because they have no ultimate, transcendent meaning. Overflowing because even though they appear to be fixed, they still contain within them alternative, denied, or suppressed definitions.' Joan W. Scott, 'Gender as a Useful Category of Historical Analysis', in Richard G. Parker and Peter Aggleton (eds), *Culture, Society and Sexuality: A Reader* (New York, 2007), pp. 61–81, p. 70.

high standard, aesthetically or technically.[59] A traditional concept of a canon is associated with something fixed, existing within established limits, and therefore often criticized as something conservative and patriarchal.[60] Yet 'canon' does not exist just as a noun; the verb 'to canonize' points to the fact that a canon must be reproduced and retold to survive. Like the phenomenon of opera production existing between the closed opera text and the openness of a performance, the concept of 'canon' straddles the open and the closed, past and present, text and performance (where performance not only means a theatrical performance, but also interpretation and the act of 'making present' in a more general sense). Hence the description of 'canon' as something closed or sealed is misleading; when dependent on re-interpretation or re-actualization, canonization also carries an openness, which is demonstrated in the canonizing, ongoing process of opera.

Working on a canonized opera thus implies that the material cannot be considered a sealed entity, but rather something open and continuously changing or adapting. As the text is reliant on actualization, it also depends on the phenomenology of the medium. Today, this fact is more evident than ever, as versions of Salome's dance are not only constantly reproduced, but also more accessible. Transferred into new forms and 'new media', opera's materiality and 'mediality' have changed dramatically: one click gives access to hundreds of different versions of 'The Dance of the Seven Veils'. Through *YouTube*'s enormous collection, but also through DVDs and television, through simulcasts or broadcasts in cinemas, what formerly would have been an oxymoron is now a certainty: today we possess an easily accessible *archive of performances*, with the potential to create new canons of (theatrical) interpretations.[61] Producers of the canonized operas will most likely have seen numerous versions, creating a background of reference and/or contrast. In addition to changes in the consumption, experience, perception and materiality of opera, mediatized versions can lead to a kind of 'operatic hermeneutics' that work across time spans and that include the visual aspect, productional contexts and particular embodiments, thus highlighting the spaces created 'in-between'. In consequence, the new mediatized existence of opera is not just *re*production, but

---

[59]   On canonization as being about both reception and reproduction, see John Guillory, 'Canon', in Frank Lentricchia and Thomas McLaughlin (eds), *Critical Terms for Literary Study* (Chicago, IL, 1995), pp. 233–49. On musical canons particularly, see Joseph Kerman, 'A Few Canonic Variations', *Critical Inquiry*, 10/1 (1983): pp. 107–25; Mark Everist, 'Reception Theories, Canonic Discourses, and Musical Value', in Nicholas Cook and Mark Everist (eds), *Rethinking Music* (Oxford and New York, 1999), pp. 378–402.

[60]   See Griselda Pollock, *Differencing the Canon: Feminist Desire and the Writing of Art's Histories* (London, 1999).

[61]   My perspective on *Salome* is, to a great extent, based on the emergence of an array of performances of the same opera text. As these extremely open and accessible archives offer the possibility to experience several variants of the same opera within a limited period of time, they have presumably changed audiences experience and consumption of opera, both in front of screens as well as in opera houses.

also production and retelling through this specific medium. As Derrida describes in his explanation of 'archive', an archive *produces* as much as it records; it is a way of making something new in the process of conservation.[62] The accessible and constantly growing archive of (mediatized) *Salome* performances confirms the productive, recreating and open process of a canon, but also demonstrates how it is bound to particularity: to individual singers and productional contexts. As emphasized in different ways through Salome's dance, it is also dependent on a perceiving and interpreting eye (and ear), either on stage, in auditoria or in front of screens, contributing to the total operatic process of making present and producing spaces.

Salome portrayed on different kinds of screens leads back to the character and her dance as some kind of frozen image (as mediatized versions of opera often have been described by the adjectives 'frozen' and 'dead').[63] When Salome dances, opera continues where words and literature end; it demonstrates its bonds to visual culture and becomes an image or a symphonic poem, revealing what has been veiled in texts and left to the imagination, but also how opera is more than representations of space and spaces of representations; it has to take place in a physical room, at a specific time and within particular bodies. This connection between the material, the representational and the imagined is actually what prevents Salome from becoming a frozen image: the premise that the production and interpretation is endless, in spite of the ends already set and established. Through the active processes of 'operatic hermeneutics' to fill and produce spaces, Salome cannot possibly be an objectified or stiff representation. Because of the operatic, open but dependent processes of canonization, she moves continuously through new material rooms, representational contexts and physical embodiments – but also through different times and media – dependent on our contribution as a curiously watching, interpreting and devoted audience and on our willingness to enter the many 'outer-spaces' of opera.

---

[62]   Jacques Derrida, *Archive Fever: A Freudian Impression*, trans. Eric Prenowitz (Chicago, IL, 1996), p. 17.

[63]   See Peggy Phelan, *Unmarked: The Politics of Performance* (London and New York, 1993); Philip Auslander, *Liveness: Performance in a Mediatized Culture* (London and New York, 1999). Discussions relating directly to opera can be found in Melina Esse, 'Don't Look Now: Opera, Liveness, and the Televisual', *The Opera Quarterly*, 26/1 (2010): pp. 81–95; Roger Parker, 'Giuseppi Verdi's *Don Carlo(s)*: "Live" on DVD', *The Opera Quarterly*, 26/4 (2010): pp. 603–14.

Chapter 6

The Dirt on Salome

Caryl Clark

> *To have dragged the sacred head of John the Baptist onto the stage, where*
> *it is abandoned to the unnatural desires of a degenerate, shameless, and*
> *wanton paramour before the eyes of the horrified audience, is the disreputable*
> *accomplishment of the English erotomaniac and aesthete Oscar Wilde.*

Max Kalbeck[1]

According to Max Kalbeck, we have Oscar Wilde and his 'sexual-pathological tendency' to blame for converting a modest biblical story into a perverted, immoral stage play. How the Salome narrative recorded in the sixth chapter of St. Mark's Gospel morphed via Wilde's imagination into a stage play of monstrous intent, eventually metastasizing into Richard Strauss's irresistibly seductive musico-drama, is now the stuff of legend. Strauss's score packs a punch of discordant and sensually decadent sounds, its aural and temporal display of shocking events and raw bodily images portrayed on stage producing an evocative allure that another early Viennese critic, Robert Hirschfeld, disgusted as he was, could not ignore: 'Where Oscar Wilde lets unpleasant thoughts drift off lightly or disappear into darkness, lest they cause us pain, the Straussian orchestra holds them fast and works them over with all the means afforded by harmonic and instrumental technique.'[2]

Explored in this chapter is another dimension of the 'sexual-pathological tendency' raised by Kalbeck. By decoupling the sexual pathology from Wilde's 'aesthete' behaviour and relocating it within the representation of Jewishness presented in the narrative itself, or more aptly, mapping it onto the individuals making up the community represented therein, I wish – with the aid of a recent powerful production – to expose other 'unnatural desires' and shameless behaviours lurking within this opera, above and beyond those displayed by Salome herself. Rather than making Salome's sexual perversity the thrust of the narrative, as

---

[1]   Max Kalbeck, *Neues Wiener Tageblatt*, 28 May 1907, cited in translation (as '*Salome*: Music Drama in One Act after Oscar Wilde, by Richard Strauss') in Bryan Gilliam (ed.), *Richard Strauss and His World* (Princeton, NJ, 1992), pp. 336–42, p. 337.

[2]   Robert Hirschfeld, *Wiener Abendpost*, 27 May 1907, cited in translation (as 'Richard Strauss's *Salome*: Premiere in Vienna at the Deutsches Volkstheater on 15 May 1907 by the Opera Society of Breslau') in Gilliam (ed.), *Richard Strauss and His World*, pp. 333–6, p. 335.

Kalbeck and many others have done, the reading offered here foregrounds another form of feminist reading, one that shifts the focus from Salome onto the elements of ethnic and familial rot residing at the core of Herod's court. That a young Jewish princess makes the bizarre request for the head of John the Baptist in exchange for dancing for her stepfather, King Herod, raises questions not only about the motivations of Salome herself, but also about the actions of those around her, including misplaced trust, patriarchal lust and mixed desires on the part of those living in this claustrophobic community. As Kalbeck rightly observed, 'unnatural desires' and wanton 'degenerate' behaviour are indeed the stuff of *Salome*; however, wantonness and degeneracy are not exclusively the domain of the title character. The 'dirt' residing within *Salome* the opera runs deep.

Typically Salome has been portrayed as a seductive *femme fatale* who poses a threat to the dominant patriarchal order. In productions extending right through the twentieth century, she emerged as a manipulative power-monger 'in the tradition of Carmen, Kundry, Dalilah, and, later, Lulu', one whose demonic beauty easily seduced a captive male audience, luring them to damnation with her eroticized, dancing body.[3] Requiring a mature, full-bodied female to perform the role vocally only complicates this characterization. How a single performer might sing the demanding vocal part while also being able to perform the 'Dance of the Seven Veils' becomes the conundrum for many a singer and director. If the eroticized dancer is understood to be *not* a voluptuous mature temptress but rather a much younger, hormonal teenager entering puberty, as was called for in the controversial production of *Salome* staged by the Canadian Opera Company (hereafter COC) in Toronto recently, the stakes are irrevocably raised.[4] For here the orientalized connotations of the *femme fatale* merge with those of a pampered, pubescent princess of Jewish origin, creating a mixture of sexual desire, ethnic difference and innocence, that, when allied to images of stimulating visuality, expose layers of textual meaning ripe for critical interpretation and revelation. Indeed, in the radical reinterpretation directed by the award-winning Armenian–Canadian film-maker, Atom Egoyan, staged in Toronto in 1996 and remounted again with minor changes in 2002, extraneous Orientalist imagery traditionally associated with the archetypal seductive woman is stripped away. The narrative is resituated to focus not only on the young princess, as attractive and seductive as

---

[3] Linda Hutcheon and Michael Hutcheon, 'Staging the Female Body: Richard Strauss's *Salome*', in Mary Ann Smart (ed.), *Siren Songs: Representations of Gender and Sexuality in Opera* (Princeton, NJ, 2000), pp. 204–21, p. 210.

[4] The Canadian Opera Company (COC) production, co–produced with Houston Grand Opera and Vancouver Opera, was premiered in Toronto at the end of September 1996, and remounted in 2002 and 2013 with different casts. For details about the earlier performances, see David J. Levin, 'Operatic School for Scandal', in Roberta Montemorra Marvin and Downing A. Thomas (eds), *Operatic Migrations: Transforming Works and Crossing Boundaries* (Aldershot, 2006), pp. 241–52, pp. 241–2 and n. 8. As discussed later in this chapter, Egoyan offers a new interpretation of the dance in his 2013 production.

she may be, but also on her dysfunctional family and the wider court community, including Herod and the five male Jews. Emphasizing Salome's youthfulness, her lithe body, her childlike playfulness, and her awakening sexual awareness and libido, alongside those who revel in her beauty, Egoyan's production of *Salome* drew a polarizing range of responses, less for its change of setting and extensive use of filmic overlay – which provoked fresh interpretations of iconic scenes – than for its savage portrayal of past sexual abuse. By trans-coding the opera to a more culturally resonant setting for postmodern audiences, Egoyan eclipses traditional narratives of the young Salome as an alluring and eroticized Orientalist princess by suggesting that the actions of this spoiled, wilful girl emerge deep from within her traumatized psyche. In other words, bodily defilement and psychic filth constitute the 'dirt on Salome'. She is victimized by the very adults charged with her protection and well-being, including her step-father, Herod, with the aid of his able-bodied henchmen, and goaded by her jealous mother, Herodias. Thus perversion resides with the elders living in the closeted community as well as with the troubled young woman. Filthy acts perpetrated by a philistine fraternity are responsible for corrupting Salome; by sadistically soiling and defiling her body, they elicit her monstrous behaviour.

The *Exotica* Backstory

Lusting after the nubile dancing female body is hardly new. Indeed, obsessive desires on the part of older men for adolescent girls have been a common theme in many films by Atom Egoyan, among them *Exotica* (1994), *The Sweet Hereafter* (1997) and *Felicia's Journey* (1999). In summing up *Exotica*, film critic Kay Armatage observes:

> The sexually violated body of one girl is found abandoned in a field; another woman, a stripper in the Exotica nightclub, routinely and indifferently performs the adolescent in schoolgirl uniform for the father of the dead girl; while a third willfully participates in another form of performance or deception, regularly "babysitting" the dead daughter for the obsessed father.[5]

In *Exotica*, a young female stripper, Christina, invokes the archetype of the innocent schoolgirl in her dance routine, a singular gesture that simultaneously heightens the dynamics between dancer and viewer (both within the diegesis and in the theatre) and the fantasies of her male viewers. When introducing her striptease act, the male announcer taunts: '… gentlemen, what is it that gives the schoolgirl her special innocence? Her sweet fragrance? Fresh flowers? Light spring rain?

---

[5]   Kay Armatage and Caryl Clark, 'Seeing and Hearing Atom Egoyan's *Salome*', in Jennifer Burwell and Monique Tschofen (eds), *Image and Territory: Essays on Atom Egoyan* (Waterloo, 2006), pp. 307–30, p. 309.

... or is it her firm young flesh inviting your every caress, enticing you to explore the deepest, most private secrets?'[6] Christina's childlike dress conjures up images of youth and innocence as well as perversity and discomfort, a double-vectored exposure that is both attractive and repulsive at the same time, simultaneously invoking pleasure in violation and the potential of paedophilia. It is little wonder then that, after seeing this film, COC general manager, Richard Bradshaw, invited the film-maker to direct *Salome* for the opera company. Translating the fetishizing of a young girl from one locale to another – from a school uniform in an exotic strip club, to seven veils in an exoticized eastern locale – was not a far stretch. Like Bradshaw, having seen *Exotica*, I was able to ponder how the lives of troubled individuals might map onto those of Salome's dysfunctional family. For I too had been captivated by the smoky, seedy, strip club scenes in *Exotica*, and Christina's cheeky dance in preppy school girl attire – short kilt and matching tie, shirt askew – with silky long hair swaying to the sound of Leonard Cohen's gruff voice declaiming 'Everybody knows' piped over the sound system.[7] How might this probing director's artistic vision translate to the dancing Salome? How would he make the transition to the opera house? Yet, ever the *provocateur*, Egoyan caught his audience off guard.

Engaging multiple perspectives is essential to reading, understanding and appreciating opera in performance. And in this particular case, Egoyan's production of *Salome* offers much to ponder, including an array of pre-recorded moving images overlaid on a live, staged set replete with costumed, singing actors engaged in acting out a musical drama. Indeed, what continues to fascinate – and haunt – me about this production is the way in which multiple methods of mediation interact within and across the production, complicating the opera's textual and visual meanings. Egoyan's added projections, images, lighting effects and a filmic choreography of the dance sequence over a minimalist set, create a rich visual overlay that invites semiotic analysis and decoding in the process of explaining submerged meanings. Always the *auteur*, film director Atom Egoyan is forever exploiting the power of the gaze in this production: of looking, and being looked at; on the prohibition of looking; on the refusal to look; on the scopic pleasure (*jouissance*) of looking and the fantasy of possession. Sophisticated video technology, film clips, live video projections, split screens, camera techniques, pseudo-home movies, superimposed images and a veiled shadow play during the dance sequence that exploits back lighting and distortion, combine with traditional aspects of operatic costuming, scenery, make-up, character and dramatic action, to compound the sensory excess and aural over-abundance so evident in the luxuriant orchestral sonorities of Strauss's *Salome*. Traced below are the primary visual inserts, which Egoyan minimally yet judiciously superimposed on the sparse sets,

---

[6]   Emma Wilson, *Atom Egoyan* (Urbana and Chicago, IL, 2009), p. 76.

[7]   As Jonathan Romney observes (here paraphrased): 'What does everybody know? There's an open secret known to all, but spoken by no one.' See his *Atom Egoyan* (London, 2003), pp. 119–21.

suggesting how adaptive technologies both redirect audience attention and impose new interpretive dimensions.

Opening Evocations, On and Off Stage

Curiously, the stage action commences before the orchestral downbeat. On a darkened stage, a shadowy figure walks along a suspended catwalk, shining a torch. In this figure's search of something (we know not what), we are alerted to themes that will unfold: suspicion, surveillance and voyeurism. In the absence of an overture, once the orchestra commences we are immediately plunged into the decadent visual and aural world of Herod's court, where a besotted young soldier, Narraboth, bathed in pale moonlight, rhapsodizes *aubade*-style about the unseen princess Salome, against the protestations of an exceedingly wary (and cross-dressed) Page.[8] Together with this now iconic opening scene, Egoyan pairs an equally evocative film sequence in which we are 'introduced' to Salome in the decadent offstage world of Herod's court: a luxurious home spa replete with massage tables, mud bath, pool and lounging area. This setting is revealed to us on a large screen overhanging the stage, and is timed to unfold progressively during Narraboth's and the Page's sumptuous musical dialogue about Princess Salome's beauty. Salome, in full-body mud wrap, is stretched out on a long white table, unmoving, looking as if she were dead. Split screen, multiple-projection images like those presented by a bank of surveillance cameras, present fragments of her unmoving, corpse-like body, reminiscent of the tantalizing snippets of musical leitmotifs presented by the gossamer-textured orchestra, rich in timbral effects. It is almost as if she were stretched out on an embalmer's preparation table, so still, so inert, so lifeless does Salome appear. (Are we witnessing a foretaste of her eulogy perhaps?) Even more disconcertingly, while hearing and learning of her beauty, we witness her voyeuristically, as if by stealth, in the process of backroom beautification. Is her much-lauded beauty only skin-deep? Are body cleansing, toning, hydrating, soothing and purification essential to the maintenance – or (self-) perception – of her (ac)claimed beauty?[9]

As the behind-scenes spa episode proceeds, repeated serial close-up images of Salome's mud-covered face emerge. White-rimmed eyes and mouth, reminiscent of Warhol-like serialized images, attest to her commodification, abstraction and alienation, further suggesting how she is viewed within the confines of the court. Indeed, her facial appearance throughout this visual sequence is reminiscent of blackface minstrel-show make-up, indicating that Salome is both a racialized and

---

[8]   The following analysis is deeply indebted to my co-authored article with film theorist and University of Toronto colleague, Kay Armatage, cited above. I wish to thank her for her insights and her friendship.

[9]   See image reproduced in Armatage and Clark, 'Seeing and Hearing Atom Egoyan's *Salome*', p. 312.

a performative figure. In the cultural background lurk images of a performative theatricality linked to the early twentieth-century music hall, cabaret and vaudeville of New York's Lower East Side. Here a disproportionate number of Jewish performers (among them Al Jolson) disguised their identity behind a mask of black cork, using theatricality as a way to mask their ethnic 'Otherness' in the process of assimilation into American society.[10] In a related gesture, Salome's offstage theatrical performance of a similarly marked body betrays deep-rooted cultural anxieties about racial inferiority, if not gender inadequacy and perceived impurity. Reinforcing this ethnic representation in the opening scene is the offstage 'noise' and din associated with the argumentative Jews quarrelling among themselves, sounded by the orchestra and commented on by nearby soldiers. Their restless, gesticulating theatricality, suggested by leaping, jabbing accompaniment gestures in the orchestra (marked 'etwas lebhafter' ['più mosso'] at Rehearsal Figure 4), provide an appropriate aural link to the ethnic representation being depicted in the video montage, in marked contrast to the princess's immobility. Salome wears the markers of her ethnicity and heritage on her body, but appears deaf to its sounds. Her dancing, theatrical body is only the stuff of hearsay at this stage. In contrast to the demonstration of male bonding emanating from the banquet hall, gender, sexuality and age dictate her (in)action while prescribing her identity.

By contrast, as if on cue, Salome's seemingly lifeless body 'awakens' from its culturally repressed slumber at the sound of John the Baptist's voice. The seemingly comatose princess suddenly opens her eyes precisely when, from a distance, Jochanaan's otherworldly voice emerges from the depths of the cistern. Penetrating her aural sphere like a divine revelation, Jochanaan's resounding disembodied voice intrudes upon Salome's space, summoning her into action. Jochanaan sings: 'When He comes the blind shall see',[11] and as if obeying some inner command, Salome's eyes open and dart about as if assessing her situation. Where is she? What is she hearing? How does this voice differ from the howling and grating ones she has been accustomed to hearing in her midst? Onstage, an attendant shines a light into the cistern from which Jochanaan's voice emerges. His voice is marked as different, and presumably not because it is allied to a foreign tongue but because of its special aurality.

Suddenly, Salome leaps off the table, and dives into the pool. Rinsing off her mud-caked body as if engaging in an act of ritualistic cleansing or rite of purification,

---

[10] By disavowing their own heritage and 'acting' or 'passing' as African Americans (white Negroism), Jewish immigrants were able to elevate their own social status vis-à-vis urban 'Others' with whom they were competing to become Americans. See Jeffrey Melnick, *A Right to Sing the Blues: African Americans, Jews and American Popular Song* (Cambridge, MA, 1999); Andrea Most, *Making Americans: Jews and the Broadway Musical* (Cambridge, MA, 2004). I am grateful to my research assistant Cynthia Smithers for bringing the former study to my attention, and for aiding my research both at the University of Toronto, and at the Archives of the Canadian Opera Company.

[11] 'Wenn er kommt, werden die Augen der Blinden den Tag sehen.'

her action might even be construed as a nascent baptismal image. Certainly Salome occupies an ambiguous position with respect to her Jewishness, attracted as she is to the prisoner Jochanaan, including his (caricatured) profession of the beliefs and tenets of Christianity, which are simultaneously new, foreign and alluring to her. While others are dismissive and uncomprehending, she at least appears open to – if not predisposed to (impressed by Egoyan's imagery) – hearing the prisoner. Her liminal position mirrors that of the brief story of Salome recounted in the Bible, which is wedged between Christian baptismal and conversion narratives in the Gospel of St. Matthew. The dirt she washes off – which we come to understand later is meant to cleanse her of her sexual defilement – is here, at least initially, understood as a marker of her Jewishness. At the conclusion of this opening visual sequence, as if to reinforce the image of purity, baptism and the cleansing of one's sins, Salome wraps herself in a white robe, exits the spa, runs out the door into a darkened woods (a preternaturally lit stage), and into view of the audience.

Thus before we even meet Salome on stage, we have been provided with much information about her both through the conversations of Narraboth and the Page, and through filmic imagery. We already understand her to be a racialized figure, an object of infinite examination and surveillance, sensually pampered, luxuriously privileged; she is a locked up and heavily guarded princess/prisoner who is able to identify with Jochanaan, that other prisoner at court. We also have a premonition of potential violence presented through the technologies of visual representation and mediation. Her mud-covered torso suggests an abject, dirty, defiled body. In the private, interior, offstage moments, Salome is anything but the beautiful young princess of legendary fame.

Upon entering the stage (in scene 2), Salome runs to her swing. A curious, inquisitive young teenager, who apparently has only recently left her girlhood behind, she is anxious to know more about this new prisoner at Herod's court. Unlike the others, she comprehends a special quality in Jochanaan's voice. Does she comprehend his words and their semantic meaning, or does she merely hear his vocalizing? Certainly she identifies with Jochanaan, and experiences the oracular quality and divination of his voice: a disembodied voice that seems to be communicating directly to her. His voice – deep, clear, and calm – is unlike the other male voices she is accustomed to hearing, and it is this difference that attracts her.

The Orphic presence of Jochanaan's voice is symbolized by a colossal visual presence, in which the aural dissolves into the visual. Huge lips, teeth, and tongue are projected on a large screen in real time. To create this visual effect, the singer is captured in the act of singing, standing a few inches away from a camera in the orchestra pit, and this image is projected larger than life onto an onstage screen. The enormity of the image of Jochanaan's mouth, however, is for us alone; it is a giant projection of what Salome hears and imagines. Its singularity, power and divine aura – qualities manifested in its musical majesty (mock or otherwise) – intrude upon the aural soundscape. This is a commanding voice, especially for one unaccustomed to deliberate and steady delivery, deep register and rhetorical nuance. Captivated by this 'new' and different voice, Salome hovers over the cistern, curious as to its source, its origin. Even after she orders the prisoner to be brought out of the cistern so she can marvel at him – eulogizing first about his body, then his hair, and finally his mouth – it is the source of his vocalizing that continues to captivate her. Although eventually repulsed by his hideous body and horrible filthy hair, Salome continues to fixate on Jochanaan's mouth. Her idealization of his mouth is then represented in her inscribing of an abstracted, idealized version of it. In tracing a large pair of red lips – uncannily reminiscent of Man Ray's famous floating lips – on a nearby wall, she is already obsessed by 'the kiss'.[12]

This lingering kiss image continues to haunt her as Jochanaan disappears from view into the cistern. As Salome staggers around the stage at the beginning of the long musical interlude (Rehearsal Figures 141–154), another large projection appears on a rear wall where Jochanaan's mouth had been. A female mud-caked body lies askew in the frame, smothered in thick lumpy dirt, reminiscent of Dead Sea mud. Rather than the aestheticized, cleansing mud of the home spa, this projection is more sinister; it is an image of impurity and defilement. As the orchestral interlude continues, the real-life Salome adopts a similar pose on the stage. Desolate and menacing, it is an image of Salome's inner state, her abject acknowledgement of her own psychic filth.

Why this troubling image of abjection? Why is Salome so obsessed with her filthy body, so self-absorbed with her dirty nakedness? What has traumatized her so? In Egoyan's interpretation, Salome's abasement results from her victimization. Sexualized violence perpetrated by her male guardians triggers her physical and mental anguish, and her subsequent actions. By exposing and clarifying the gendered power imbalance between male parent and female child, and other parameters of female vulnerability, this production blames Salome's transgressive desire for Jochanaan squarely on the misogynistic and paedophilic actions of Herod and his courtiers. As we slowly come to understand, a brutalized and debased Salome, suffering in silence, acts out against intolerable injustices, seeking revenge against those who wield the power in her world: Jewish men.

Jewish Barbarism

There is no way of getting around it: Strauss's representation of Jews in *Salome* is deeply problematic. As Sander Gilman has noted, in setting Wilde's text, Strauss not only signalled his break with Wagnerism, he also identified the cultural avant-garde with Jewishness. Aware that in setting Wilde's play to music in Germany he was writing an 'Orient- und Judenoper', one in which the characters of the opera would be understood as 'stage Jews' with all their intimation of disease

---

[12]   A black and white image of the lips is reproduced in Armatage and Clark, 'Seeing and Hearing Atom Egoyan's *Salome*', p. 316.

and difference, Strauss was able to capitalize on early twentieth-century society's perception of the perverted sexuality of both homosexual and Jew. As Gilman explains, the perverted discourse of the Jew – his language (Yiddish), tone, articulation, jargon, and gesturing, in other words, *Mauscheln* – is inexorably linked with the polluted language of sexual pathology and the homosexual.[13] Salome's perversion, manifested as sexual hysteria through her sadistic desire 'to possess a fetish, the severed head of a man who rejected her' was understood to have 'its origin in the trauma of her attempted seduction by her stepfather, Herod.'[14] The supposed predisposition of the Jewish race – male and female – for hysteria, understood in late-nineteenth-century terms as arising from 'inbreeding', lies at the core of the opera. Perverted Jewish sexuality and criminal incest are intertwined and embedded within both Wilde's play and Strauss's opera.

In Wilde's play, the Jews are presented as engaging in a particularly 'noisy' form of discourse. In Strauss's opera, this characterization is translated into a similarly noisy and discordant musical language. In the opening scene of the opera, for instance, we are unceremoniously introduced to the bickering offstage Jews, the quarrelsome Pharisees, whose 'howling' clamour contrasts with the luxuriant, shimmering orchestral soundscape associated with the radiant moonlight and the young princess's beauty. The noisiness of the arguing Jews, depicted initially by the orchestra, is later manifested in the banquet hall (scene 4) by a quintet of male singers (the only ensemble in the opera), who partake in a gargantuan parody of Jewish speech and behaviour. Arguing among themselves about the identity of the prisoner and his powers as compared with those of God, the Five Jews participate in a raucous display of pseudo-knowledge, sophistry and pedestrian nit-picking.

Herod too is linked to this caricature. Indeed, the leitmotif allied to offstage quarrelling and Jewish hysteria introduced in the opening scene accompanies Herod's hasty arrival onstage alongside Herodias in scene 4. His short, stuttered enquiries about Salome's whereabouts contrast starkly with those of others, including Narroboth's highly emotional utterances heard earlier, Herodias's dispassionate ones, and Jochanaan's expansive – if overly serious and even pedantic – diatonic pronouncements.[15] Abrupt modulations, unstable whole-tone

---

[13] Sander L. Gilman, *Disease and Representation: Images of Illness from Madness to AIDS* (Ithaca, NY, 1988).

[14] Ibid., p. 168.

[15] As Bryan Gilliam notes: 'the general public failed to understand Strauss's lack of sympathy for John the Baptist and, as late as the 1930s, the composer believed he still needed to explain that he had composed Jochanaan "as a clown", because "a preacher in the desert, especially one who feeds on locusts, seems infinitely ridiculous to me. Only because I had already caricatured the five Jews and also poked fun at Father Herod did I feel I had to follow the law of contrast and write a pedantic–Philistine motif for four horns to characterize Jochanaan".' See Bryan Gilliam, 'Strauss and the sexual body: the erotics of humour, philosophy, and ego-assertion', in Charles Youmans (ed.), *The Cambridge Companion to Richard Strauss* (Cambridge, 2010), pp. 269–79, p. 276.

melodies, high tenor register, and a wayward, restless and rapid vocal delivery associate the Tetrarch with 'nervosität' and representations of the highly strung, effeminate Jewish male. These symptoms of hysteria and neurasthenia map onto his lust and incestuous desire for Salome.[16] Wracked with hallucinations, perceptions of strange howling sounds and paranoia, Herod clings to normality by a slender thread. Indeed, his closest relatives on stage are not his wife Herodias, or his step-daughter Salome, but his fellow Jews; they are members of his tribe, his band of brothers.

Strauss's caricature of the five disputing Jews easily builds on this stereotype. This quintet of four high tenors and a bumbling comic bass, utilizes high tessitura, hemiola effects, Dorian mode (associated with Jewish folksong), and the nasal sound of an accompanying oboe – all within the context of a skittish scherzo – to reinforce the stereotype musically. Initially they debate with Herod about his refusal to release the prisoner, Jochanaan, making their arguments one after another in an orderly, if awkward, manner. Jagged melodies and shifting, asymmetrical metres mark their successive statements (Rehearsal Figures 188–204). But as the debate progresses and the discussion grows more heated and more animated, any vestiges of civilized conversation begin to crumble as all five reiterate their arguments one on top of the other. Eventually, they all speak simultaneously, underscored by increasing orchestral activity and dynamic levels, resulting in a cacophonous morass of competing contrapuntal lines and textual unintelligibility.[17] Their argumentative style, assuming the form of selfish, animalistic behaviour lacking in emotional depth and feeling, sets them apart. But despite the apparent confusion, they understand one another within their fraternal circle. Although communicating incoherently and blatantly stereotypically to those observing them, they are communicating with and to one another, clearly comprehending the intent of one another's gestures and arguments.

Herodias blurts out a call for silence, eventually breaking up the boisterous babble. But it is Herod who continues this behaviour subsequently, aping their style in the highest tenor register of all. His vocal line leaping about erratically and frenetically, he is the very physical embodiment of his nervous, superstitious, degenerate physicality. Following the quintet, he responds to Jochanaan's 'comforting diatonicism' with 'jarring dissonance'; for Gilman,

---

[16]   See Anne L. Seshadri, 'The Taste of Love: Salome's Transfiguration', *Women & Music*, 10 (2006): pp. 22–44, pp. 31–2.

[17]   Cleverly hidden within the tumultuous texture and screaming clamour is the fourth Jew's observation about the Greeks and Gentiles not being circumcised ['beschnitten'], which occurs on a high B, the highest vocalized pitch in the entire passage. As Gilman observes, in the late-nineteenth century, the act of circumcision was associated 'with the act of castration, the unmanning of the Jew by making him a Jew.' Sander L. Gilman, 'Strauss, the Pervert, and Avant Garde Opera of the Fin de Siècle', *New German Critique*, 43 (1988): pp. 35–68, p. 57.

'Herod is (musically) no more than another Jew.'[18] And it is this ethnic, sexual and behavourial link that Egoyan makes so palpable in his production, by marking the Jewish brotherhood fraternally and professionally.

In Egoyan's production, all five Jews are linked to the medical profession. Clad in white laboratory coats, they are seen administering medication to the Tetrarch, suggesting that we are to understand them as doctors or apothecaries, professions long associated with Jewish men.[19] But these professionals also bear the taint of chicanery and quackery. For inside their pristine lab coats they carry large caches of drugs, their garments concealing what appear to be illicit and illegal substances, which they dispense to their pathetic patient at will. We witness them offering Herod what appears to be cocaine, and injecting him with medication to control his agitation and anxiety, much as a hit of heroin acts upon a drug addict (see Plate 5). All suggests that Herod's hallucinations and spectral hauntings are not so much the responses of a weak and fearful ruler but the chemically induced ravings of a drug addict experiencing symptoms of being high or in withdrawal. Depicting the Five Jews as high-class drug pushers to the wealthy Tetrarch forges a link between 'the Jewish Occupation' and unethical behaviour. By engaging in fraudulent and illegal acts, together they condone one another's actions. This brotherhood thrives on illicit behaviour.

Herod, their patient, is the sixth Jew in all but name. Manipulated and 'treated' by pseudo-medical practitioners/pharmacists – pill-pushing and needle-wielding 'healers' – Herod comes across as the weakest member of this male fraternity. Engaged in actions of reciprocal dependency, and understanding one another implicitly, they are bound up in each other's crimes. Herod and his henchmen speak the same fraternal language in word and deed, their actions suggesting that, when together, they comprehend one another clearly and act in consort, as the traumatic explanation offered in the 'Dance of the Seven Veils' reveals.

All is 'Revealed'

Salome's dance has been pivotal (as discussed throughout this volume) not only to productions of the opera, but in countless visual and filmic interpretations from the earliest days of cinema. Dance, striptease, sexualized performance, erotic titillation, nudity, hyperbolized kitsch are all images and sensations associated with the spectacle of looking at the female body and the power of the male gaze. As Lawrence Kramer and Linda and Michael Hutcheon have observed, Salome

---

[18]   Ibid.

[19]   For an overview of this history, see John M. Efron, *Medicine and the German Jews: A History* (London and New Haven, CT, 2001).

accrues power during the dance precisely through being the object of that gaze, which in turn allows for her unequivocal demand for the head of Jochanaan.[20]

Egoyan's version of the erotic dance spins the apparatuses of looking into an unusual new realm. Rather than putting the spectacle of the diva's body on display, the director turns Salome into a prop. Seated on her iconic swing, a symbol of her youthfulness (or her pole-dancing prowess?), she is hoisted up into the flies as the famous dance music begins, her dress unfurling to become a giant scrim covering the front of the stage near the proscenium. Onto this large screen, which is made up of seven pieces of cloth sewn together, a startling multivalent version of the 'dance' ensues. Akin to other modes of visual representation encountered thus far, this representation too is fragmentary, hallucinatory, gestural, and it tells another story altogether. Indeed, it deepens the psychopathology of the central character while delimiting the complexity of her character. All along, Egoyan has prepared us for the possibility that Salome's 'pathology originates in some offstage space and medium as well', as David Levin observes: 'here the by now clichéd notion that Salome is the child of her psychoanalytically rife environment is retooled for the twenty-first century.'[21]

Allied to an orchestral echo of Salome's youthful leitmotif is an image of a young girl on a swing, facing the camera and smiling broadly. Similar to a home-movie or amateur video that we are all familiar with, especially nowadays with *YouTube*, this film sequence introduces us to an earlier, much younger Salome. Innocent and carefree, this Salome suggests a simpler, happier time: the wind gently blows through her fine hair as she swings back and forth, back and forth, in the sunshine.

Soon thereafter we see a blindfolded young girl alone in the woods, reminiscent of countless fairy tales, and the peril they portend. And sure enough, as Salome begins walking (on a treadmill), and a forest landscape moves eerily and independently in the background (the two images superimposed one over the other), Herod emerges downstage in front of the scrim, torch in hand, following her. The shaft of light, always a controlling element in cinema, suggests knowledge, power and penetration; in this narrative, dominated as it is by the danger of the gaze, coupled with the safety of blindness, lurks the anxiety of the unknown. When the child suddenly removes her blindfold and gazes on the grown-up Salome, the true dance begins.

Commencing at the waltz theme in C♯ minor, a shadow play of a pseudo-dance unfolds behind a backlit screen. Hidden from plain view, and masked by the dress-cum-scrim, denying audience members direct access to the spectacle, a ghostly spectre of a dance ensues. From our perspective, it appears that the dancer's seemingly naked body is performing for Herod and the other male Jews.

---

[20] Lawrence Kramer, 'Culture and musical hermeneutics: The Salome complex', *Cambridge Opera Journal* 2/3 (1990): pp. 269–94, p. 272 and fn. 8; Hutcheon and Hutcheon, 'Staging the Female Body', pp. 204–21.

[21] Levin, 'Operatic School for Scandal', p. 243.

The backlighting transforms the actors on stage into silhouettes, mere shadows projected in two dimensions across a gauze-like screen: a low-tech yet high-impact circuit of access and denial of vision, visibility and mediation. Herod's henchmen appear either larger than life or diminishing in size depending on their position vis-à-vis the light source. As Salome's dancing actions become ever-more frenzied, her tiny, sharply focussed silhouette in the foreground is dwarfed by those of her pursuers, who appear as hulking monsters on the screen (see Figure 6.1). The power imbalance in numbers and size increases the sense of danger. As the music builds towards its bombastic conclusion, the girl is hoisted up, swirled round over the heads of the men, and then thrown to the floor where she is gang raped by Herod and his men. Out of sight of the others at court, the unthinkable happens, and the audience, the horrified voyeurs to this despicable act of violence, sits dumbstruck in its seats, its complicity made evident through its very act of silence.

For the 2013 revival, Egoyan collaborated with Clea Minaker, a Montreal-based shadow designer and puppeteer, to re-imagine the dance sequence. Together they incorporated subtle changes that work to dissipate the depiction of sexual assault. While Egoyan's original film images are retained, their effect is softened by two major innovations: first, the addition of a carousel of dancing ballerinas projected onto the scrim on which the film narrative of the young Salome unfolds; and secondly, a retooling of the original choreography and gang rape scene now filtered through Minaker's gossamer design aesthetic. Like the child's swing, the miniature carousel of ballerinas Salome plays with downstage left prior to the dance is further testimony to her youth. Suggestive of miniature music-box ballerinas, these little whirling white figurines provide a measure of agency to Salome even as they portend her fate. Later, when lit from below and projected larger than life onto the scrim, these shadowy figures create a sense of beauty, sensuality and wonder in conjunction with the menacing image of the darkened forest and leering glare of the lurking Herod, foreshadowing the trapped dancer and sexual violence to come. With the commencement of the behind-the-scenes shadow play (at the move to C♯ minor), further enhancements ensue. Here, the dance no longer unfolds in front of a single large, direct light source; rather, moving lights behind the scrim pan in and out following the frenetic figure in a flickering fashion, making her movements less visible, the actions of her attackers less direct, and the rape less literal, less illustrative. The whole effect is more distancing viscerally and emotionally. Instead of bludgeoning the viewer, Egoyan and Minaker offer a reinterpretation that is more nuanced, and possibly even more powerful for having been rendered more suggestive.[22]

---

[22]   As Egoyan and Minaker explain in a recent interview, rather than the focus of the scene being about finding some justification for Salome's horrific behaviour, 'this time, the dance is composed for the image; it's not a dance with light on it. We're in her mind, we're on her body, we're with her movement'. See J. Kelly Nestruck, 'Salome: Take Three', *The Globe and Mail*, 18 April 2013.

Figure 6.1 A scene from the Canadian Opera Company's production of
      Salome, 2002
Source: Photo by Michael Cooper.

Is it any wonder that Salome seeks revenge? As an abuse survivor, can we blame her for seeking reprisal? At the very end of the scene, at the point where in traditional productions Salome might posture suggestively over the opening to the cistern, the image returns again to the essential question of the gaze. It devolves into an extreme close-up of a human eye, or iris, at the centre of which is projected the initial image of the little girl smiling broadly at the camera, after which the final octaves of the dance tumble down helter-skelter through the orchestra, and the screen-dress collapses. Is her gaze triumphant? Is it accusatory? Is the child-Salome smiling out at the camera already the victim of domestic abuse? How long, might we ask, has this been going on? Clearly, irrevocably, the homosocial bonds formed by the Jewish men in her midst have created a climate tolerant of acts of powerful domination and control. Aggression and humiliation, submission and perversity, lying and concealment, sadomasochism and sexual assault; they are all part of a despicable arsenal of intimidation and sexual control employed by a loathsome male brotherhood. In an attempt to overcome their own perceived inadequacies and insecurities, and their own depressive behaviours, Herod and his male compatriots work together to mutually empower one another by marking their own masculinity. Fraternal brotherhoods function this way.[23] Hiding behind their own sexual insecurities and dependences, the six Jews, under Herod's weak and drug-crazed leadership, mark their own tenuous grasp of masculinity by engaging in acts of violent sexual assault and depravity, encouraged by a code of brotherly silence, support and sexual gratification. Could there be a more provocative testament of perversion?

Radical stagings such as this one are commonplace today. As Mary Ann Smart, David Levin, Clemens Risi and many others have observed, inventive stagings and director-driven opera productions (*Regietheater*) are the new norm.[24] Restagings of canonic operas are now requiring that we study opera *in* and *as* performance, what Carolyn Abbate has termed the 'drastic', or the 'doing' of opera.[25] In order to embrace opera's liveness and multiple avenues of mediation, it is necessary to invent yet again a new set of analytical tools, ones that take into account assumptions about opera's contingencies, its performative aspects and its intermedial dimensions, in order to understand more deeply how opera communicates, how a work changes over time and accrues new meanings, what an opera has meant at various times in history, and how audiences experience opera (i.e., how individuals receive what is transmitted to them, and what they might

---

[23] The classic text here is Eve Kosofsky Sedgwick, *Between Men: English literature and male homosocial desire* (New York, 1985). On the politics of incest in Egoyan's films, see Melanie Boyd, 'To Blame her Sadness: Representing Incest in Atom Egoyan's *The Sweet Hereafter*', in Burwell and Tschofen (eds), *Image and Territory*, pp. 275–93.

[24] David J. Levin, *Unsettling Opera: Staging Mozart, Verdi, Wagner, and Zemlinsky* (Chicago, IL, 2007).

[25] Carolyn Abbate, 'Music – Drastic or Gnostic?', *Critical Inquiry*, 30/3 (2003): pp. 505–36.

take away). Increasingly this means we have to understand how opera is mediated through technology, whether in HD-Broadcasts 'live' from the Metropolitan Opera in New York, transmitted and mediated through the videographer's art (with simultaneous translation via supertitles), or in revisionist stagings, what David Levin terms 'strong' productions in *Unsettling Opera*. As Gundula Kreuzer and Ryan Minor, the organizers of the joint conference 'Beyond Opera: Staging Theatricality' held at Stony Brook and Yale in April 2010, observed, today we have a new 'ecosystem' for opera. Like Baroque stage machinery, new technologies employed in opera create new modes of production mechanics, materiality and interaction that are continually opening up new interpretive dimensions. Developing in our midst is a musicology of presence.

The new technologies and devices employed by Egoyan in the COC's production of *Salome* open up hitherto unsuspected interpretive potentialities. What is fascinating, however, is the ways in which these new interpretive mediations employed by Egoyan resonate with aspects of the Dresden premiere. As Anne Seshadri notes, audiences at the premiere understood the work as a 'Jewish opera', and the inhabitants of Herod's court as 'the unchanging racialized Other'.[26] In contrast, some saw Salome as transcending her Jewishness, and by the opera's end as possibly even undergoing a transfiguration, ending with her conversion to Christianity (thus necessitating her martyr-like death). Nearly a century later, aspects of Egoyan's production resonate with and complicate these observations and interpretations. While reinforcing Salome's Jewish ethnicity, his production also exploits traditional imagery to offer other possibilities: indeed, the dirt on her body marks not only her ethnicity, but also her bodily defilement and loss of virginity to the powerful yet misguided men charged with her care. Rather than being reduced to a seductive *femme fatale* figure or a hysterically decadent woman, Egoyan's Salome emerges as a youthful and sympathetic character, an adolescent who is tragically molested and abused both physically and psychologically. Her pettiness, petulance and stubbornness, which may be understood as markers of Jewish difference, are here also allied to a sexually defiled body; as such, Salome is to be understood as an abused young woman who cannot be fully responsible or accountable for her actions. Guilt must also reside with her patriarchal masters, who defile her body while engaging in oppressive ritualistic acts of homosocial bonding. And this is where Egoyan's production succeeds in pushing the boundaries of the art form, by exposing and problematizing aspects of Jewish identity, or identities, latent in the work. Having been implicated in these crimes of silence enacted on the innocent, the audience is forced to ask itself at the opera's end: what other misdemeanours might we be guilty of hiding behind a veil of secrecy? The simplicity of the filmic mediation layered over the opera is employed to profound ends in this provocative production of misplaced passion and possession. This is indeed a *Salome* for our times.

---

[26]   Seshadri, 'The Taste of Love', p. 24.

Chapter 7
Outrageous Salome:
Grace and Fury in Carmelo Bene's *Salomè* and Ken Russell's *Salome's Last Dance*

Tristan Grünberg

My business as an artist was with Ariel. You set me to wrestle with Caliban.

Oscar Wilde, *De Profundis*[1]

Salome on Screen: Sensuality and Censorship

Since her first appearance on the stage, Oscar Wilde's Salomé has continuously found new playgrounds, from Aubrey Beardsley's illustrations to Richard Strauss's opera. Cinema, whose birth is contemporary to the premiere of the play, also chose Salome to be one of its favourite heroines. Thus every decade has brought to the screen new adaptations of Wilde's play, whether Hollywood blockbuster or avant-garde film.

In 1918, J. Gordon Edwards directed the first feature-length *Salome*. The film, now lost, starred Theda Bara, well known for being the first true *vamp* of the history of cinema.[2] The only photographs and posters remaining from the production show her covered in jewels and translucent veils, both seductive and dangerous, sophisticated and savage. A few years later, in 1923, Alla Nazimova, Russian actress turned Hollywood star, produced an experimental version of *Salome*, adapted from Oscar Wilde, inspired by Aubrey Beardsley's aesthetics and directed by Charles Bryant. Extremely modern and erotic, the film was judged scandalous, thus ending Nazimova's career on the screen. In these times of moral censorship, Salome had to make herself discreet, only appearing in toned-down versions where her scorching sensuality was to be condemned nevertheless.

In the 1950s, the Hollywood studios found new interest in filming Biblical episodes. From *The Robe* (Henry Koster, 1953) to *The Ten Commandments* (Cecil B. DeMille, 1956), from *Ben Hur* (William Wyler, 1959) to *Solomon and Sheba* (King Vidor, 1959), these blockbusters drew large audiences to the movie

---

[1]   Oscar Wilde, 'De Profundis', in *Complete Works of Oscar Wilde* (London and Glasgow, 1948, reprinted 1977), pp. 873–957, p. 939.

[2]   In 1915, she appeared as a *femme fatale* named 'The Vampire' in *A Fool There Was* (Frank E. Powell, USA).

theatres. But it was time for Salome to make a new and dashing appearance. In 1953, directed by Wilhelm Dieterle, *Salome* saw Rita Hayworth – whose fiendish strip-tease in *Gilda* (1946) made her a perfect fit for the part of the oriental dancer – put Salome back on her pedestal with an epic and memorable 'Dance of the Seven Veils',[3] Hayworth at the peak of her sensuality. But this 'excessive' display of eroticism is finally repressed, as Salome atones for the beheading of John the Baptist. Betraying the true essence of Salome, the only woman in the New Testament who does not provide a promise of redemption, the epilogue of the film shows the former sinner, all dressed in white, suddenly touched by divine grace as she listens to Jesus spreading the Word.

Whether she is blacklisted or turned into a repentant figure, Salome, or her representation, has asserted herself as a symptom of society's moral standards. Both rebellious and submissive to men's desire, Salome has been perceived as much as a proto-feminist as the exemplary personification of a devilish woman.[4] Indeed, as she is not afraid to express her desires and refuses to obey the laws of men, she can be read and staged as a feminist icon. But the deadly outcome of her impulses and the way in which she uses Herod's lust to lead Jokanaan towards his end is typical of the vamp's modus operandi. Thus branded with the stamp of depravity, she dives with delight into the lake of fire and brimstone, proclaiming herself a truly transgressive figure. As such, the 1970s underground European cinema, characterized by its rebellion against sexual repression and academic cinema, welcomed her with open arms. From Germany (Werner Schroeter and Götz Friedrich) to Spain (Rafael Gassent and Pedro Almodovar), from France (Pierre Koralnik and Teo Hernandez) to England (Clive Barker), Oscar Wilde's play and main character became an ethical and aesthetic emblem of avant-garde cinema.

Indeed, the character of Salome finds a new relevance each time the fight against moral order and middle-class 'good taste' is awakened. Fundamentally excessive and subversive, sexually and morally ambiguous, she is able to reverse moral values and the balance of power. In Oscar Wilde's play, ambivalence prevails each time Salome's figure is seen through the lustful or the hateful gaze: between violence and naivety, harmony and chaos, she is, in the eyes of the young Syrian or of Jokanaan, 'the shadow of a white rose in a mirror of silver',[5] as much as the 'daughter of Babylon'.[6] Her power and her mystery lie in her ability to reconcile these opposing qualities.

---

[3]   The Armenian–Canadian director Atom Egoyan, strongly impressed by the figure of Salome, used this scene in *Felicia's Journey* (1999, Canada) where it reflects upon the main character's sadistic impulses. For details of Egoyan's vision of Salome, see Caryl Clark's chapter in this volume.

[4]   See Petra Dierkes-Thrun, *Salome's Modernity: Oscar Wilde and the Aesthetics of Transgression* (Ann Arbor, 2011), pp. 161–96.

[5]   Oscar Wilde, 'Salomé', in *Complete Works*, pp. 552–75, p. 553.

[6]   Ibid., p. 558.

This true essence of Wilde's *Salomé* was never better transposed to the screen than by Carmelo Bene and Ken Russell, two of the most unusual European directors. At different times, in different countries and, most of all, within different aesthetics, both directors gave Salome a cinematographic existence by capturing, through filmic means, her animal grace and ancient fury. Thus, this chapter will examine the ways in which Carmelo Bene's *Salomè* portrays the figures of Temptation and Punishment, leading the Biblical episode into the land of myth and tragedy, while Ken Russell's *Salome's Last Dance*, vacillating between Transgression and Sacrifice, dives into farce and the grotesque.

As much as these two films have in common – Oscar Wilde's story, words and characters used as their main canvas, their poetics of excess (both visual and sound), their use of colours as an expression of desire and death in progress, their display of artificiality, their explicit staging of sexual ambiguity (if not ambivalence) – they also take different paths within Salome's tale, always highlighting her incredible and frightful eroticism. If reversal and masquerade are central in both films, each of them makes different use of Wilde's play, comprehended as a living material, waiting to be shaped.

Carmelo Bene (1937–2002) was an Italian playwright and director who deserted the stage from 1967 to 1974, years during which he devoted himself to the cinema. *Salomè*, released in 1972, was his fourth film, and the story was freely adapted from that of the Irish poet. Indeed, Bene was engaged in a true enterprise of deconstruction of the play. First of all, Salome and Jokanaan become secondary characters, whereas Herod, interpreted by Bene himself, takes the centre of this cinematographic stage. One of the consequences of this change is that the two climactic and iconic episodes of Salome's dance and of Jokanaan's beheading are absent, or rather they appear only in disguise. Moreover, new characters haunt the film, as a poetic and oracular echo to the tale. Thus, the film starts with a sensual duo where a silent woman, covered in jewels, tries to seduce a Christian hermit who only succeeds in resisting the temptress thanks to his love of God (see Plate 6).[7] This scene, that seems to play out in advance Salome's seductive plea to Jokanaan, is extracted from an unfinished play by Oscar Wilde, *La Sainte Courtisane*, in which Myrrhina, an Alexandrian noblewoman, charms Honorius before being converted by his faith. Finally, Jesus Christ himself, who is only mentioned in the play, appears on several occasions in the film, wearing impressive vampire fangs at his Last Supper. This game of duplication and disappearance, of displacement and condensation – heir to Wilde's symbolism – emphasizes the violence of temptation, the symptoms of which are the multiple burns marking bodies, faces and film, as both expressions of a forbidden desire and an inevitable punishment.

---

[7]   'There is no love but the love of God', says Honorius in Oscar Wilde's 'La Sainte Courtisane or The Woman Covered with Jewels', in *Complete Works*, pp. 701–5, p. 704. Wilde's play was inspired by Anatole France's novel *Thaïs* (1890).

Ken Russell (1927–2011), English screen and television director, spent his whole cinematographic career filming transgressive characters. From biopics (*The Music Lovers*, *Valentino*) to science-fiction (*Billion Dollar Brain*, *Altered States*), from melodramas (*Women in Love*, *Whore*) to gothic and fantasy movies (*The Devils*, *Gothic*, *The Lair of the White Worm*), his films always question the boundaries between sanity and madness, reality and the supernatural, harmony and disorder, and how they are crossed. This recurrence has led to the qualification of his work as baroque, decadent, fiendish or even kitsch. Oscar Wilde's play and character, with their capacity to reverse values all the way to sacrilege or the grotesque, naturally drew Russell's attention. In 1988, he directed *Salome's Last Dance*, an adaptation which vacillates between true loyalty to the play and its clever *mise en abîme*. Indeed, if Russell chose to depict the essential theatricality of Wilde's *Salomé*, he also offered its reverse angle, blurring the frontiers between Art and Reality. The film starts as Oscar Wilde himself, still glowing from the triumph of *Lady Windermere's Fan* and accompanied by his lover Lord Alfred Douglas, walks into a London brothel where a surprise awaits him. He sits on a comfortable sofa while the master of the house teases his curiosity, as he promises the poet the first staging of his infamous *Salomé*. In front of Wilde, the curtains open, revealing an eccentric troupe, made up of prostitutes and maids, ready to perform for the author.

The prologue, as a frame to the play, sets in place the many borders to be trespassed throughout the film. Indeed, the distance between the stage and the auditorium, the fourth wall, is strongly asserted yet easily passable in one direction or the other. In this carnival atmosphere, masks are swapped and fall, leading to the inevitable sacrifice: life catches up with fiction, for as Salome dies and the play ends, Oscar Wilde is left in the hands of policemen, arrested on charges of gross indecency and the corruption of minors. In Russell's movie, transgression is at the centre of the act of representation, as an erotic prelude to sacrifice. If Carmelo Bene's *Salomè* sentences its characters and spectators to divine punishment for succumbing to temptation, Ken Russell's grotesque adaptation of Wilde's play reveals the carnal violence that lies beneath the charming surface of the 'beautiful coloured musical' piece that is *Salomé*.[8] In fact, as both directors show us, it is in the very colours and melody of Wilde's words that eroticism makes its way to the stage, whether theatrical or cinematographic.

Wilde's Red Omen: Colours of Desire

Oscar Wilde's *Salomé* is a play in black, white and red. Indeed, it takes place during a night when the moon, pale as 'a woman rising from a tomb', shines brightly, fighting back the darkness that surrounds the Palace of Herod.[9] This white

---

8   Wilde, 'De Profundis', p. 939.
9   Wilde, 'Salomé', p. 552.

light signals the values attached to the princess Salome: virginal and fatal, pure and demonic, her whiteness completes and opposes the Tetrarch's 'sombre look'.[10] Beside these monochrome characters, the mortal enemies Queen Herodias and the prophet Jokanaan express their duality by showing a black and white surface. When she first appears on stage, Herodias is described as 'she who wears a black mitre sewn with pearls'.[11] Salome, in her seductive yet hateful plea to Jokanaan, praises his body's whiteness and the blackness of his hair:

> Thy body is white like the lilies of a field that the mower hath never mowed. Thy body is white like the snows that lie … on the mountains of Judaea, and come down into the valleys. The roses in the garden of the Queen of Arabia are not so white as thy body. … Thy body is hideous. It is like the body of a leper. It is like a plastered wall where vipers have crawled; like a plastered wall where the scorpions have made their nest. It is like a whitened sepulchre full of loathsome things. It is horrible, thy body is horrible. It is of thy hair that I am enamoured, Jokanaan. Thy hair is like clusters of grapes, like the clusters of black grapes that hang from the vine-trees of Edom in the land of the Edomites. … The long black nights, when the moon hides her face, when the stars are afraid, are not so black. The silence that dwells in the forest is not so black. There is nothing in the world so black as thy hair. … Let me touch thy hair.[12]

Thus, through Salome's lips and Wilde's pen, colours reveal their ability to signify opposite values, from beauty to monstrosity, from attraction to terror. The black and white screen of bodies and set, giving birth to dreams and nightmares, is gradually torn by words and actions, sensual desire and imminent deaths. From these symbolic or real wounds flows a red liquid – whether wine or blood – that stains floors and skin, making the connection between horror and ecstasy, leaving the field open to eroticism. Georges Bataille, in his fundamental work on eroticism, precisely defines it as the result of a tear, a fracture, a wound. He writes:

> In human life …, sexual violence causes a wound that rarely heals of its own accord; it has to be closed, and will not even remain closed without constant attention based on anguish. Primary anguish bound up with sexual disturbance signifies death. The violence of this disturbance reopens in the mind of the man experiencing it, who also knows what death is, the abyss that death once revealed. The violence of death and sexual violence, when they are linked together, have this dual significance. On the one hand the convulsions of the flesh are more acute when they are near to a black-out, and on the other a black-out, as long as there is enough time, makes physical pleasure more exquisite. Mortal anguish

---

10   Ibid., p. 553.
11   Ibid.
12   Ibid., pp. 558–9.

does not necessarily make for sensual pleasure, but that pleasure is more deeply felt during mortal anguish.[13]

Jokanaan's mouth, that 'band of scarlet on a tower of ivory' that Salome desires to kiss so eagerly, is the first visual symptom of this overspill of violence.[14] This flash of red is immediately followed by a spill of blood, as the young Syrian, rejected by the princess, commits suicide right before her eyes. The stain of blood, which will never be erased or cleaned, leading Herod to slip and Salome to dance on it, is the herald of a red omen that will finally tint the whole stage. The blood of the young Syrian is like the spot on Lady Macbeth's hands,[15] never to be washed away by water, never to be covered with perfumes, only extending its empire. The roses of Herod's garland burn his forehead and turn into 'stains of blood'[16] as the moon becomes 'red as blood',[17] as prophesized by Jokanaan.

All these explosions of passionate colours are the foreshadowing of other bloody epiphanies to come, including the two most fascinating and iconic episodes of Salome's tale: the 'Dance of the Seven Veils' and the beheading of Jokanaan, where eroticism and violence reach their climax. Coloured bursts build up to these two 'opening numbers', where veils fall before heads roll, where Salome's nudity is offered to Herod's lust in exchange for the prophet's life. But both scenes suddenly deprive the audience and the reader of this expected visual overflow. Instead, Wilde, after losing himself in the thorough descriptions of Salome's charms, infamously and laconically indicates merely 'Salomé dances the dance of the seven veils'.[18] Herod and the soldier, usually quick to relate every detail of the dancer's figure or attitude, remain surprisingly silent as Salome unfolds her naked body. It is as if this choreography dumbfounds the audience and the author who are entirely captivated by the sight of Salome's beauty. On the contrary, the horror of Jokanaan's decapitation is unseen, set offstage but heard and recounted by the bloodthirsty princess:

> There is a silence, a terrible silence. Ah! something has fallen upon the ground. I heard something fall. It was the sword of the headsman. He is afraid, this slave. He has let his sword fall. He dare not kill him. He is a coward, this slave![19]

---

[13]   Georges Bataille, *Erotism: Death and Sensuality* (New York, 1962), p. 104.

[14]   Wilde, 'Salomé', p. 559.

[15]   'What, will these hands ne'er be clean? – No more o' that, my lord, no more o' that; you mar all with this starting. ... Here's the smell of the blood still. All the perfumes of Arabia will not sweeten this little hand. O, o, o!' William Shakespeare, *Macbeth: Texts and Contexts*, William C. Carroll (ed.) (Boston, MA and New York, 1999), p. 97.

[16]   Wilde, 'Salomé', p. 568.

[17]   Ibid., p. 569.

[18]   Ibid., p. 570.

[19]   Ibid., p. 573.

Finally, as Salome is left alone with the severed head for her final seduction scene, all light is put out, drying up the torrent of colours which expressed the violence of desire. 'Manasseth, Issachar, Ozias, put out the torches. I will not look at things, I will not suffer things to look at me. Put out the torches! Hide the moon! Hide the stars!', Herod says before ordering the murder of Salome.[20] Oscar Wilde's play is clearly a story of the gaze, of the eyes alternately over-stimulated and bedazzled. The gaze is the means of temptation, yet prohibited. The words, endlessly repeated by Herodias or her Page, 'You are always looking at her. You look at her too much.' or 'You must not look at her!', act as a leitmotif, resuming this ambivalence.[21] Thus Herod says to Salome:

> It is true, I have looked at you all evening. Your beauty has troubled me. Your beauty has grievously troubled me, and I have looked at you too much. But I will look at you no more. Neither at things, nor at people should one look. Only in mirrors should one look, for mirrors do but show us masks.[22]

In Wilde's play the ancient prohibition of the gaze (from Orpheus to Noah) replaces the Christian prohibition of touch ('Noli me tangere'). This slippage from Biblical tale to ancient myth is also revealed through the tragic use of colours, in the poet's play as well as in Carmelo Bene's and Ken Russell's adaptations.

Temptation and Punishment

If Oscar Wilde's colour range is very subtle, playing with shade as well as sharp contrast, Carmelo Bene's is much more garish. The visual rhythm of *Salomè* is made of multiple scansions, bordering on hysteria, endlessly wounding the characters and the film itself. The first images reveal this proximity between visual and physical violence, nudity and sacrifice, pleasure and pain: the camera never stops its free movements as it captures the sight of naked women turning their backs on a stained-glass sun, and being whipped by a beater made of soft, multicoloured feathers. A flush appears on the whiteness of their skin prefiguring the red overflow which will contaminate the whole picture: flush of desire, as Salome's profane body is revealed; flush of shame as Herod's royal body is tempted; flush of blood, as Jokanaan's sacred body is sacrificed.

By moonlight, water turns red, like Herod's wine, like Jokanaan's blood. This confusion is affirmed as Herod's feast becomes the setting for Jesus's Last Supper. The same Jesus wears ostensible fangs as he institutes the ritual of the Eucharist where his blood, symbolized by wine, is given to be drunk. Thus, the carnal appetites, which encompass sexual desire and a hunger for flesh, become

---

[20]   Ibid., p. 574.

[21]   Ibid., pp. 553, 561.

[22]   Ibid., p. 571.

extremely ghoulish. As night falls, the many colours of the theatrical set, costumes and make-up become fluorescent. The light that shines on a nude Salome is not the moonlight anymore, but the light of desire, coming from within, characterized by its scarlet nuance. Indeed, Herod's eyes, suddenly red as fire, reflect the passion that inflames his veins. And this colour, whether wine, blood, stained glass, flowers, light, draperies or flames, manifests itself in every shot. When the camera adopts the Tetrarch's point of view, the whole picture is suddenly tinged with red. The editing, syncopated since the beginning of the film, becomes even faster as the promise of Salome's dance approaches. The viewer's eyes suffer from this succession of flickering images, but not as much as the characters, whose heads are literally severed by close-ups and incessant cuts.

But this arousal of desire does not lead to the expected ending. Indeed, as Salome agrees to dance for Herod and the music starts, the oriental dancer disappears from the film just as she slipped away in Wilde's description, giving centre stage to Jesus. This anachronistic, misplaced Christ disrobes and, naked, lies on a fluorescent cross. The Son of Man grabs the hammer and nails of his martyrdom and crucifies himself (see Plate 7). Every blow echoes as the blood on Jesus's feet starts to drip. This sacrifice, which is a true offering of Christ's nude and suffering body, comprises and symbolizes both Salome's unveiling and Jokanaan's execution, both completely absent from Bene's movie.

Between visual excesses and defects, *Salomè* is indeed the site of an epiphany and of an eclipse. The light itself becomes the means of divine punishment. The moonlight which gently beamed down on Salome changes into a scorching sun. Herod, exhausted by his outburst of carnal passion, lies down, under transparent fabrics. Salome reappears completely naked, against the light, and starts a reverse 'Dance of the Seven Veils'. She softly lifts each layer of material covering Herod's body but does not stop, even when the last one is gone (see Plate 8). Indeed, the blazing sun burns not only Herod's eyes but also his skin, which becomes another veil ready to be removed. As Salome peels off his dried-up make-up and his burnt-up skin – revealing his true face behind the theatrical mask – the sun becomes brighter and the image, at first tinged with orange shade, turns to the clearest light, blinding both Herod and the spectator (see Plate 9).

The Tetrarch cries a tear of pure white, followed by tears of blood, last witnesses of a life that seems to desert the film. The last layer to suffer the light's burning effect is the image itself. Indeed, the last shot fades to white until it appears as virginal and as mortuary as the princess Salome herself. In the end, the film becomes the last victim of the vampiric appetites it captured. In her book on vampirism, psychoanalyst Pérel Wilgowicz defines one of the vampire's fundamental characteristics as 'an eye that bites'.[23] The gaze is a way for this fascinating creature to attract and draw all life from his prey. In *Salomè*, alternately

---

[23]   Pérel Wilgowicz, *Le Vampirisme: de la Dame blanche au Golem: essai sur la pulsion de mort et sur l'irreprésentable* (Meyzieu, 1991), p. 66.

red with desire and blood, then whitened to death, the gaze bites as well as being bitten.

Thus, Herod is punished by the very means of his sin: for wanting to see his step-daughter's nudity, he will endure the bite of the sun, which burns his eyes and consumes his body. In Wilde's play, a curtain of darkness falls over the stage. In Bene's adaptation, the final light is blinding and leads this interpretation into the land of myth. Here Herod follows the path of Tiresias who was cursed with blindness after stumbling upon Athena, bathing naked. He also re-enacts the fate of Semele, Zeus's mistress who burned to death when she asked the father of the Gods to reveal himself in all his glory. The tale is told in the third book of Ovid's *Metamorphoses*, here in Ted Hughes's vivid translation:

> Yet he did what he could to insulate
> And filter / The nuclear blast / Of his naked impact – / Such as had demolished Typhoeus / And scattered his hundred hands.
> He chose / A slighter manifestation / Fashioned, like the great bolts, by the Cyclops / But more versatile – known in heaven / As the general deterrent.
> Arrayed in this fashion / Jove came to the house of Cadmus' daughter. / He entered her bedchamber, / But as he bent over her sleeping face / To kiss her
> Her eyes opened wide, saw him / And burst into flame. / Then her whole body lit up / With the glare / That explodes the lamp –
> In that splinter of a second, / Before her blazing shape / Became a silhouette of sooty ashes / The foetus was snatched from her womb.[24]

In Wilde's play, words are able to seduce and hurt, to caress and wound, to heal and kill. The poet reaffirmed this idea when he wrote in *The Ballad of Reading Gaol*: 'Yet each man kills the thing he loves, / By each let this be heard, / Some do it with a bitter look, / Some with a flattering word. / The coward does it with a kiss, / The brave man with a sword!'[25] In Carmelo Bene's *Salomè*, the gaze is invested with the powers of both a kiss and the sword. It is through manipulation of the gaze that Honorius falls for Myrrhina, that Salome seduces Herod. It represents the eyes that always want to see beyond, under the veils and under the skin. Even the eye of the camera cannot help but split bodies and faces.

Jokanaan bears the brunt of it, he whose unspoiled beauty and chastity designate him as an ideal object for desire and sacrifice. Salome's unsatisfied lust towards him leads her to see even deeper, as she demands his execution. If her gaze and caresses cannot reach the prophet, the sword of the executioner will. Like Venus's carnal and pagan body, whose nudity is problematized by Georges Didi-Huberman as an appeal to see beyond, Jokanaan's sacred and glorious body is to be stained by any means possible. 'The greater the beauty of the facade, the

---

[24]   Ted Hughes, *Tales from Ovid* (London, 1997), pp. 98–9.

[25]   Oscar Wilde, 'The Ballad of Reading Gaol', in *Complete Works*, pp. 843–60, p. 844.

deeper the stain inside, the more heartrending also the possibility of opening, of a wound. ... There is no image of the body without the imagination of its opening', writes Didi-Huberman.[26] His words about the ancient goddess apply equally to the Biblical prophet, object of Salome's dark desire.

In the Italian director's film, the temptation of 'opening' is a visual melody, conducted by spasmodic editing and punctuated by bursts of colour. This melody is as enchanting as the sirens' music, which lures its victims before ringing like a knell. In the end, temptation turns the tables and makes the masks fall, as Herod becomes the main victim of his visual appetites.

Profundity of the Grotesque

In *Salome's Last Dance*, Ken Russell's cinematographic adaptation of the play, a similar reversal seems to be prevented from the very outset, when identities are clearly defined as dual and artificial. Salome's terrible seduction, Jokanaan's sacrificial righteousness, Herod's incestuous desire and Herodias's thirst for blood are just costumes put on for a show. Indeed, the boundaries between the stage, where *Salomé*'s first performance is about to happen, and the auditorium, where the sole spectator Oscar Wilde is quietly seated, are firmly upheld. The frame is ostensible and keeps the rules of theatre and the rules of life separate. A blue veil is used as a curtain and every actor is introduced to Wilde before donning a costume and getting into character. Lord Alfred Douglas plays Jokanaan, Rose, the humble servant, Salome; Lady Alice plays Herodias and Alfred Taylor, master of this house of pleasure, Herod.

But the very place where this performance is to unfold leads us to imagine that the boundaries have been set only to be crossed. For the premiere of *Salomé* is not staged in a theatre, but in a brothel where Wilde is a familiar patron. In opposition to the rigours of Victorian society, this whorehouse allows the satisfaction of prohibited desires, behind closed doors. A place of transgression, far away from moral censorship, it is the ideal shelter for Salome's carnal explosion. Indeed, it is an explosion already foreseen, as the play takes place on Guy Fawkes Night: the fireworks lighting up London's dark-blue sky and the effigies being torched are a sign of the ancient sacrifice about to be re-enacted.

The same contrast of colour invades the brothel: a halo of blue dreamy light shines on the stage in contrast to the red voluptuous decor of the auditorium. In a prologue to the play, Jokanaan, covered in blue make-up, appears locked in a cage like a wild animal. Music starts, and three topless female guards dance and tease him. From the outset, the prophet is the victim of a sadistic desire which is

---

[26] 'Plus grande est la beauté du devant, plus profonde est la souillure du dedans, plus déchirante aussi la possibilité d'ouverture, de blessure ... Il n'y a pas d'image du corps sans l'imagination de son ouverture.' Georges Didi-Huberman, *Ouvrir Vénus* (Paris, 1999), pp. 96–9.

very much enjoyed by the author. The shot/reverse shot shows the simultaneous rise of pain and of pleasure, which climaxes when Jokanaan's decency is violated by a phallic spear. A light flashes on the face of both Jokanaan and Wilde as a parallel visual orgasm. But the illusion is revealed as the poet's attention is drawn towards the source of this brightness: from the auditorium, a photographer has just captured this erotic vision. A first tear in the play's narrative and chronological unity, this artificial lightening disrupts the illusion and allows Wilde to congratulate the operator, embodied by Ken Russell himself, who quickly puts his fake beard back on. Thus, the distinction between performance and audience spaces starts to diminish. This transgression of the rules of the theatre is only at its beginning and is reiterated when Salome, for her first entrance, comes out of the wings to join Oscar Wilde on the sofa. The young Syrian and the Page leave the stage and follow her, but she definitely prefers her author's company. Instead of addressing her suitor, she whispers in Wilde's ear. The camera gets closer to the unusual couple, paying no more attention to the stage. Only Jokanaan's voice, both offscreen and offstage, succeeds in awakening Salome's curiosity and bringing her back to the boards. From this moment on, the frontiers prove to be easily crossed.

This burst of theatre into the realm of 'real life' leads characters and spectators into a true masquerade, where disguise is as revealing as concealing. From now on, everyone tests and jeopardizes the fragile threshold between illusion and reality. The performance of *Salomé* expands its field, takes over the whole room and encompasses all characters in the tragic episode: the auditorium and the wings become an extension of the stage, and everybody, Oscar Wilde included, is ordered to wear a mask until the end. Actually, the poet assumes many different identities: alternately desired and desiring, he takes on Salome's and Herod's costumes before finally appearing as Jokanaan himself. As an echo to Salome's lustful declaration to the prophet, Wilde is seduced by the Page while the blue moonlight contaminates the whole brothel.

Yet suddenly, the theatrical system is reversed: Salome and her mother, on stage, become the amused witnesses of a show happening in the audience. As the music starts, Herod joins Oscar Wilde and the guards in the auditorium. The Tetrarch dances to exhaustion and falls on the sofa, driving Wilde out of his seat and provoking general hilarity. Salome descends the stairs from the stage to dance for her King, while Wilde goes backstage with the Page. Deprived of its only spectator, the play goes on, compelled to lead tragedy to its end. As in Bene's film, Salome's thirst for blood, as she demands the head of Jokanaan, turns the light red. Every other character deserts the stage and invades the auditorium, while Herod tries to convince his step-daughter to renounce her request. But the executioner accomplishes his task and Salome is left alone with Jokanaan's severed head. For the occasion, Wilde re-enters the room and surveys the morbid duo. Finally, the moonlight fades away as Herod orders Salome's execution.

This epilogue, which ends the play, reinstates the frontiers between illusion and reality: Oscar Wilde applauds and joins Jokanaan's severed head on stage, Lord Alfred Douglas comes back to life and reproaches his lover's infidelity. But the poet replies: 'Come, come. Jealousy is not part of a prophet's make-up. And yours, my dear, is just a little overdone, if I may be permitted a tiny criticism.' The revelation of the artifice seems to end the masquerade, and yet Wilde suddenly launches into declaiming Salome's text and is about to kiss Jokanaan's mouth when he is interrupted by the actors coming out of the dressing rooms. But Wilde's congratulations do not last long, as two policemen enter the room and arrest the poet on charges of gross indecency. As he gets into the police van, Wilde questions the accuracy of the casting: 'Alfred, I think Bosie [Lord Alfred Douglas] was miscast. If you want a revival, he really should play Salome and I should play the prophet.' Thus, the transgression of the boundaries between life and art demands a final sacrifice and sentences Wilde to wear the martyr's mask for life.

The epilogue thus echoes the firmly established public and critical confusion between Salome's and Wilde's morality.[27] Thomas Prasch writes, 'The deliberate conflation of life and art in Russell's film interestingly corresponds to the dominant tropes in recent critical accounts of *Salome*, which similarly cannot resist playing the play's decadent themes against the problems in Wilde's personal life.'[28] The author concludes: '... breaking that fourth wall re-signals the interpretation of life and work in Wilde, and reinforces the way the play stages his own martyrdom ...'.[29] Petra Dierkes-Thrun draws a similar conclusion:

> Ken Russell twists the historical chronology of *Salomé*'s censorship and Wilde's arrest so as to suggest a direct relation between Wilde's art and Wilde's life ... . Through the intricate intertwining of onstage and offstage people and events, *Salome's Last Dance* hence establishes a strong allegorical association between the dramatic plot of *Salomé* and Wilde's own life and suggests that *Salomé* provides a direct window into the author's homosexuality.[30]

As artificial as they may appear, Russell's *mise en abîme* and chronological shortcuts transform the play into an artistic mirror in which Wilde's tragedy is reflected. If this carnival performance of *Salomé* allows every transgressive reversal, it also reveals the power of artifice as often more real than reality itself. Charles Baudelaire affirmed not only the beauty of artifice but also its ability to lead into sacred territory:

> Woman is quite within her rights, indeed she is even doing a sort of duty, when she devotes herself to appearing magical and supernatural; she must surprise and

---

[27]   For discussion of *Salomé*'s reception in the early twentieth century, see Clair Rowden's Introduction and Sandra Mayer's chapter in this volume.

[28]   Thomas Prasch, 'Behind the Last Veil: Forms of Transgression in Ken Russell's *Salome's Last Dance*', in Kevin M. Flanagan (ed.), *Ken Russell: Re-viewing England's Last Mannerist* (Plymouth, 2009), pp. 195–210, p. 196.

[29]   Ibid., p. 203.

[30]   Dierkes-Thrun, *Salome's Modernity*, pp. 162, 165.

charm; as an idol, she must adorn herself in order to be adored. Thus she must borrow from all the arts the means to elevate herself above Nature, the better to conquer hearts and catch the attention. It matters very little that the trickery and artifice are known to all, so long as their success is assured and their effect always irresistible.[31]

[La femme est bien dans son droit, et même elle accomplit une espèce de devoir en s'appliquant à paraître magique et surnaturelle; il faut qu'elle étonne, qu'elle charme; idole, elle doit se dorer pour être adorée. Elle doit donc emprunter à tous les arts les moyens de s'élever au-dessus de la nature pour mieux subjuguer les cœurs et frapper les esprits. Il importe fort peu que la ruse et l'artifice soient connus de tous, si le succès en est certain et l'effet toujours irrésistible.]

Echoing the French poet's words, Ken Russell's film uses artifice as a way to conquer depth and beauty. William Tydeman and Steven Price have described Russell's use of artifice as 'often close to the surface', and condemned it as 'witless bad taste', without even considering it as a true aesthetic tool.[32] While often blatant, theatrical, even laughable, Russell's artifice is not as shallow as it seems. From plastic pools of blood to bodies covered in blue or golden make-up, from sheet metal used as thunder to flatulence as a manifestation of the wind, the artifice is always both excessive and unconcealed. As such, it is not an illusionist's trick but an aesthetic means to an artistic end.

At the end of the performance, Oscar Wilde congratulates Alfred Taylor and says: 'I was delighted to find that I'd written yet another comedy.' Indeed, the excess of tragic and comic effects in *Salome's Last Dance* means that laughter rings hollow. Thus, the grandiloquent death of Salome, pierced by a javelin, reveals its monstrous character as we learn that it was not feigned, and that the actress played her part to the death. Once again, Ken Russell's poetic liberties make Salome's and Wilde's destiny collide, under the auspices of the grotesque. About his own tragedy, Wilde wrote:

I remember I used to say that I thought I could bear a real tragedy if it came to me with purple pall and a mask of noble sorrow, but that the dreadful thing about modernity was that it put Tragedy into the raiment of Comedy, so that the great realities seemed commonplace or grotesque or lacking in style. … Everything about my tragedy has been hideous, mean, repellent, lacking in style. Our very dress make us grotesques. We are the zanies of sorrow. We are clowns whose

---

[31]   Charles Baudelaire, 'Le peintre de la vie moderne', in *Ecrits sur l'art*, Le Livre de Poche (Paris, 1999), pp. 503–52, p. 543. Translated by Clair Rowden.

[32]   William Tydeman and Steven Price, *Wilde: Salome*, Plays in Production (Cambridge and New York, 1996), p. 172.

hearts are broken. We are specially designed to appeal to the sense of humour.
... Of all possible objects I was the most grotesque.[33]

In his essay 'On the Essence of Laughter', Baudelaire problematized the excessive, absolute, profound and savage essence of the grotesque, and the often 'insane and excessive mirth' which it provokes.[34] He also distinguished between the comic as an imitation of reality, and the grotesque, which he elevated to the realm of 'creation'. In *Salome's Last Dance*, the grotesque has a favourite field of expression: carnal desire. Russell chooses not only to stage Salome's lust for love and blood, but he emphasizes it to the point of exuberance. The dancer appears as a man-eating creature, not only metaphorically. In Wilde's play, inspired by Solomon's *Song of Songs*, Salome compares Jokanaan's body, hair and mouth to delicate and flavoursome fruits: 'clusters of black grapes that hang from the vine-trees of Edom', or 'a pomegranate cut with a knife of ivory'.[35] In the film, as she says those words, she licks her lips as a prelude to her kiss or her bite. Indeed, Salome's hunger is at the same time erotic and sadistic, she craves food as much as sex, and when attempting to seduce Herod, appears in every shot with items of food to her mouth, from a suggestive banana to a giant red lollipop.

Indeed, Salome's intention towards Jokanaan is not so much to smother him with kisses as to devour his body. In Russell's film, Jokanaan's means of transportation from his prison to the stage is a dumbwaiter. It is from the dumbwaiter that he appears to Salome for the first time, and it is the way in which his severed head is served to her. Finally, Jokanaan succumbs to Salome's cannibal appetite: 'Ah! thou wouldst not suffer me to kiss thy mouth, Jokanaan. Well! I will kiss it now. I will bite it with my teeth as one bites a ripe fruit.'[36] And, as she kisses his not-yet-cold mouth, the camera gets closer, intimately recording the way her kisses change to bites. Then, she turns food critic: 'I have kissed thy mouth, Jokanaan. ... There was a bitter taste on thy lips. Was it the taste of blood ...? But perchance it is the taste of love ... . They say that love hath a bitter taste ... .'[37] But as Herod and Herodias, frightened by such a sight, leave the stage, she sits on the prophet's head as to incorporate it. Salome's sexuality asserts itself as clearly transgressive, with regard to both the sacred and the taboo. As she breaks both prohibitions, her sacrifice is demanded by Herod to restore moral order.

But when Salome expires, Jokanaan's severed head becomes a grotesque figure: it starts talking and moving while remaining a prisoner of the silver platter. This episode of the talking head recalls Baudelaire's description of a grotesque English pantomime, where Pierrot is guillotined:

---

[33]   Wilde, 'De Profundis', pp. 936–7.

[34]   'une hilarité folle, excessive'. Charles Baudelaire, 'De l'essence du rire', in *Ecrits sur l'art*, pp. 281–303, p. 293.

[35]   Wilde, 'Salomé', p. 559.

[36]   Ibid., p. 573.

[37]   Ibid., p. 575.

After having struggled and bellowed like an ox that smells the slaughter-house, Pierrot at last bowed to his fate. His head was severed from his neck, a great red and white head, which rolled noisily to the prompter's box, showing the bleeding circle of the neck, the split vertebrae and all the details of a piece of butcher's meat recently dressed for the counter. But then, all of a sudden, the shortened trunk, moved by an irresistible obsession for theft, got up, triumphantly made its own head disappear as if it were a ham or a bottle of wine, and far more sensibly than the great Saint Denis, stuffed it into its pocket![38]

[Après avoir lutté et beuglé comme un bœuf qui flaire l'abattoir, Pierrot subissait enfin son destin. La tête se détachait du cou, une grosse tête blanche et rouge, et roulait avec bruit devant le trou du souffleur, montrant le disque saignant du cou, la vertèbre scindée, et tous les détails d'une viande de boucherie récemment taillée pour l'étalage. Mais voilà que, subitement, le torse raccourci, mû par la monomanie irrésistible du vol, se dressait, escamotait victorieusement sa propre tête, comme un jambon ou une bouteille de vin, et, bien plus avisé que le grand saint Denis, la fourrait dans sa poche!]

Moreover, Baudelaire adds: 'Therefore, with the English actors' special talent for hyperbole, all these monstrous pranks took on an uncommonly striking reality.'[39] What is true for English actors seems apt for British playwrights and directors who, like Oscar Wilde and Ken Russell, proved that there is nothing as deep as skin-deep. As Lord Henry Wotton says in *The Picture of Dorian Gray*:

People say sometimes that Beauty is only superficial. That may be so. But at least it is not so superficial as Thought is. To me Beauty is the wonder of wonders. It is only shallow people who do not judge by appearances. The true mystery of the world is the visible, not the invisible … .[40]

Russell's aesthetic path, which continuously leads from terror to laughter, reveals the monstrous and tragic face of the grotesque, both artificial and excessive, superficial and profound, yet always absolute. This 'skilful deconstruction' of the rules of representation also applies to Bene's artistry, described by José Guinot as a 'perversion of genre', 'subversion of acting', 'formal discordance' with a 'baroque dimension of metamorphosis and ostentation'.[41]

---

[38]   Baudelaire, 'De l'essence du rire', p. 298. Translated by Clair Rowden.

[39]   'Aussi, avec le talent spécial des acteurs anglais pour l'hyperbole, toutes ces monstrueuses farces prenaient-elles une réalité singulièrement saisissante.' Ibid., pp. 298–9. Translated by Clair Rowden.

[40]   Wilde, 'The Picture of Dorian Gray', in *Complete Works*, pp. 17–167, p. 32.

[41]   José Guinot, 'Le Théâtre du grotesque', in Jean-Paul Manganaro (ed.), *Carmelo Bene, dramaturgie* (Paris, 1977), pp. 1–3, pp. 2–3.

Salomé's Ambiguities: Androgyny and Homoeroticism

Carmelo Bene's *Salomè* and Ken Russell's *Salome's Last Dance* both use the grotesque as a way to reveal concealed desires. From passionate colours to syncopated editing, from endless masquerade to constant reversals, from vampire temptation to cannibal feast, both films stage the transgressive expression of repressed impulses. By moonlight, in Herod's palace, incestuous and sadistic desires are revealed and satisfied. Fantasies turn to tragicomic reality, leaving the stage and the picture covered in blood and corpses. Next to these explicit expressions of desire, one other remains much more discreet. Mixed with fear and admiration, worship and sacrilege, Herod's actions towards Jokanaan are truly enigmatic. Much has been written about Herod's sexuality, from his incestuous desire and castration anxiety,[42] to his homoerotic attachment to Jokanaan.[43] If the Tetrarch imprisons the prophet, it is as much a means of keeping him away from society as of keeping him close. Herod, whose weakness and cowardice are legendary, only finds courage when he opposes his wife's will to have Jokanaan executed. The bond that ties the King to the prophet also makes Herod almost betray his promise to Salome. When the dancer asks for Jokanaan's head, he replies: 'I have sworn by my gods. I know it well. But I pray you, Salomé, ask of me something else. Ask of me the half of my kingdom, and I will give it to you. But ask not of me what you have asked.'[44]

The Tetrarch's reluctance is explained by his fear of divine punishment: 'This man comes perchance from God. He is a holy man. The finger of God has touched him. God has put into his mouth terrible words.'[45] Ready to deny his royal word and faith, to alienate his powerful spouse and court, Herod asserts his deep and irrational attachment to the prophet. These loving feelings, disguised as idealistic admiration and superstitious fear, reveal their true carnal face when staged by Carmelo Bene and Ken Russell.

Indeed, in both films, sexual ambiguity prevails, through the figure of androgyny. Interrogating Salome's representations in literature, paintings, opera and films, Linda and Michael Hutcheon observe: 'But while Salome might well have been, to use Lawrence Kramer's term, "everyone's favorite *fin-de-siècle* dragon lady", this is a *femme fatale* with a difference: as Ken Russell captured well in his film, *Salome's Last Dance*, she is an adolescent and a virgin.'[46] Stratton also describes Russell's Salome as a 'sexually precocious pubescent' girl, 'both

---

[42] Jon Stratton, *The Desirable Body: Cultural Fetishism and the Erotics of Consumption* (Manchester, 1996).

[43] Murielle Gagnebin, *Pour une esthétique psychanalytique: L'artiste, stratège de l'inconscient* (Paris, 1994).

[44] Wilde, 'Salomé', p. 570.

[45] Ibid., p. 571.

[46] Linda Hutcheon and Michael Hutcheon, *Bodily Charm: Living Opera* (Lincoln and London, 2000), p. 94.

androgynous in her puberty and sexually alluring'.[47] It is in this very ambivalence that Salome's sexuality asserts its specificity. Russell's choice of Imogen Millais-Scott for the part of Salome heightens this ambiguity: her frail and androgynous body blurs the frontier between girl and woman,[48] male and female.

Thus Salome's sexuality cannot be obviously defined, wavering between a virginal passion and sadistic impulses.[49] But just as moral identities are split and reversed, sexual characters are able to transform and unite, a possibility made all the easier by the fragility of Salome's and Herodias's femininity and the unassured nature of Jokanaan's and Herod's virility. Thus, in the play, feminine desire is clothed in the traditionally masculine values of aggressiveness and violence, while men's sexuality is branded with passiveness. In Carmelo Bene's *Salomè*, women appear as tempting creatures, half-animal, half-goddesses. Their beauty is artificial, made of pearls and jewels, glitter and mirrors. But behind – or underneath – this display of shimmering finery, their sexual identity is much more troubled. Indeed, Salome's nudity, which should reflect her extreme femininity, only reveals a boyish figure and shaved head (see Plate 8). Herodias's costume, made of feathers, translucent veils and long red hair, also maintains the confusion as she finally appears as a Renaissance angel in the style of Filippino Lippi, whose sexual identity is nothing but uncertain. Herod himself, whose face, eyes and body are covered in delicate make-up, ends up taking Salome's place as he performs a scorching 'Dance of the Seven Veils', offering both his nudity and his life.

In Russell's *Salome's Last Dance*, such inversions blur the lines between stereotypical femininity and virility. Jokanaan appears as a sexual toy in the hands of his lustful female guards. From the Page to the prophet, men who awaken desire are entirely covered in make-up, whether blue or golden, which transforms them into fetishes, both sacred and acquirable. Here, make-up unites the theatricality and the seduction; it is an artifice as Baudelaire understands it. Thus, red blusher on Herod's cheeks is as much part of his dramatic mask or a means of travesty, as an expression of flushing desire. In opposition to men's fragility and sensitivity, women assert a violent and insatiable desire as an expression of their power. Herodias flirts with every man on Herod's guard, while Salome trades her nudity

---

[47]   Stratton, *The Desirable Body*, p. 101.

[48]   Moreover, Salome's 'deviant' sexual appetites correspond to Sigmund Freud's problematized definition of child sexuality, driven by unrepressed pre-genital impulses: her oral fixation reconciles her endless desire to kiss Jokanaan and her final wish to bite him. See Sigmund Freud, *Three Essays on the Theory of Sexuality*, trans. James Strachey (New York, 1962). Originally published in 1905.

[49]   Linda and Michael Hutcheon affirm: '... the Salome of the opening is young and beautiful; she is an impulsive spoiled child who must have her own way, a pampered princess who lives very much in her own world, as befits the narcissism of the young. Yet it is the same pubescent girl who develops an obsessive passion to kiss the lips of Jochanaan.' Hutcheon and Hutcheon, *Bodily Charm*, p. 95.

for Jokanaan's life. The Queen's and princess's androgynous figures contrast with the warders' extreme femininity, allowing them to be both desired and desiring.

But, as veils fall, the ambiguous sexual identity, embodied by the carnal yet idealistically androgynous figure, gives way to sexual ambivalence. In Bene's as in Russell's film, this ambivalence is always addressed to Herod, disclosing his homosexual desires. Thus, the objects of the Tetrarch's lust – his wife Herodias and his step-daughter Salome – exchange their extreme femininity for a much more complex identity. In *Salomè*, as Jokanaan's voice prophesizes the coming of Jesus, Herodias is suddenly embodied by two characters, a woman dressed as an angel, wearing white wings behind her back, and a man with a black moustache in a multicoloured turban. Both share Herodias's part and lines, warning Herod against the prophet's fearful words. Even though offscreen, Jokanaan's figure finds its way into the shot, as Herod's eyes seem to be filled with his image. Indeed, the Tetrarch is forever prone to hallucinations, or omens. He is the only one to hear the beating of wings in the air, to see his red roses turn to stains of blood, to feel his wreath turn to fire.

As much as the sight of Salome, Jokanaan's voice seems to trigger these burning visions which are both sensual and dangerous. Ken Russell expresses this visual and ambivalent arousal, as Salome dances the 'Seven Veils'. Her face and body hidden under vaporous blue veils and positioned down stage, Salome begins her choreography to Edvard Grieg's *In the Hall of the Mountain King*. Cloaked in ubiquity, Salome makes the Tetrarch's head turn as she strips and teases him. The music quickens and the dancer splits in two before tearing off her last veil. But instead of the expected vision, it is a man's nudity which is revealed to the audience. A flash of light catches this climatic epiphany, which enlightens again a concealed homosexual desire. It is only after a reverse shot of Herod's troubled face that Salome finally appears in her female form, before being covered up. But, for a quick yet revealing moment, the object of Herod's desire was neither his step-daughter's nor his wife's nudity, but the naked body of a man offered to his lustful gaze. 'Marvelous, marvelous', he exclaims as the music stops and Salome comes closer to demand Jokanaan's head. The expression of his desire is instantly repressed and the prophet's body, after being hallucinated and undressed by his eyes, is offered up and executed by Salome's will. Enduring the same fate as Jokanaan, Salome is sentenced to death after awakening Herod's concupiscence. True to Wilde's words, the Tetrarch 'kills the thing he loves', whether prophet or dancer.

Unlike Alla Nazimova's *Salome*, where travesty is a way to 'emphasize the homoerotic and camp elements of Wilde's play',[50] Russell's and Bene's adaptations provide an even deeper ambiguity. Even after all the veils have been taken off, the desired body still cannot be perceived as male or female, since it is both. This specific conception, developed by both directors, takes us back to

---

50   Dierkes-Thrun, *Salome's Modernity*, p. 147.

ancient times when human nature 'was not the same as now but a different sort.' In his *Symposium*, Plato writes:

> First of all, the races of human beings were three, not two as now, male and female; for there was also a third race that shared in both, a race whose name still remains, though it itself has vanished. For at that time one race was androgynous, and in looks and name it combined both, the male as well as the female; but now it does not exist except for the name that is reserved for reproach.[51]

There is no doubt that Carmelo Bene's and Ken Russell's stagings of *Salomé* turn the Jewish princess into a mythological figure of ancient times. Androgynous, both ingenuous and perverse, desired as much as desiring, luminous as much as blinding, revolutionary woman and demonic temptress, she trespasses every moral, sexual, ethical and aesthetical border, leading men and spectators into the land of myth, reviving the grace and fury of ancient goddesses.

In 1964, Susan Sontag dedicated her 'Notes on Camp' to Oscar Wilde,[52] and described camp sensibility as essentially unnatural, artificial and exaggerated. Whether she is painted by Caravaggio, given voice by Oscar Wilde, drawn by Aubrey Beardsley, directed on stage by Visconti, and on film by Carmelo Bene and Ken Russell, Salome inspires every artist who finds beauty in outrage, truth in artifice, violence in stylization, and profundity in the grotesque.

---

[51]   Plato, *Symposium*, trans. Seth Bernardete (Chicago, IL, 2001), p. 19.

[52]   Susan Sontag, 'Notes on Camp', in *Against Interpretation and Other Essays* (London, 2009), pp. 275–92. Originally published in *Partisan Review*, 31/4 (Fall 1964): pp. 515–30.

Primary Printed Sources

A Working Relationship: The Correspondence between Richard Strauss and Hugo von Hofmannsthal, trans. Hanns Hammelmann and Ewald Osers (New York: Random House, 1961).

Ackté, Aino, *Muistojeni kirja* (Helsinki: Otava, 1925).

Ackté, Aino, *Taiteeni taipaleelta* (Helsinki: Otava, 1935).

Allan, Maud, *My Life and Dancing* (London: Everett & Co, 1908).

Antropp, Theodor, 'Wiener Theater', *Österreichische Rundschau*, 33 (1912): 478–9.

Appia, Adolphe, *Music and the Art of the Theatre*, trans. Robert W. Corrigan and Mary Douglas Dirks, foreword by Lee Simonson, ed. Barnard Hewitt (Coral Gables, FL: University of Miami Press, 1962).

Archer, William, 'Mr. Oscar Wilde's New Play', in Karl Beckson (ed.), *Oscar Wilde: The Critical Heritage* (London: Routledge, 1997).

Bakhtin, Mikhail, 'Forms of Time and Chronotope in the Novel', in Michael Holquist (ed.), *The Dialogic Imagination*, trans. Caryl Emerson and Michael Holquist (Austin, TX: University of Texas Press, 1981).

Barthes, Roland, 'Le Corps de la Musique', in *L'Obvie et l'obtus: Essais critiques III* (Paris: Editions du Seuil, 1982).

Roland Barthes, 'La Mort de l'auteur', in Eric Marty (ed.), *Roland Barthes Œuvres complètes, Tome III, 1966-1973* (Paris: Editions du Seuil, 1994). [Originally published in English as 'The Death of the Author', in *Aspen Magazine*, 5–6 (Autumn/Winter 1967).]

Barthes, Roland, *The Responsibility of Forms: Critical Essays on Music, Art and Representation*, trans. Richard Howard (Oxford: Blackwell, 1986).

Baudelaire, Charles, 'De l'essence du rire', in *Ecrits sur l'art*, Le Livre de Poche (Paris: Librairie générale française, 1999).

Baudelaire, Charles, 'Le peintre de la vie moderne', in *Ecrits sur l'art*, Le Livre de Poche (Paris: Librairie générale française, 1999).

Baudelaire, Charles, 'Richard Wagner and the Tannhäuser in Paris', *The Painter of Modern Life and Other Essays*, trans. Jonathan Mayne (London: Phaidon Press Ltd., 1995).

Beauvoir, Simone de, *Pour une morale de l'ambiguité* (Paris: Gallimard, 1947).

Beauvoir, Simone de, *Pyrrhus et Cinéas* (Paris: Gallimard, 1944).

Beauvoir, Simone de, *The Second Sex*, trans. Constance Borde and Sheila Malovany-Chevallier, introduction by Judith Thruman (New York: Knopf Doubleday Publishing Group, 2010 [1949]).

Becker, Marie Luise, 'Salome in der Kunst des letzten Jahrtausends', *Bühne und Welt*, 4/1 (1901/1902): 201–9.

Becker, Marie Luise, 'Salome – Darstellerinnen auf der modernen Bühne', *Bühne und Welt*, 9/1 (1906/1907): 439–47.

Beecham, Sir Thomas, *A Mingled Chime. An Autobiography* (London: Arrow Books, 1961 [1944]).

Benjamin, Walter, 'The Task of the Translator', *Illuminations*, trans. Harry Zohn, ed. Hannah Arendt (New York: Schocken Books, 1969).

Best Works of Aubrey Beardsley (New York: Dover, 1990).

Bridge, Ursula (ed.), *W.B. Yeats and T. Sturge Moore: Their Correspondence, 1901–1937* (London: Routledge and Kegan Paul, 1953).

Concerts de Danse. N. Trouhanowa (Paris: Imprimerie Maquet, 1912).

Craft, Robert (ed.), *Stravinsky: Selected Correspondence, Volume II* (London and Boston, MA: Faber and Faber, 1984).

Daffner, Hugo, *Salome, ihre Gestalt in Geschichte und Kunst: Dichtung – Bildende Kunst – Musik* (Munich: Hugo Schmidt, 1912).

Derrida, Jacques, *Archive Fever: A Freudian Impression,* trans. Eric Prenowitz (Chicago: University of Chicago Press, 1996).

Dukas, Paul, *Chroniques musicales sur deux siècles 1892–1932* (Paris: Editions SEFI, 1948; Editions Stock, 1980).

Duncan, Isadora, *La Danse de l'avenir*, ed. and trans. Sonia Schoonejans (Bruxelles: Editions Complexe, 2003).

Ellis, Havelock, *Studies in the Psychology of Sex, Volume 1* (Rockville, MD: Wildside Press, 2008 [1900]).

Ellmann, Richard (ed.), *The Artist as Critic: The Critical Writings of Oscar Wilde* (New York: Random House, 1969).

Flaubert, Gustave, 'Hérodias', in *Trois Contes*, Le Livre de Poche (Paris: Librairie générale française, 1983).

Fokine, Michel, *Fokine: Memoirs of a Ballet Master*, trans. Vitale Fokine, ed. Anatole Chujoy (Boston and Toronto: Little Brown, 1961).

Freud, Sigmund, *Three Essays on the Theory of Sexuality*, trans. James Strachey (New York: Basic Books, 1962 [1905]).

Garden, Mary and Louis Biancolli, *Mary Garden's Story* (New York: Simon and Schuster, 1951).

Glazounow [Glazunov], Alexandre, *Introduction et la Danse de Salomée [sic] d'après le Drame "Salomée" [sic] de Oscar Wilde* (Leipzig: M.P. Belaïeff, 1912).

Hirschfeld, Robert, 'Richard Strauss's *Salome*: Premiere in Vienna at the Deutsches Volkstheater on 15 May 1907 by the Opera Society of Breslau', in Bryan Gilliam (ed.), *Richard Strauss and His World* (Princeton, NJ: Princeton University Press, 1992). [Originally published in *Wiener Abendpost*, 27 May 1907.]

Hughes, Ted, *Tales from Ovid* (London: Faber and Faber, 1997).

Humières, Robert d', *Théâtre II: Pièces orientales* (Paris: Mercure de France, 1924).

Huysmans, Joris-Karl, *Against Nature (A Rebours)*, trans. Robert Baldick (Harmondsworth: Penguin, 1959).

Joyce, James, 'Oscar Wilde: The Poet of "Salomé"', in Ellsworth Mason and Richard Ellmann (eds), *The Critical Writings of James Joyce* (London: Faber and Faber, 1959).

Kalbeck, Max, '*Salome*: Music Drama in One Act after Oscar Wilde, by Richard Strauss', in Bryan Gilliam (ed.), *Richard Strauss and His World* (Princeton, NJ: Princeton University Press, 1992). [Originally published in *Neues Wiener Tageblatt*, 28 May 1907.]

Kalisch, Alfred, 'Richard Strauss: the man', in Ernest Newman, *Richard Strauss* (London and New York: John Lane, 1908).

Laforgue, Jules, 'Salomé', *Moralités légendaires* (Paris: Librairie de la 'Revue Indépendante', 1887).

Lindner, Anton, 'Von den Wiener Theatern 1903/04', *Bühne und Welt*, 6/1 (1903/1904): 344–7.

Mallarmé, Stéphane, *Œuvres complètes*, Henri Mondor and G. Jean-Aubry (eds) (Paris: Gallimard, Bibliothèque de la Pléïade, 1945).

Mikhail, E.H. (ed.), *Oscar Wilde: Interviews and Recollections*, 2 vols. (Basingstoke: Macmillan, 1979).

Nordau, Max, *Entartung*, 2 vols. (Berlin: C. Duncker, 1982–1893).

Oscar Wilde: Œuvres, Jean Gattégno (ed.), Bibliothèque de la Pléiade (Paris: Editions Gallimard, 1996).

Pater, Walter, *The Renaissance* (Charleston, SC: BiblioBazaar, 2007).

Plato, *Symposium*, trans. Seth Bernardete (Chicago, IL: University of Chicago Press, 2001).

Pound, Ezra, *Instigations of Ezra Pound together with an essay on the Chinese Written Character by Ernest Fenollosa* (New York: Boni and Liveright, 1920).

Richard Strauss & Romain Rolland: Correspondence, Rollo Myers (ed.) (London: Calder and Boyars, 1968).

Richter, Helene, 'Oscar Wildes künstlerische Persönlichkeit', *Englische Studien*, 45 (1912): 201–57.

Schmitt, Florent, *La Tragédie de Salomé*, full score (Paris: Durand, 1912).

Schuh, Willi (ed.), *A Confidential Matter: The Letters of Richard Strauss and Stefan Zweig, 1931–1935*, trans. Max Knight (Berkeley, CA: University of California Press, 1977).

Shakespeare, William, *Macbeth: Texts and Contexts*, William C. Carroll (ed.) (Boston, MA and New York: Bedford/St. Martin's, 1999).

Strauss, Richard, *La Légende de Joseph*, texte de Cte Harry de Kessler et de Hugo von Hofmannsthal, musique de R. Strauss (op. 63), partition complète pour piano seul, avec texte détaillé, arrangée par Otto Singer (Berlin and Paris: A. Fürstner, 1914).

Strauss, Richard, *Recollections and Reflections*, trans. L.J. Lawrence, ed. Willi Schuh (London: Boosey & Hawkes, 1953). Originally published in German in 1949.

Strauss, Richard, *Salome*, Opera in One Act (Melville, NY: Belwin Mills, n.d.).

Strauss, Richard, *Salome*, Richard Strauss Edition, Complete Stage Works, full score (Vienna: Verlag, Dr. Richard Strauss, 1996).

Wagner, Richard, 'Staging notes on *Der fliegende Holländer*' in Thomas Grey (ed.), *Richard Wagner: Der fliegende Holländer*, Cambridge Opera Handbooks (Cambridge: Cambridge University Press, 2000).

Wilde, Oscar, 'De Profundis', in *Complete Works of Oscar Wilde* (London and Glasgow: Collins, 1948, rpt. 1977).

Wilde, Oscar, 'La Sainte Courtisane or The Woman Covered with Jewels', in *Complete Works of Oscar Wilde* (London and Glasgow: Collins, 1948, rpt. 1977).

Wilde, Oscar, *Salomé*, drawings by Aubrey Beardsley (Boston, MA: Branden, 1996).

Wilde, Oscar, 'Salomé', in *Complete Works of Oscar Wilde* (London and Glasgow: Collins, 1948, reprinted 1977).

Wilde, Oscar, 'The Ballad of Reading Gaol', in *Complete Works of Oscar Wilde* (London and Glasgow: Collins, 1948, rpt. 1977).

Wilde, Oscar, 'The Censure and Salomé', in E.H. Mikhail (ed.), *Oscar Wilde: Interviews and Recollections, Volume 1* (Basingstoke: Macmillan, 1979),

Wilde, Oscar, *The Complete Letters of Oscar Wilde*, Merlin Holland and Rupert Hart-Davis (eds) (London: Fourth Estate, 2000).

Wilde, Oscar, *The Letters of Oscar Wilde*, Rupert Hart-Davis (ed.) (London: Rupert Hart–Davis Ltd., 1962).

Wilde, Oscar, 'Pen Pencil and Poison', in Richard Ellmann (ed.), *The Artist as Critic: The Critical Writings of Oscar Wilde* (New York: Random House, 1969).

Wilde, Oscar, 'The Picture of Dorian Gray', in *Complete Works of Oscar Wilde* (London and Glasgow: Collins, 1948, rpt. 1977).

Wilde, Oscar, *The Portable Oscar Wilde*, Richard Aldington and Stanley Weintraub (eds) (New York: Penguin Books, 1981).

Wilde, Oscar, 'The Soul of Man under Socialism', in *Complete Works of Oscar Wilde* (London and Glasgow: Collins, 1948, reprinted 1977).

Wilde, Oscar, 'The Truth of Masks', in *Complete Works of Oscar Wilde* (London and Glasgow: Collins, 1948, rpt. 1977).

Primary Press Sources

Aderer, Adolphe, 'Premières Représentations', *Le Petit Parisien*, 7 May 1910.

Anon., 'Dress rehearsal of "Salome"', *The Morning Leader*, 8 December 1910.

Anon., 'Music and Musicians. Dr Strauss's "Salome"', *The Morning Post*, 28 November 1910.

Anon., '"Salome" at Covent Garden. The grand rehearsal. Mme Ackté & the blood-stained sword', *The Daily News*, 8 December 1910.

Anon., '"Salome." Foreglimpse at what the audience will see to-night', *The Star*, 8 December 1910.

Anon., '"Salome" rehearsal. The light side of opera. Incidents at Covent Garden', *Pall Mall Gazette*, 8 December 1910.

Anon., 'Salome to-night. The event of the opera season. Rehearsal comedies', *The Sketch*, 8 December 1910.

Anon., 'Spectacles & Concerts. La Réouverture de l'Olympia', *Le Figaro*, 23 August 1909.

Anon., 'The head problem in Salome. Censor sanctions a new arrangement', *The Morning Leader*, 30 December 1910.

Bauer, Henry, 'Les Premières Représentations', *L'Echo de Paris*, 13 February 1896.

Boschot, Adolphe, 'La Musique', *L'Echo de Paris*, 7 April 1919.

Bristol Times, The, 9 December 1910.

Brussel, Robert, 'De la Musique et de la danse. Les concerts de Mlle Trouhanowa', *La Revue musicale S.I.M.*, 15 May 1912.

Brussel, Robert, 'Les Théâtres', *Le Figaro*, 23 April 1910.

Burckhard, Max, 'Wilde's "Salome" im Volkstheater', *Die Zeit*, 13 December 1903.

Carrère, Max, 'La critique musicale', *Bonsoir*, 8 April 1919.

C.K., 'Production of "Salome"', *The Morning Leader*, 8 December 1910.

Curzon, Henri de, 'La Semaine. Paris. Concert de danse de Mlle Trouhanowa', *Le Guide musical*, 23 April 1912.

Daily Mail, 9 December 1910.

Daily News, The, 13 December 1910.

Daily Telegraph, The, 19 November 1910.

Daily Telegraph, The, 23 November 1910.

Daily Telegraph, The, 3 December 1910.

Debay, Victor, 'La "Salomé" de Richard Strauss à L'Opéra', *Le Courrier musical*, 15 May 1910.

Debay, Victor, 'Vers l'erreur', *Le Courrier musical*, 15 May 1912.

Deutsches Volksblatt, 13 December 1903.

Deutsches Volksblatt, 29 December 1906.

Duncan, Isadora, 'Les Idées d'Isadora Duncan sur la Danse', *La Revue musicale S.I.M.*, 15 March 1912.

Evening News, The, 23 November 1910.

Evening Standard, 23 November 1910.

Evening Standard, 9 December 1910.

Galbat, Marcel, 'Les Concerts de danse de Mlle Trouhanowa', *Comœdia*, 19 April 1912.

Gauthier-Villars, Henry, *Comœdia*, 10 November 1907.

Gauthier-Villars, Henry, Louis Schneider and Louis Handler, 'Théâtre national de l'Opéra. Salomé', *Comœdia*, 7 May 1910.

Hevesi, Ludwig, '"Salome"', *Fremden–Blatt*, 15 December 1903.

Hirschfeld, Robert, '"Salome" von Richard Strauß', *Wiener Abendpost*, 27 May 1907.

Holden, Anthony, 'Don't go and lose your head …', *The Observer*, 24 February 2008, http://www.guardian.co.uk/music/2008/feb/24/classicalmusicandopera. livereviews, accessed 10 February 2011.

Hurcourt, Louis d', 'Soirées parisiennes', *La Patrie*, 8 July 1919.

Illustrated Sporting and Dramatic News, 3 December 1910.

Illustrirtes Wiener Extrablatt, 13 December 1903.

Irish Times, The, 9 December 1910.

Jacobsohn, Siegfried, 'Oskar Wilde', *Die Zeit*, 19 November 1902.

Jullien, Adolphe, 'Revue musicale', Feuilleton du *Journal des Débats*, *Le Journal des Débats*, 15 May 1910.

Kraus, Karl, '"Salome"', *Die Fackel*, 5/150 (1903): 1–14.

Lady's Pretorial, The, 10 December 1910.

Lalo, Pierre, 'La Musique', Feuilleton du *Temps*, *Le Temps*, 28 December 1905.

Lalo, Pierre, 'La Musique', Feuilleton du *Temps*, *Le Temps*, 15 May 1907.

Lalo, Pierre, 'La Musique', Feuilleton du *Temps*, *Le Temps*, 9 April 1919.

Lancashire Evening Post, 31 December 1910.

Linor, Georges, 'Les Ballets Russes au Théâtre des Champs-Elysées', *Comœdia*, 14 June 1913.

Liverpool Post, 9 December 1910.

Malherbe, Henry, 'La Renaissance du ballet français', *Musica*, 140 (May 1914).

Manchester Guardian, The, 9 December 1910.

M.K. [Maurice Kufferath], 'Salomé', *Le Guide musical*, 24 March 1907.

Morning Leader, The, 30 December 1910.

Morris, Steven, 'Importance of not being Salome', *The Guardian*, 17 July 2000.

Mortier, Pierre, 'Mademoiselle Natacha Trouhanowa', *Le Théâtre*, 1 July 1909.

Nestruck, J. Kelly, 'Salome: Take Three', *The Globe and Mail*, 18 April 2013.

Neues Wiener Journal, 13 December 1903.

Neues Wiener Journal, 29 December 1906.

Neues Wiener Tagblatt, 13 December 1903.

Newman, Ernest, 'Strauss's "Salome"', *The Nation*, 17 December 1910.

Nozière [Fernand Weil], 'Le Théâtre', *Gil Blas*, 9 May 1907.

Onlooker, The, 10 December 1910.

Pillois, Jacques, 'A Propos d'un Concert de Danse', *Le Courrier musicale*, 1 May 1912.

Pohl, Otto, 'Feuilleton', *Arbeiter–Zeitung*, 19 December 1903.

Reichspost, 15 December 1903.

Reichspost, 1 January 1907.

Reynold's Weekly Newspaper, 11 December 1910.

Ross, Robert, 'Salomé', *The Saturday Review*, 27 May 1905.

Schneider, Louis, 'Au Théâtre municipal du Châtelet. Les Concerts de Danse de Mlle Trouhanowa. La mise en scène et les décors', *Comœdia*, 24 April 1912.

Schneider, Louis, 'Salomé', *Le Théâtre*, 202 (May 1907).

Schütz, Friedrich, 'Oskar Wilde', *Neue Freie Presse*, 15 December 1903.

Strapontin, 'Paris la Nuit', *Gil Blas*, 23 August 1909.

Times, The, 23 November 1910.

Tout-Paris, 'Bloc-Notes Parisien. Les Concerts de danse de Mlle Trouhanowa', *Le Gaulois*, 18 April 1912.

Vaterland, Das, 13 December 1903.

Vuillemin, Louis, 'Théâtre municipal de la Gaité-Lyrique. Salomé', *Comœdia*, 23 April 1910.

Secondary Sources

Abbate, Carolyn, *In Search of Opera*, Princeton Studies in Opera (Princeton, NJ: Princeton University Press, 2001).

Abbate, Carolyn, 'Music – Drastic or Gnostic?', *Critical Inquiry*, 30/3 (2003): 505–36.

Abbate, Carolyn, 'Opera; or, the Envoicing of Women', in Ruth A. Solie (ed.), *Musicology and Difference* (Berkeley, CA: University of California Press, 1992).

Abbate, Carolyn, *Unsung Voices: Opera and Musical Narrative in the Nineteenth Century* (Princeton, NJ: Princeton University Press, 1991).

Albright, Daniel, 'Golden Calves: the Role of Dance in Opera', *The Opera Quarterly: Sound Moves*, 22/1 (Winter 2006): 22–37.

Alloula, Malek, *Le Harem Colonial: images d'un sous-érotisme* (Paris: Garance, 1981).

Apter, Emily, 'Acting Out Orientalism: Sapphic Theatricality in Turn-of-the-Century Paris', in Elin Diamond (ed.), *Performance and Cultural Politics* (New York and London: Routledge, 1996).

Armatage, Kay and Caryl Clark, 'Seeing and Hearing Atom Egoyan's *Salome*', in Jennifer Burwell and Monique Tschofen (eds), *Image and Territory: Essays on Atom Egoyan* (Waterloo: Wilfrid Laurier University Press, 2006).

Auslander, Philip, *Liveness: Performance in a Mediatized Culture* (London and New York: Routledge, 1999).

Bataille, Georges, *Erotism: Death and Sensuality* (New York: City Light Books, 1962).

Becker-Leckrone, Megan, 'Salome©: The Fetishization of a Textual Corpus', *New Literary History*, 26/2 (1995): 239–60.

Beizer, Janet L., *Ventriloquized Bodies: Narratives of Hysteria in Nineteenth-Century France* (Ithaca, NY and London: Cornell University Press, 1994).

Bentley, Toni, *Sisters of Salome* (New Haven, CT: Yale University Press, 2002).

Berenson, Edward, *The Trial of Madame Caillaux* (Berkeley, CA: University of California Press, 1992).

Berger, Klaus, *Japonisme in Western Painting from Whistler to Matisse*, trans. David Britt (Cambridge and New York: Cambridge University Press, 1992).

Bernheimer, Charles, *Decadent Subjects: The Idea of Decadence in Art, Literature, Philosophy, and Culture of the* Fin de Siècle *in Europe*, T. Jefferson Kline and Naomi Schor (eds) (Baltimore, MD and London: The John Hopkins University Press, 2002).

Bhabha, Homi K., *The Location of Culture* (London and New York: Routledge, 1994).

Bizot, Richard, 'The Turn-of-the-Century Salome Era: High- and Pop-Culture Variations on the Dance of the Seven Veils', *Choreography and Dance*, 2 (1992): 71–87.

Blackburn, Robert, '"The unutterable and the dream": Aspects of Wilde's Reception in Central Europe 1900–1922', *Irish Studies Review*, 11 (1995): 30–35.

Bloom, Lisa, 'Contest for meaning in body politics and feminist conceptual art: revisioning the 1970s through the work of Eleanor Antin', in Amelia Jones and Andrew Stephensons (eds), *Performing the Body/Performing the Text* (London and New York: Routledge, 1999).

Borower, Djawid Carl, *Struktur und Wandel der Wiener Theaterzensur im politischen und sozialen Kontext der Jahre 1893 bis 1914* (University of Vienna: unpublished MA thesis, 1986).

Boyd, Melanie, 'To Blame her Sadness: Representing Incest in Atom Egoyan's *The Sweet Hereafter*', in Jennifer Burwell and Monique Tschofen (eds), *Image and Territory: Essays on Atom Egoyan* (Waterloo: Wilfrid Laurier University Press, 2006).

Brook, Peter, *The Shifting Point: Theatre, Film, Opera 1946–1987* (New York: Theatre Communications Group, 1994).

Bucknell, Brad, 'On "Seeing" Salome', *English Literary History*, 60/2 (1993): 503–26.

Butler, Judith, *Gender Trouble: Feminism and the Subversion of Identity* (New York: Routledge, 1990).

Caddy, Davinia, 'On Ballet at the Opéra, 1909–1914, and *La Fête chez Thérèse*', *Journal of the Royal Musical Association*, 133/2 (2008): 220–69.

Caddy, Davinia, *The Ballets Russes and Beyond: Music and Dance in Belle-Époque Paris* (Cambridge and New York: Cambridge University Press, 2012).

Calico, Joy H., 'Staging Scandal with *Salome* and *Elektra*', in Rachel Cowgill and Hilary Poriss (eds), *The Arts of the Prima Donna in the Long Nineteenth Century* (London and New York: Oxford University Press, 2012).

Carnegy, Patrick, *Wagner and the Art of the Theatre: The Operas in Stage Performance* (New Haven, CT: Yale University Press, 2006).

Carpenter, Tethys, 'Tonal and Dramatic Structure', in Derrick Puffett (ed.), *Richard Strauss: Salome*, Cambridge Opera Handbooks (Cambridge: Cambridge University Press, 1989).

Cave, Richard Allen, 'Wilde's plays: some lines of influence', in Peter Raby (ed.), *The Cambridge Companion to Oscar Wilde* (Cambridge: Cambridge University Press, 1997).

Cherniavsky, Felix, *The Salome Dancer: The Life and Times of Maud Allan* (Toronto: McClelland and Stewart, 1991).

Clément, Catherine, *Opera or the Undoing of Women*, trans. Betsy Wing (London: Virago Press, 1989).

Cleto, Fabio (ed.), *Camp: Queer Aesthetics and the Performing Subject. A Reader* (Edinburgh: Edinburgh University Press, 1999).

Conrad, Peter, *Romantic Opera and Literary Form*, Quantum Books (Berkeley, CA: University of California Press, 1977).

Cook, Nicholas, *Analysing Musical Multimedia* (Oxford: Clarendon Press, 1998).

Coudroy-Saghaï, Marie-Hélène, 'L'infortunée *Namouna* d'Edouard Lalo: une œuvre de précurseur', in Jean-Christophe Branger (ed.), *Musique et chorégraphie en France de Léo Delibes à Florent Schmitt* (Saint-Etienne: Publications de l'Université de Saint-Etienne, 2010).

Cusick, Suzanne G., 'On a Lesbian Relation with Music: A Serious Effort Not to Think Straight', in Philip Brett, Elizabeth Wood and Gary C. Thomas (eds), *Queering the Pitch: New Gay and Lesbian Musicology* (New York and London: Routledge, 1994).

Darnton, Robert, *The Great Cat Massacre and Other Episodes in French Cultural History* (London: Penguin Books, 1984).

Davis, Eugene, 'Oscar Wilde, *Salome*, and the German Press, 1902–1905', *English Literature in Transition 1880–1920*, 44/2 (2001): 149–80.

Dellamora, Richard, 'Traversing the Feminine in Oscar Wilde's *Salomé*', in Thaïs E. Morgan (ed.), *Victorian Sages and Cultural Discourses: Renegotiating Gender and Power* (New Brunswick, NJ and London: Rutgers University Press, 1990).

Després, Aurore, 'Place et fonction de la danse dans la synthèse des arts sur la scène', in Pascal Lécroart (ed.), *Ida Rubinstein: une utopie de la synthèse des arts à l'épreuve de la scène* (Besançon: Presses Universitaires de Franche-Comté, 2008).

Diamond, Elin, 'The Shudder of Catharsis in Twentieth-Century Performance', in Andrew Parker and Eve Kosofsky Sedgwick (eds), *Performativity and Performance* (London and New York: Routledge, 1995).

Didi-Huberman, Georges, *Ouvrir Vénus* (Paris: Gallimard, 1999).

Dierkes-Thrun, Petra, *Salome's Modernity: Oscar Wilde and the Aesthetics of Transgression* (Ann Arbor, MI: University of Michigan Press, 2011).

Dijkstra, Bram, *Idols of Perversity: Fantasies of Feminine Evil in Fin-de-Siècle Culture* (Oxford and New York: Oxford University Press, 1986).

Dimova, Polina Dimcheva, *'Beautiful, Colored Musical Things': Metaphors and Strategies for Interartistic Exchange in Early European Modernism* (Berkeley, CA: University of California, ProQuest, UMI Dissertations Publishing, 2010, 3526569).

Donohue, Joseph, 'Distance, Death and Desire in Salome', in Peter Raby (ed.), *The Cambridge Companion to Oscar Wilde* (Cambridge: Cambridge University Press, 1997).

Dorra, Henri (ed.), *Symbolist Art Theories: A Critical Anthology* (Berkeley, CA and London: University of California Press, 1994).

Downes, Stephen, *Music and Decadence in European Modernism: The Case of Central and Eastern Europe* (Cambridge: Cambridge University Press, 2010).

Eells, Emily, 'Naturalizing Oscar Wilde as an homme de lettres: The French Reception of Dorian Gray and Salomé (1895–1922)', in Stefano Evangelista (ed.), *The Reception of Oscar Wilde in Europe*, The Athlone Critical Traditions Series: The Reception of British and Irish Authors in Europe (London: Continuum, 2010).

Eells, Emily, 'Transposing Wilde's Salomé: The French operas by Strauss and Mariotte', in Andrew Radford and Victoria Reid (eds), *Franco-British Cultural Exchanges, 1880–1940: Channel Packets* (Basingstoke and New York: Palgrave Macmillan, 2012).

Efron, John M., *Medicine and the German Jews: A History* (London and New Haven, CT: Yale University Press, 2001).

Ellmann, Richard, *Oscar Wilde* (London: Penguin, 1988).

Ellmann, Richard, *Yeats: The Man and the Masks* (New York and London: W.W. Norton and Company, 1948, reissued 1999).

Esse, Melina, 'Don't Look Now: Opera, Liveness and the Televisual', *The Opera Quarterly*, 26/1 (2010): 81–95.

Evans, David T., *Phantasmagoria: A Sociology of Opera* (Aldershot and Vermont: Ashgate/Arena, 1999).

Everist, Mark, 'Reception Theories, Canonic Discourses, and Musical Value', in Nicholas Cook and Mark Everist (eds), *Rethinking Music* (Oxford and New York: Oxford University Press, 1999).

Fauser, Annegret, 'Visual Pleasures, Musical Signs: Dance at the Paris Opéra', in Bryan Gilliam (ed.), *Music, Image, Gesture, The South Atlantic Quarterly*, 104/1 (Winter 2005): 99–124.

Féral, Josette, 'Introduction: Towards a Genetic Study of Performance – Take 2', *Theatre Research International*, 35 (2008): 223–33.

Findlater, Richard, *Banned! A Review of Theatrical Censorship in Britain* (London: MacGibbon & Kee, 1967).

Fischer-Lichte, Erika, *The Transformative Power of Performance: A New Aesthetics* (London: Routledge, 2008).

Fletcher, Ian, *Aubrey Beardsley* (Boston, MA: Twayne Publishers, 1987).

Foster, Susan Leigh, 'Pygmalion's No-Body and the Body of Dance', in Elin Diamond (ed.), *Performance and Cultural Politics* (New York and London: Routledge, 1996).

Foucault, Michel, 'Of Other Spaces', trans. Jay Miskowiec, *Diacritics: A Review of Contemporary Criticism*, 16/1 (1986): 22–7.

Frank, Joseph, *The Idea of Spatial Form* (New Brunswick, NJ: Rutgers University Press, 1991).

Frankel, Nicholas, *Oscar Wilde's Decorated Books* (Ann Arbor, MI: University of Michigan Press, 2000).

Frisch, Walter, *German Modernism: Music and the Arts* (Berkeley, CA: University of California Press, 2005).

Gagnebin, Murielle, *Pour une esthétique psychanalytique: L'artiste, stratège de l'inconscient* (Paris: Presses universitaires de France, 1994).

Garafola, Lynn, *Legacies of Twentieth-Century Dance* (Middletown, CT: Wesleyan University Press, 2005).

Garber, Marjorie B., *Vested Interests: Cross-Dressing and Cultural Anxiety* (New York: Routledge, 1991).

Gilliam, Bryan (ed.), *Richard Strauss and His World* (Princeton, NJ: Princeton University Press, 1992).

Gilliam, Bryan, 'Strauss and the sexual body: the erotics of humour, philosophy, and ego–assertion', in Charles Youmans (ed.), *The Cambridge Companion to Richard Strauss* (Cambridge and New York, Cambridge University Press, 2010).

Gilman, Sander L., *Disease and Representation: Images of Illness from Madness to AIDS* (Ithaca, NY: Cornell University Press, 1988).

Gilman, Sander L., *Jewish Self-Hatred: Anti-Semitism and the Hidden Language of the Jews* (Baltimore, MD: Johns Hopkins University Press, 1986).

Gilman, Sander L., 'Strauss and the Pervert', in Arthur Groos and Roger Parker (eds), *Reading Opera* (Princeton: Princeton University Press 1988).

Gilman, Sander L., 'Strauss, the Pervert, and Avant Garde Opera of the Fin de Siècle', *New German Critique*, 43 (1988): 35–68.

Gilman, Sander L., *The Jew's Body* (New York: Routledge, 1991).

Gilman, Sander L., et al., *Hysteria Beyond Freud* (Berkeley, CA: University of California Press, 1993).

Goldovsky, Boris, *Bringing Opera to Life: Operatic Acting and Stage Direction* (New York: Appleton-Century-Crofts, 1968).

Grigoriev, Serge, *The Diaghilev Ballet 1909–1929*, trans. Vera Bowen (London: Constable, 1953).

Guest, Ivor, *Le Ballet de l'Opéra de Paris: trois siècles d'histoire et de tradition*, trans. Paul Alexandre (Paris: Théâtre national de l'Opéra: Flammarion, 1976).

Guillory, John, 'Canon', in Frank Lentricchia and Thomas McLaughlin (eds), *Critical Terms for Literary Study* (Chicago, IL: University of Chicago Press, 1995).

Guinot, José, 'Le Théâtre du grotesque', in Jean-Paul Manganaro (ed.), *Carmelo Bene, dramaturgie* (Paris: Centre International de Dramaturgie, 1977).

Gutsche-Miller, Sarah, 'Le ballet-pantomime sur la scène des Folies-Bergère: *Fleur de lotus* (1893) et les conventions du ballet populaire', in Jean-Christophe Branger (ed.), *Musique et chorégraphie en France de Léo Delibes à Florent Schmitt* (Saint-Etienne: Publications de l'Université de Saint-Etienne, 2010).

Guy, Josephine and Ian Small, *Studying Oscar Wilde: History, Criticism, and Myth* (Greensboro, NC: ELT Press, 2006).

Harvey, David, *The Condition of Postmodernity: An Enquiry into the Origins of Cultural Change* (Oxford: Blackwell, 1989).

Heisler Jnr., Wayne, 'Kitsch and the Ballet *Schlagobers*', *The Opera Quarterly: Sound Moves*, 22/1 (Winter 2006): 38–64.

Heisler Jnr., Wayne, *The Ballet Collaborations of Richard Strauss* (Rochester, NY: University of Rochester Press, 2009).

Hepokoski, James, 'Operatic Stagings: Positions and Paradoxes. A Reply to David Levin', in Fabrizio Della Seta, Roberta Montemorra Marvin and Marco Marica (eds), *Verdi 2001: Atti del Convegno Internazionale, Parma, New York, New Haven, 24 gennaio–1 febbraio 2001* (Firenze: Olschki, 2003).

Hoare, Philip, *Wilde's Last Stand: Decadence, Conspiracy & The First World War* (Trowbridge: Duckworth, 1997).

Holden, Raymond, *Richard Strauss. A Musical Life* (New Haven, CT and London: Yale University Press, 2011).

Holloway, Robin, '*Salome*: art or kitsch?', in Derrick Puffett (ed.), *Richard Strauss: Salome*, Cambridge Opera Handbooks (Cambridge: Cambridge University Press, 1989).

Holman, Michael and Jean Boase-Beier, 'Introduction: Writing, Rewriting and Translation through Constraint to Creativity', in Boase-Beier and Holman (eds), *The Practices of Literary Translation: Constraints and Creativity* (Manchester: St. Jerome Publishing, 1999).

Höslinger, Clemens, '*Salome* und ihr österreichisches Schicksal 1905 bis 1918', *Österreichische Musikzeitschrift*, 32 (1977): 300–309.

Huart, Annabelle d' and Nadia Tazi, *Harems* (Paris: Chêne, Hachette, 1980).

Hucher, Yves, *Florent Schmitt* (Paris: Editions Le Bon Plaisir/Librarie Plon, 1953), re-edited (Paris: Editions d'Aujourd'hui, 1983).

Hutcheon, Linda and Michael Hutcheon, *Bodily Charm: Living Opera* (Lincoln and London: University of Nebraska Press, 2000).

Hutcheon, Linda and Michael Hutcheon, 'Staging the Female Body: Richard Strauss's *Salome*', in Mary Ann Smart (ed.), *Siren Songs: Representations of Gender and Sexuality in Opera* (Princeton, NJ: Princeton University Press, 2000).

Jay, Martin, *Downcast Eyes: The Denigration of Vision in Twentieth-Century French Thought* (Berkeley, CA: University of California Press, 1993).

Jefferson, Alan, *The Operas of Richard Strauss in Britain 1910–1963* (London: Putnam, 1963).

Johnston, John, *The Lord Chamberlain's Blue Pencil* (London: Hodder & Stoughton, 1990).

Jullian, Philippe, *Oscar Wilde*, trans. Violet Wyndham (New York: The Viking Press, 1969).

Kaye, Richard A., 'Sexual Identity at the Fin de Siècle', in Gail Marshall (ed.), *The Cambridge Companion to the Fin de Siècle* (Cambridge: Cambridge University Press, 2007).

Kennedy, Michael, *Richard Strauss* (Oxford: Oxford University Press, 1995).

Kerman, Joseph, 'A Few Canonic Variations', *Critical Inquiry*, 10/1 (1983): 107–25.

Kittler, Friedrich A., 'Opera in the Light of Technology', in Beate Allert (ed.), *Languages of Visuality: Crossings Between Science, Art, Politics and Literature* (Detroit, MI: Wayne State University Press, 1996).

Koestenbaum, Wayne, *The Queen's Throat: Opera, Homosexuality, and the Mystery of Desire* (New York and London: Poseidon Press, 1993).

Kohlmayer, Rainer, 'From Saint to Sinner: The Demonization of Oscar Wilde's *Salomé* in Hedwig Lachmann's German Translation and in Richard Strauss's

Opera', in Mary Snell-Hornby, Zuzana Jettmarová and Klaus Kaindl (eds), *Translation as Intercultural Communication. Selected Papers from the EST Congress – Prague 1995* (Amsterdam and Philadelphia, PA: John Benjamins, 1997).

Kohlmayer, Rainer and Lucia Krämer, '*Bunbury* in Germany: Alive and Kicking', in Stefano Evangelista (ed.), *The Reception of Oscar Wilde in Europe*, The Athlone Critical Traditions Series: The Reception of British and Irish Authors in Europe (London: Continuum, 2010).

Koritz, Amy, 'Salomé: Exotic Woman and the Transcendent Dance', in Antony H. Harrison and Beverly Taylor (eds), *Gender and Discourse in Victorian Literature and Art* (DeKalb, IL: Northern Illinois University Press, 1992).

Kramer, Lawrence, 'Culture and musical hermeneutics: the Salome complex', *Cambridge Opera Journal*, 2/3 (1990): 269–94.

Kramer, Lawrence, *Interpreting Music* (Berkeley, CA: University of California Press, 2010).

Kramer, Lawrence, *Opera and Modern Culture: Wagner and Strauss* (Berkeley, CA: University of California Press, 2004).

Kristeva, Julia, *Desire in Language: A Semiotic Approach to Literature and Art*, Leon S. Roudiez (ed.) (New York: Columbia University Press, 1980).

Kristiansen, Morten, 'Strauss's road to operatic success: *Guntram, Feuersnot*, and *Salome*' in Charles Youmans (ed.), *The Cambridge Companion to Richard Strauss* (Cambridge and New York: Cambridge University Press, 2010).

Lefebvre, Henri, *The Production of Space*, trans. Donald Nicholson-Smith (Oxford: Blackwell, 1991).

Leinsdorf, Erich, *The Composer's Advocate: A Radical Orthodoxy for Musicians* (New Haven, CT: Yale University Press, 1981).

Lesnig, Günther, '100 Jahre *Salome*: die ersten 50 Jahre', *Richard Strauss–Blätter*, 54 (2005): 52–145.

Levi, Giovanni, 'On microhistory', in Peter Burke (ed.), *New Perspectives on Historical Writing* (Pennsylvania, PA: The Pennsylvania State University Press, 2008).

Levin, David J., 'A Picture-Perfect Man? Senta, Absorption, and Wagnerian Theatricality', *The Opera Quarterly*, 21/3 (2006): 486–95.

Levin, David J., 'Operatic School for Scandal', in Roberta Montemorra Marvin and Downing A. Thomas (eds), *Operatic Migrations: Transforming Works and Crossing Boundaries* (Aldershot: Ashgate, 2006).

Levin, David J., *Unsettling Opera: Staging Mozart, Verdi, Wagner, and Zemlinsky* (Chicago, IL: University of Chicago Press, 2007).

Lindenberger, Herbert Samuel, *Opera in History: From Monteverdi to Cage* (Stanford, CA: Stanford University Press, 1998).

Locke, Ralph P., 'Unacknowledged Exoticism in Debussy: The Incidental Music for *Le martyre de saint Sébastien* (1911)', *Musical Quarterly*, 90/3–4 (2007): 371–415.

Lorent, Catherine, 'Florent Schmitt et l'Orient', *Salammbô: Un film de Pierre Marodon d'après Flaubert. Musique de Florent Schmitt*, Été Florent Schmitt. Avignon, Opéra de Paris Garnier, Montpellier, La Roque d'Anthéron (Paris: Sacem, L'Avant-Scène Opéra, July 1991).

Loxley, James, *Performativity* (London and New York: Routledge, 2007).

Lucas, John, *Thomas Beecham. An Obsession with music* (Woodbridge: The Boydell Press, 2008).

Marvin, Roberta Montemorra, 'The Censorship of Verdi's Operas in Victorian London', *Music & Letters*, 82/4 (2001): 582–610.

Mawer, Deborah, *The Ballets of Maurice Ravel: Creation and Interpretation* (Aldershot: Ashgate, 2006).

Mayer, Sandra and Barbara Pfeifer, 'The Reception of Oscar Wilde and Bernard Shaw in the Light of Early Twentieth-Century Austrian Censorship', *Platform*, 2/2 (2007): 59–75.

McCarren, Felicia, 'Stéphane Mallarmé, Loie Fuller, and the Theater of Femininity', in Ellen W. Goellner and Jacqueline Shea Murphy (eds), *Bodies of the Text: Dance as Theory, Literature as Dance* (New Brunswick, NJ: Rutgers University Press, 1995).

McCarthy, John A., 'Zensur und Kultur: "Autoren nicht Autoritäten!"', in John A. McCarthy and Werner von der Ohe (eds), *Zensur und Kultur, Censorship and Culture: Zwischen Weimarer Klassik und Weimarer Republik mit einem Ausblick bis heute* (Tübingen: Niemeyer, 1995).

McClary, Susan, *Feminine Endings: Music, Gender, and Sexuality* (Minneapolis, MN: University of Minnesota Press, 1991).

McClatchie, Steven, 'Bayreuth, Wagnerism, and *Der fliegende Holländer*', in Thomas Grey (ed.), *Richard Wagner: Der fliegende Holländer*, Cambridge Opera Handbooks (Cambridge: Cambridge University Press, 2000).

Melnick, Jeffrey, *A Right to Sing the Blues: African Americans, Jews and American Popular Song* (Cambridge, MA: Harvard University Press, 1999).

Meltzer, Françoise, *Salome and the Dance of Writing: Portraits of Mimesis in Literature* (Chicago, IL: University of Chicago Press, 1987).

Minors, Helen Julia, 'Paul Dukas's *La Péri* (1911–12): A Problematic Creative– Collaboration', *Dance Research*, 27 (2009): 227–52.

Mitchell, Timothy, 'Orientalism and the Exhibitionary Order', in Nicholas Mizoeff (ed.), *The Visual Culture Reader* (London: Routledge, 1998).

Most, Andrea, *Making Americans: Jews and the Broadway Musical* (Cambridge, MA: Harvard University Press, 2004).

Nicholson, Steve, *The Censorship of British Drama 1900–1968*, vol. I: 1900–1932 (Exeter: University of Exeter Press, 2003).

Owens, Craig, 'The Medusa Effect, or, The Spectacular Ruse', in Scott Bryson et al. (eds), *Beyond Recognition: Representation, Power and Culture* (Berkeley, CA: University of California Press, 1992).

Parker, Roger, 'Giuseppi Verdi's *Don Carlo(s)*: "Live" on DVD', *The Opera Quarterly*, 26/4 (2010): 603–14.

Parker, Roger, *Remaking the Song: Operatic Visions and Revisions from Handel to Berio*, Ernest Bloch lectures (Berkeley, CA: University of California Press, 2006).

Pasler, Jann, 'Florent Schmitt', in Stanley Sadie (ed.), John Tyrrell (exec. ed.), *The New Grove Dictionary of Music and Musicians*, second edition, 29 vols (London: Macmillan, 2001).

Pasler, Jann, *Writing Through Music: Essays on Music, Culture, and Politics* (Oxford: Oxford University Press, 2008).

Pennino, John, 'Mary Garden and the American Press', *The Opera Quarterly*, 6/4 (1989): 61–75.

Phelan, Peggy, *Unmarked: The Politics of Performance* (London and New York: Routledge, 1993).

Picard, Timothée, 'Modèle de la danse et synthèse des arts chez les artistes ayant collaboré avec Ida Rubinstein', in Pascal Lécroart (ed.), *Ida Rubinstein: une utopie de la synthèse des arts à l'épreuve de la scène* (Besançon: Presses Universitaires de Franche-Comté, 2008).

Pierrot, Jean, *L'Imaginaire décadent 1880–1900* (Paris: Presses Universitaires de France, 1977).

Pollock, Griselda, *Differencing the Canon: Feminist Desire and the Writing of Art's Histories* (London: Routledge, 1999).

Porges, Heinrich, *Wagner Rehearsing the 'Ring': An Eye-Witness Account of the Stage Rehearsals of the First Bayreuth Festival*, trans. Robert L. Jacobs (Cambridge and New York: Cambridge University Press, 1983).

Prasch, Thomas, 'Behind the Last Veil: Forms of Transgression in Ken Russell's *Salome's Last Dance*', in Kevin M. Flanagan (ed.), *Ken Russell: Re-viewing England's Last Mannerist* (Plymouth: Scarecrow Press, 2009).

Praz, Mario, *The Romantic Agony*, trans. Angus Davidson (Oxford and New York: Oxford University Press, 1970).

Puffett, Derrick (ed.), *Richard Strauss: Salome*, Cambridge Opera Handbooks (Cambridge: Cambridge University Press, 1989).

Reid, Charles, *Thomas Beecham: an Independent Biography* (London: Victor Gollancz, 1962).

Revel, Jacques (ed.), *Jeux d'échelles: La micro-analyse à l'expérience* (Paris: Gallimard & Le Seuil, 1996).

Revel, Jacques, *Un parcours critique: Douze exercises d'histoire sociale* (Paris: Editions Galaade, 2006).

Ricoeur, Paul, *Memory, History, Forgetting*, trans. Kathleen Blamey and David Pellauer (Chicago, IL: The University of the Chicago Press, 2006).

Robinson, Paul, 'A Deconstructive Postscript: Reading Libretti and Misreading Opera', in Arthur Groos & Roger Parker (eds), *Reading Opera* (Princeton, NJ: Princeton University Press, 1988).

Romney, Jonathan, *Atom Egoyan* (London: British Film Institute, 2003).

Rosenthal, Harold, *Two Centuries of Opera at Covent Garden* (London: Putnam, 1958).

Ross, Alex, 'Strauss's place in the twentieth century', in Charles Youmans (ed.), *The Cambridge Companion to Richard Strauss* (Cambridge: Cambridge University Press, 2010).

Rowden, Clair, 'Loïe Fuller et Salomé: les drames mimés de Gabriel Pierné et de Florent Schmitt', in Jean-Christophe Branger (ed.), *Musique et chorégraphie en France de Léo Delibes à Florent Schmitt* (Saint-Etienne: Publications de l'Université de Saint-Etienne, 2010).

Rowden, Clair, *Republican Morality and Catholic Tradition at the Opera: Massenet's* Hérodiade *and* Thaïs (Weinsberg: Musik-Edition Lucie Galland, 2004).

Rowden, Clair, '*Salome* and modern opera: a Parisian perspective', in Günter Brosche and Jürgen May (eds), *Richard Strauss–Jahrbuch 2011*, herausgegeben von der Internationalen Richard Strauss–Gesellschaft in Wien und dem Richard Strauss–Institut in Garmisch-Partenkirchen (Tutzing: Hans Schneider, 2011).

Rühm, Gerhard, 'oscar wildes "salome" und meine deutsche nachdichtung', *Protokolle*, 4 (1982): 141–52.

Rutherford, Jonathan, 'The Third Space: Interview with Homi Bhabha', in Jonathan Rutherford (ed.), *Identity, Community, Culture, Difference* (London: Lawrence & Wishart, 1990).

Said, Edward W., *Orientalism* (New York: Vintage Books, 1978).

Saladin, Linda A., *Fetishism and the Femme Fatale: Gender, Power, and Reflexive Discourse* (New York: Peter Lang, 1993).

Satzinger, Christa, *French Influences on Oscar Wilde's The Picture of Dorian Gray and Salome* (Lewiston, NY: Edwin Mellen Press, 1994).

Sayler, Oliver M., *Max Reinhardt and his Theatre* (New York and London: Benjamin Blom, 1968).

Schroeder, Horst, *Additions and Corrections to Richard Ellmann's 'Oscar Wilde'*, second edition, revised and enlarged (Braunschweig: privately printed, 2002).

Schroeder, Horst, *Alice in Wildeland* (Braunschweig: privately printed, 1994).

Scott, Joan W., 'Gender as a Useful Category of Historical Analysis', in Richard G. Parker and Peter Aggleton (eds), *Culture, Society and Sexuality: A Reader* (New York: Routledge, 2007).

Sedgwick, Eve Kosofsky, *Between Men: English Literature and Male Homosocial Desire* (New York: Columbia University Press, 1985).

Seshadri, Anne L., 'The Taste of Love: Salome's Transfiguration', *Women & Music*, 10 (2006): 24–44.

Severi, Rita, 'Oscar Wilde, La Femme Fatale and the Salomé Myth', in Anna Balakian and James J. Wilhelm (eds), *Proceedings of the Xth Congress of the International Comparative Literature Association* (New York: Garland, 1985).

Shellard, Dominic and Steve Nicholson with Miriam Handley, *The Lord Chamberlain Regrets ... A History of British Theatre Censorship* (London: The British Library, 2004).

Showalter, Elaine, *Sexual Anarchy: Gender and Culture at the Fin de Siècle* (New York: Viking Penguin, 1990).

Siegel, Jonah, *Desire and Excess: The Nineteenth-Century Culture of Art* (Princeton, NJ: Princeton University Press, 2000).

Silverman, Kaja, *The Acoustic Mirror: The Female Voice in Psychoanalysis and Cinema* (Bloomington, IN: Indiana University Press, 1988).

Small, Ian, *Oscar Wilde: Recent Research* (Greensboro, NC: ELT Press, 2000).

Smart, Mary Ann, 'The Silencing of Lucia', *Cambridge Opera Journal*, 4/2 (July 1992): 119–41.

Smyth, Ethel, *Beecham and Pharaoh* (London: Chapman & Hall, 1935).

Soja, Edward W., 'Thirdspace: Expanding the Scope of the Geographical Imagination', in Philip Sarre, John Allen and Doreen Massey (eds), *Human Geography Today* (Cambridge: Polity Press, 1999).

Sontag, Susan, *Against Interpretation and Other Essays* (London: Penguin Books, 2009).

Spackman, Barbara, 'Interversions', in Liz Constable, Dennis Denisoff and Matthew Potolsky (eds), *Perennial Decay* (Philadelphia, PA: University of Pennsylvania Press, 1999).

Spitaler, Franz, *Die Wiener Erstaufführung der* Salome*: Ein Beitrag zur Geschichte der Rezeption Oscar Wildes in Österreich* (University of Vienna: unpublished MA thesis, 1990).

Sprengel, Peter and Gregor Streim, *Berliner und Wiener Moderne: Vermittlungen und Abgrenzungen in Literatur, Theater, Publizistik* (Vienna: Böhlau, 1998).

Stratton, Jon, *The Desirable Body: Cultural Fetishism and the Erotics of Consumption* (Manchester: Manchester University Press, 1996).

Tanitch, Robert, *Oscar Wilde on Stage and Screen* (London: Methuen, 1999).

Taruskin, Richard, *Music in the Early Twentieth Century*, The Oxford History of Western Music (Oxford and New York: Oxford University Press, 2009).

Taruskin, Richard, *The Danger of Music and Other Anti-Utopian Essays* (Berkeley, CA: University of California Press, 2009).

Thomas, David Wayne, 'The "Strange Music" of *Salome*: Oscar Wilde's Rhetoric of Verbal Musicality', *Mosaic*, 33/1 (2000): 15–38.

Tookey, Helen, '"The fiend that smites with a look": The Monstrous/Menstruous Woman and the Danger of the Gaze in Oscar Wilde's *Salomé*', *Literature and Theology*, 18/1 (2004): 23–37.

Townsend, Julie, 'Staking Salomé: The Literary Forefathers and Choreographic Daughters of Oscar Wilde's "Hysterical and Perverted Creature"', in Joseph Bristow (ed.), *Oscar Wilde and Modern Culture: The Making of a Legend* (Athens, OH: Ohio University Press, 2008).

Turnbull, Michael T.R.B., *Mary Garden* (Portland, OR: Amadeus Press, 1997).

Tydeman, William and Steven Price, *Wilde: Salome*, Plays in Production (Cambridge and New York: Cambridge University Press, 1996).

Wagner, Peter (ed.), *Icons, Texts, Iconotexts: Essays on Ekphrasis and Intermediality* (Berlin and New York: De Gruyter, 1996).

Wilgowicz, Pérel, *Le Vampirisme: de la Dame blanche au Golem: essai sur la pulsion de mort et sur l'irreprésentable* (Meyzieu: Césura Lyon Edition, 1991).

Wilson, Emma, *Atom Egoyan* (Urbana and Chicago, IL: University of Illinois Press, 2009).

Wilson, F.A.C., *W.B. Yeats and Tradition* (London: Victor Gollancz, 1958).

Worth, Katharine, *Oscar Wilde* (London and Basingstoke: Macmillan, 1983).

Youmans, Charles, 'Strauss and the nature of music', in Charles Youmans (ed.), *The Cambridge Companion to Richard Strauss* (Cambridge: Cambridge University Press, 2010).

Zagona, Helen Grace, *The Legend of Salome and the Principle of Art for Art's Sake* (Genève: Droz, 1960).

Index

Wilde, *Salomé*, Strauss, *Salome* and all the character names from Wilde's play/Strauss's opera are omitted from this index.

Abbate, Carolyn 8–11, 40–41, 45n81, 91, 139–40, 169
Ackté, Aino 4n5, 10, 12, 99–132, Plate 3
Allan, Maud 3, 50–52, 72, 75, 84n53, 96n108, 105n30, 106, 119–20, 131
Almodóvar, Pedro 172
Annunzio, Gabriele d'
    Le Martyre de saint Sébastien 96n108
    La Pisanelle ou la Mort parfumée 95
Anti-Semitism 61, 63–4, 162–5
Antin, Eleanor 96–7
Antropp, Theodor 50
Apollotheater, Vienna 51
Appia, Adolphe 84, 138, 147
Apter, Emily 7, 96n108
Archdeacon, Albert 103–6, 117–18, 129–30
Armatage, Kay 157, 159n8
Astruc, Gabriel 72, 73n14
Asquith, Herbert H. (Prime Minister) and Mrs. Margot 106, 131
Athena 179

Badet, Régine 72
Bakhtin, Mikhail 135n4
Bakst, Léon 92, 93n93, 95n101, 96n108
Ballets Russes 71, 73, 77n26, 82, 91n80, 92–6
Balzac, Honoré de 63
Bara, Theda 171
Barker, Clive 172
Barthes, Roland 11n55, 142
    The Death of the Author 11, 13
Baudelaire, Charles 21, 63, 182–5, 187
Beardsley, Aubrey 20, 22–3, 25–7, 31n55, 34–9, 45n80, 47, 139, 171, 189
Beauvoir, Simone de 141, 152
Becker, Marie Luise 49–50, 61

Becker-Leckrone, Megan 15, 17, 133n1
Beecham, Thomas 100–110, 117–18, 120–22, 124–6, 128, 131
Bellincioni, Gemma 10
Bene, Carmelo
    Salomè 171, 173–4, 177–80, 181, 185–9, plates 6–9
Bernhardt, Sarah 4, 25
Bernheimer, Charles 8n38, 9n45, 33
Bhabha, Homi K. 136n8
Bijou Theatre, London 53, 105n30
Boni, Aïda 73n14
Botticelli, Sandro 93n91, 133
Bradshaw, Richard 158
Breslau State Theatre 52, 99, 155n2
Bréval, Lucienne 75–6, 84–5, 95
Brook, Peter 146–7
Brookfield, Charles (Examiner of Plays) 130
Bruneau, Alfred 89n71, 92
Bryant, Charles 171
Burckhard, Max 67
Burrian, Carl 99
Butler, Judith
    Gender Trouble: Feminism and the Subversion of Identity 5

Calico, Joy H. 2
Campbell-Bannerman, Sir Henry (Prime Minister) 101
Canadian Opera Company, Toronto 156, 158, 168, 170, Plate 5
Caravaggio, Michelangelo Merisi da 189
Carltheater, Vienna 50–51
Charcot, Jean-Martin 91, 145
Charpentier, Gustave 92
Chicago Grand Opera 99

Cischini, Franz Josef Ritter von 57, 59
Clément, Catherine 12
Clustine, Ivan 83n46, 92, 96
Cohen, Leonard 158
Concert-Goer's Club (Royal Academy of
    Music, London) 110
Concerts Colonne 78n33, 88
Conrad, Peter 137n12, 143,
Cook, Nicholas 142
Corinth, Lovis 60
Costa, Franz 128
Court Opera House, Vienna 51, 59, 99
Craig, Gordon 79, 83–4
Cusick, Suzanne 97

Daffner, Hugo 50, 67
Dali, Salvador 146–7
Dance of the Seven Veils 6–10, 13, 15, 21,
    23–4, 33, 34, 36, 39, 50–52, 72–6,
    78–9, 81–3, 85, 87–9, 91–6, 99n3,
    100, 105–6, 108, 116, 120, 122,
    126, 133–7, 139–46, 148–54, 156,
    158, 165–9, 172–3, 176, 178, 181,
    187–8
Darlay, René 9–10
Dawson, Sir Douglas (Comptroller) 102–3,
    105–7, 109–12, 118–19, 120n82,
    121–2, 125, 129–32
Debussy, Claude 92
    Khamma 96n108
    Le Martyre de saint Sébastien 96n108
    Pelléas et Mélisande 92
Dellamora, Richard 15
Delsaux, Jeanne 95
Delvin, Es 148
DeMille, Cecil B.
    The Ten Commandments 171
De Nederlandse Opera, Amsterdam 133–4,
    Plate 4
Derrida, Jacques 5, 154
Destinn, Emmy 72–3, 84
Dethomas, Maxime 79, 86, 95, Plate 2
Deutsche Oper, Berlin 145
Deutsches Volkstheater, Vienna 52, 56–9,
    61, 67n73, 99, 155n2
Diaghilev, Serge 6n32, 88n66, 94n100
Didi-Huberman, Georges 179–80

Dierkes-Thrun, Petra 4n17, 9n47, 12, 49,
    68n82, 75n16, 96, 172n4, 182,
    188n50
Dieterle, Wilhelm
    Salome 172
Dijkstra, Bram 19n11, 29n44, 33
D'Oisly, Maurice 128
Donohue, Joseph 53
Douglas, Lord Alfred 26–7, 31, 174, 180–82
Dukas, Paul 92
    La Péri 76–7
Duncan, Isadora 72, 91, 94
Dürer, Albrecht 24

Edwards, J. Gordon
    Salome 171
Eells, Emily 1n1, 9n46, 10n49
Egoyan, Atom 13, 64n60, 156–9, 161–2,
    165–70, 172n3, Plate 5
    Exotica 157–8
    Felicia's Journey 157, 172n3
    The Sweet Hereafter 157, 169n23
Ellmann, Richard 15, 24, 26n37, 27n40
Ewing, Maria 146, 150
Eysoldt, Gertrud 61, 83, 84n53

Fauser, Annegret 82
Fellner, Richard 61
Flaubert, Gustave
    Hérodias (from *Trois Contes*) 9–10, 21,
        24, 26n37, 76, 93, 95n105, 96, 133
    Salammbô 95n105
Fokine, Mikhail 71–2, 92–3, 94, 96n108
Foucault, Michel 91n81, 135n4, 136n8,
    151–2
France, Anatole
    Thaïs 173n7
Fremstad, Olive 99, 102
Freud, Sigmund 2, 137n13, 148, 187n48
Friedrich, Götz 144–5, 148, 150, 172
Froelich, Bianca 99n3
Fuller, Loïe 3–4, 72, 77–8, 81n40, 82, 84,
    88–90, 95–6
Fürstner, Adolph 3, 75

Garafola, Lynn 93n92, 97
Garber, Marjorie 15, 136n10

Garden, Mary 10, 75–6, 99–100
Gassent, Rafael 172
Gauthier-Villars, Henry 76–7, 89–90
Gautier, Théophile 63
George, Stefan 60
Gérôme, Jean-Léon
    The Snake Charmer 144
Ghirlandaio, Domenico 24
Giacometti, Paolo
    Giuditta/Juditha 109
Gide, André 28, 34
Gilliam, Bryan 45n80, 163n15
Gilman, Sander 2, 64n64, 162–3, 164–5
Glazunov, Alexander 4, 72n8, 92–3
Glossy, Carl 56–7
Gorky, Maxim 58
Grand Café, Paris 24
Gray, John 25–6
Grewe, Felix Paul 28
Grieg, Edvard
    In the Hall of the Mountain King 188
Grünfeld, Heinrich 2
Guerra, Nicolas 95
Guinot, José 185
Guszalewicz, Alice 16–18

Habsburg Monarchy 54, 56, 64
Hall, Sir Peter 146, 150
Hammerstein I, Oscar 99
Hari, Mata 51
Hartl, Papa 104, 120
Hartwig, Adele 61
Harvey, David 135n4, 135n5, 135n6
Hayworth, Rita 172
Heine, Heinrich
    Atta Troll 21, 26, 133
Heisler Jnr, Wayne 5–6, 73, 92n85
Hernandez, Teo 172
Herzl, Theodor 64
Higgins, Dick 19n9
Hirschfeld, Robert 68, 69n84, 155
Hofmannsthal, Hugo von 6n32, 39, 82n45, 84n52
Hofoper, Dresden 2
Holden, Anthony 148–9
Holden, Raymond 111n56
Holland, Merlin 17

Holloway, Robin 6n33, 150
Humières, Robert d'
    La Tragédie de Salomé 72, 77–82, 85, 87, 94n100, 95–6, Plate 2
Hutcheon, Linda and Hutcheon, Michael 7n37, 8, 83, 165–6, 186, 187n49
Huysmans, Joris-Karl
    A Rebours 9, 19n10, 20n13, 22, 24, 36, 96

Indy, Vincent d' 97n113
    Istar 76
Isola, frères 75–6

Jacobsohn, Siegfried 60, 84n53
Jesus Christ 20, 84, 87, 114, 118n78, 172, 173, 177–8, 188, Plate 7
Jolson, Al 160
Josephus
    Antiquities of the Jews 112n61, 137n11
Joyce, James 55

Kalbeck, Max 155–6
Kalisch, Alfred 101, 110–19, 132
Kamerny Theater, Moscow 94
Karsavina, Tamara 4, 72, 94–5
Kemp, Lindsay 17
Kessler, Harry von 82n45
Kleines Theater, Berlin 1–2, 55, 60
Klimt, Gustav 66
Koestenbaum, Wayne 12
Kohlmayer, Rainer 67, 84n53
Konwitschny, Peter 133–4, 135, 149, 150, Plate 4
Koralnik, Pierre 172
Korn, Erich
    Nachtmar 61
Koster, Henry
    The Robe 171
Kousnezoff, Marie 94
Krafft-Ebing, Richard von 60
Kramer, Lawrence 8, 19n10, 19n11, 83, 87, 116, 124, 129n107, 142n36, 146n44, 165–6, 186
Kraus, Ernst 121, 128
Kraus, Karl 61, 64
Kreuzer, Gundula 170

Kristiansen, Morten 2–3

Lachmann, Hedwig 2, 27, 49, 59, 67–8
Laforgue, Jules
    Moralités légendaires 5n21, 22
Lalo, Edouard
    Namouna 91
Lechleichner, Franz 147
Lefebvre, Henri
    The Production of Space 13, 135–6, 151
Leo, Franco Plate 7
Levi, Giovanni 132
Levin, David 134n2, 166, 169, 170
Lindner, Anton 27, 60
Lippi, Filippino 187
Lord Chamberlain, Lord Althorp/Lord
    Spencer 4, 100–112, 117–20, 122,
    124–5, 129–32
Lucas, John 101, 103, 104
Lueger, Karl 64
Lugné-Poë, Aurélien 1
Luini, Bernardino 24
Luna, Donyale Plate 8

Macbeth, Lady 176
McClary, Susan 8–9
McVicar, David 133, 135, 148–50
Maeterlinck, Maurice 4, 27, 66
    La Princesse Maleine 28
Mahler, Alma 39n73
Mahler, Gustav 51
Malfitano, Catherine 145
Mallarmé, Stéphane 71, 136n10
    Hérodiade 21, 95n105
Manhattan Opera House 99
Man Ray 162
Marberg, Lili 61–2
Mariotte, Antoine
    Salomé 3, 72, 75–6, 85, 90–91, 95
Marvin, Roberta Montemorra 100n7, 109,
    112
Massenet, Jules 91–2
    Hérodiade 21–2, 95, 112, 133
    Thaïs 104
Mayer, Daniel 103–4
Mazarin, Mariette 73n14
Mérode, Cléo de 72
Metropolitan Opera, New York 99, 170

Metzger, Ottilie 121, 128
Meyerhold, Vsevolod 92–3, 95n101
Michael, Nadja 148–9
Millais-Scott, Imogen 187
Milliet, Paul and Henri Grémont [Georges
    Hartmann]
    Hérodiade 95
Minaker, Clea 167
Minor, Ryan 170
Minors, Helen Julia 76n23, 77
Modernism 4–6, 11, 34n68, 45n80, 82,
    87n63, 96–7
Montesquiou, Robert de 93
Moreau, Gustave 10, 96, 133
    L'Apparition & *Salomé dansant devant
    Hérode* 9, 19n10, 21, 22, 24,
    95n105, Plate 1
Morgan, John Pierpont 99
Moulin Rouge, Paris 24
Munte, Lina 1, 9–10, 83

Nash, Vaughan 106–7
Nazimova, Alla 171, 188
Nestroy, Johann 60
Neues Theater, Berlin 55, 60, 61, 83n50
Newman, Ernest 110, 111, 131
New Stage Club 53
Nicholson, Steve 102, 122n90
Nietzsche, Friedrich 31, 71
Nijinsky, Vaslav 82
Noah 177
Nordau, Max 61
    Entartung 61n54

Odilon, Helene 61
Olympia, Paris 92
Opéra, Paris 3, 75, 97
Orchestre Lamoureux 76
Orientalism 77, 89, 96, 143–4, 150
Orpheus 140, 141, 161, 177
Ovid
    Metamorphoses 179
Owens, Craig 7

Pacino, Al
    Wilde Salomé 13
Palace Theatre, London 52, 119
Paterism (Walter) 15, 17, 21, 34n68

Petzl-Demmer, Elly 128
Philadelphia Opera Company 99
Pierné, Gabriel 78n33
    Salomé 78n32, 95
Pillois, Jacques 88
Pioch, Georges 89
Plato 30
    Symposium 189
Pohl, Otto 66–7
Porges, Heinrich 138
Pougy, Liane de 72
Pound, Ezra
    Our Tetrarchal précieuse 5n21
Powell, Frank E.
    A Fool There Was 171n2
Prasch, Thomas 182
Praz, Mario 19n11, 22n20
Price, Steven 19n10, 28n41, 83n50, 84n53,
    93n93, 105n30, 140n29, 183

Ransome, Arthur 28
Rappe, Signe 128
Ravel, Maurice
    Adélaïde, ou le langage des fleurs
        (*Valses nobles et sentimentales*) 76,
        79n38
Redford, George Alexander (Examiner
    of Plays) 102–3, 107, 108, 111,
    130–31
Regieoper/Regietheater 152, 169
Reinhardt, Max 1–2, 3n11, 27, 55, 60, 61,
    83–4, 138–9
Rémy, Marcel 50–51, 75n16
Renvall, Heikki 104, 107–8, 116–17,
    120–21, 123, 125–6
Revel, Jacques 131–2
Richter, Helene 68
Ricketts, Charles 25–6
Ricoeur, Paul 132
Rimsky-Korsakov, Nikolai Andreyevich
    91n80, 93n94
Risi, Clemens 169
Robinson, Paul 12
Roerich, Nicolas 82
Rolland, Romain 23, 73, 75
Ross, Robert 36n70, 53
Rossetti, Dante Gabriel 27–8
Rouché, Jacques 76

Rouen Cathedral 21
Royal Academy of Music, London 110
Royal Opera House, Covent Garden,
    London 4, 100–101, 103–4,
    109–10, 117–19, 120, 123, 125–7,
    128n106, 129, 133, 146–9
Rubens, Peter Paul 24
Rubinstein, Ida 4, 72, 92–7
Rühm, Gerhard 68–9
Russell, Ken
    Altered States 174
    Billion Dollar Brain 174
    Gothic 174
    Salome's Last Dance 17, 173–4, 177,
        180–89
    The Devils 174
    The Lair of the White Worm 174
    The Music Lovers 174
    Valentino 174
    Whore 174
    Women in Love 174

Saint Mark's Gospel 1, 9, 20, 63, 112n61,
    137n11, 155
Saint Matthew's Gospel 1, 9, 20, 63,
    112n61, 137n11, 161
Satterlee, Mrs. 99
Schmitt, Florent
    Le Tragédie de Salomé 3–4, 72, 76,
        77–82, 87–91, 94–6, Plate 2
Schneider, Louis 76
Schroeder, Horst 17
Schroeter, Werner 172
Schumann, Robert 142
Schütz, Friedrich 61, 63–4
Scott, Joan Wallach 152n58
Secession Art Hall, Vienna 51
Semele 179
Seshadri, Anne L. 2, 170
Séverac, Déodat de 94
Shacklock, Constance 147
Showalter, Elaine 17
Silvestre, Armand and C.H. Meltzer
    Salomé 78n32, 95
Smart, Mary Ann 91n81, 169
Smyth, Ethel 101–2, 105
Smyth Pigott, Edward F. (Examiner of
    Plays) 52

Soja, Edward 151
Solomon
    Song of Songs 184
Sontag, Susan
    Notes on Camp 5–6, 96n106, 189
Spackman, Barbara 36
Stradella, Alessandro
    San Giovanni Battista 133
Stanzioni (Massimo Stanzione) 24
Stratas, Theresa 144, 150
Stratton, Jon 186–7
Strauss, Richard
    Ariadne auf Naxos 110
    Der Rosenkavalier 110
    Elektra 6, 39, 101, 110
    Josephslegende/La Légende de Joseph
        6n32, 82n45, 94n99
    Schlagobers 92n85
Stravinsky, Igor
    Le Sacre du Printemps/The Rite of
        Spring 82, 88
Street, George (Examiner of Plays) 105n30
Sturge Moore, T. 4n20
Symbolism 4, 8, 19, 21, 53, 60, 78, 82n45,
    96, 138–40, 173

Taruskin, Richard 152
Tear, Robert Plate 5
Théâtre du Châtelet, Paris 3, 93, 95n101
Théâtre de la Comédie-Parisienne, Paris 1,
    78n32, 95, 105n30
Théâtre de la Gaîté, Paris 75
Théâtre de l'Œuvre, Paris 1, 78n32, 83
Théâtre des Variétés, Paris 3n13, 75
Thomas Beecham Opera Company 103–5,
    117–18
Thulden, Theodoor van 24
Tils, Ludwig 58–9
Tiresias 179
Titian (Tiziano Vecelli) 24
Trouhanowa, Natalia 4, 12, 72–97
Tydeman, William 19n10, 28n41, 83n50,
    84n53, 93n93, 105n30, 140n29, 183

Verande, Louis 122
Verdi, Giuseppe 112
    Nabucco 109

Verhaeren, Emile
    Hélène de Sparte 94
Verhunk, Franchette 10, 99
Veruschka (von Lehndorff) Plate 6
Vidal, Paul 100n6, 103n22
Vidor, King
    Solomon and Sheba 171
Vinci, Leonardo da 24
Visconti, Luchino 189

Wagner, Peter 19n9
Wagner, Richard 2–3, 21, 25n33, 45n80,
    71, 77n27, 90n78, 91–2, 162
    Der Fliegende Holländer/The Flying
        Dutchman 104, 107, 138n16
    Gesamtkunstwerk 20–21, 136, 138–40
    Lohengrin 21, 104
    Tannhäuser 104
    Tristan und Isolde 2–3, 45n80
Wedekind, Frank 58
Weigl, Petr 145
Whitehill, Clarence 104, 117, 122, 126–8
Wilde, Oscar
    De Profundis 24, 33, 67, 140n28, 171,
        174, 183–4
    La Sainte Courtisane or The Woman
        Covered with Jewels 173
    Lady Windermere's Fan 174
    Pen Pencil and Poison 34
    The Ballad of Reading Gaol 33–4, 179
    The Decay of Lying 33
    The Importance of Being Earnest 60
    The Picture of Dorian Grey 32, 66,
        185
    The Soul of Man under Socialism 54
    The Truth of Masks 138n19
Wilgowicz, Pérel 178
Wittich, Marie 2
Worth, Paris 120, 129, Plate 3
Wyler, William
    Ben Hur 171

Yeats, William Butler 4–5
    A Full Moon in March 4
    The King of the Great Clock Tower 4
Youmans, Charles 6–7, 45n80
YouTube 153, 166

Zeus 179
Zweig, Stefan 40n75